The Nigrescent Beyond

Mexico, the United States, and the Psychic Vanishing of Blackness

✦

Ricardo A. Wilson II

NORTHWESTERN UNIVERSITY PRESS
EVANSTON, ILLINOIS

Northwestern University Press
www.nupress.northwestern.edu

Printed in the United States of America

10 9 8 7 6 5 4 3 2 1

Library of Congress Cataloging-in-Publication Data

Names: Wilson, Ricardo A. II, author.
Title: The nigrescent beyond : Mexico, the United States, and the psychic vanishing of blackness / Ricardo A. Wilson II.
Description: Evanston, Illinois : Northwestern University Press, 2020. | Includes bibliographical references and index.
Identifiers: LCCN 2020005896 | ISBN 9780810142046 (paperback) | ISBN 9780810142053 (cloth) | ISBN 9780810142060 (ebook)
Subjects: LCSH: Blacks—Race identity—Mexico—History. | African Americans—Race identity—History. | Mexican literature—History and criticism. | American literature—History and criticism. | Blacks in literature. | Race relations in literature. | Mexico—Race relations—History. | United States—Race relations—History.
Classification: LCC F1392.B55 W57 2020 | DDC 305.896072—dc23
LC record available at https://lccn.loc.gov/2020005896

The Nigrescent Beyond

For Meredith and Tanner, and in memory of my mother:

none of this is without you

CONTENTS

ACKNOWLEDGMENTS

My thanks begin with Gianna Mosser, who saw promise in this project and brought it to Northwestern University Press when it was still coalescing, and with Trevor Perri, Maia Rigas, and the rest of the staff for shepherding the manuscript to the finish line. Thank you to Arlette Hernández for helping to source the image for the cover and to Washington and Lee University for its generosity.

It is an incredible privilege to acknowledge the following individuals for enabling me to understand myself as a scholar and for their uniquely empowering mentorship over the years: Gerard Aching, Nahum Chandler, Roberto Ignacio Díaz, Michelle Gordon, Erin Graff Zivin, Peggy Kamuf, Anne McKnight, Tim Murray, Pani Norindr, Elmo Terry-Morgan, and Tryon Woods. Thank you to Nada Ayad and Carlos Yu-Kai Lin for being so helpful with the early iterations of this work during our time together at USC. Without the resources I received as a postgraduate fellow in the Society for the Humanities and Africana Studies at Cornell, this book would not have found its form. To my dear friends and colleagues at Cornell and Washington and Lee who were so instrumental as this project developed, I owe each of you a debt of gratitude for your critical eye and ongoing encouragement: Edward Adams, Annetta Alexandridis, Craig Campbell, Ted DeLaney, Paula Epps-Cepero, Lucie Fielding, Maria Flood, Virginia Garrett, Chris Gavaler, Genelle Gertz, Leah Green, Kelly Grotke, Stephen Hastings-King, Miguel Ángel Hernández, Sarah Horowitz, Mohamed Kamara, Wan-Chuan Kao, Suzanne Keen, Taryn Mattice, Seth Michelson, Diego Millan, Deborah Miranda, Sandy O'Connell, Holly Pickett, Steve Potter, Carina Ray, Riché Richardson, Michelle Rothenberger, Samantha Sheppard, Elizabeth Spragins, Beth Staples, T. J. Tallie, Taylor Walle, Rebecca Wanzo, and Lesley Wheeler.

Finally, Sue, Craig, Toby, Naomi, Gabrey, Langston, Geoff, Charlotte, Ciara, and Dad, your unconditional support sustains me, and I love you for it.

INTRODUCTION

Contemporary conversations revolving around ideas of blackness in the postrevolutionary Mexican context cannot escape the gravity of the future. Eduardo Urzaiz's 1919 novel *Eugenia: Esbozo novelesco de costumbres futuras*, a work that both centers on and critiques the eugenics movement and the drive toward a perfect society, may be seen to represent a certain starting point in this regard. Published six years prior to José Vasconcelos's world-building *La raza cósmica*, it brings to life Villautopia, the capital of the Subconfederation of Central America, in the year 2218. Born in Cuba and raised in Mérida, Mexico, Urzaiz was a physician with expertise in both obstetrics and psychiatry. He was an early supporter of birth control and coeducation and played a substantial leadership role at all levels of the then-developing educational system in the Yucatán.[1] This diversity of thought finds space in *Eugenia*, an elusive work framed as a love story where the value of modernization and an aesthetically grounded philosophy of procreation, the role of indigeneity in this future, and the concept of utopia itself are left productively unsettled. As such, the work forces a valuable contemplation. However, despite the somewhat nuanced and progressive nature of the futuristic sketch it provides, an idea of blackness rests on solid and antiquated ground. In Urzaiz's imagination, Booker T. Kuzubé and Lincoln Mandínguez, two pejoratively named black doctors from the fictionalized Hottentot nation in Africa, come to Villautopia to learn of its eugenic practices and prevent "the evolutionary stagnation of their race."[2] And here we hear the anachronistic echo of Vasconcelos's straight-faced visioning of a fifth race synthesized from what he understood as White, Black, Native American, and Asian components that shaped Mexican racial thought (and Latin American thought more broadly). As many who study Latin America know, it is a synthesis that in many ways constrains the indigenous component and disappears the black.

Urzaiz's black doctors are described, "like those of their race," as having "formidable cannibal-like teeth" and a developed custom of "sleeping anywhere at any time."[3] And while much of the legible world has been remade by Urzaiz (there exist the Confederation of the Americas and the Euro-Asian Confederation, for example), the system of "Africa" does not contain the possibility of such revision. So here, after a series of scenes that make up only a few pages of the novel, ends the narrative's investment in any idea of blackness. It is either a blindness to or, if reading generously, a spot-on description of the cultural moment. In either case, there is no relief or subtlety to produce a vacillation or a rethinking in regard to the role of blackness in this (almost) aesthetically pure future. And while some of the scholarship surrounding *Eugenia* does address these few scenes, and this includes the work done by the editors and translators of the important 2016 English critical edition, this scholarship does not go much beyond noting that the representation of blackness by Urzaiz was clearly influenced by the eugenics movement.[4] It is a scholarship apparently conditioned by a relative loss for words when interrogating what may lie beneath the surfacing of these representatives of Hottentot. And while my concern in the pages that follow is not with *Eugenia* as an object, the novel's narrative does demand that a future blackness be not only nonexistent within the bounds of what one might argue to be a surrogate Mexico but manifested beyond this border as irrevocably backward in nature. This demand very much aligns with my interest in understanding Mexico as a space that collectively understands itself, and is largely understood by those looking in, as devoid of any substantial blackness. In other words, it is helpful to start with the fact that we have caught up with the vanishings of Urzaiz's futures.

For a clue as to the extent of this vanishing, what I understand in the work to come as a psychic vanishing within the collective conscious of the Mexican nation, one could read Brian Hamnett's latest edition of *A Concise History of Mexico* (2019). In its five hundred pages, there is one sentence dedicated to the relation between Mexico and its history of African slavery: "Earlier use of negro slavery did not have a lasting significance in New Spain."[5] This marker of absence is located in a one-hundred-plus-page portion of the book dealing with periods where blacks played a very visible role in Mexican society. Sentiments like this exist even though there has been a rise in Afro-Mexican scholarship, particularly over the last twenty years, that presents a dramatically different picture.

We know, for example, that prior to 1640 New Spain was the largest recipient of enslaved Africans in the New World.[6] And while Brazil, Cuba, the United States, and other nations within the hemisphere would go on to dwarf these numbers, this is not to suggest that slavery in early New Spain was insignificant. Ben Vinson notes that in 1553 the Viceroy Luis de Velasco was lamenting that there were then "possibly more than 20,000 negroes and mulattos . . . in the colony, far outnumbering the white population."[7] And in 1646, over 35,000 Africans and more than 116,000 more people of African descent were registered in New Spain.[8] In 1810, 10 percent of the population of the colony was considered Afro-descendant.[9] Though Mexico would abandon a racialized *sistema de castas*, where Europeans, indigenous, and Africans (and their various mixtures) were so recorded in legal discourse in an attempt to maintain social order and separation, the nation would become no longer tenable in the late nineteenth century because of rebellion from both factions of the elite and the mixed-race masses. In response to this rampant instability, the nation was reformed in the Mexican Revolution and the mestizo (the imagined indigenous-Spanish subject) produced as its organizing symbol. This transfer was largely symbolic, as a very similar power structure maintained its authority over the new mestizo masses. However, even within that then-new symbolic order which recognized Mexico's pluricultural composition, any idea of blackness went unregistered.[10]

Afro-Mexican studies had what is regarded as its commemorative moment in 1946 with the publishing of Gonzalo Aguirre Beltrán's *La población negra de México, 1519–1810: Estudio etnohistórico*. The great majority of the scholarship that has followed in its wake has fallen within the domain of history and anthropology with a focus on the colonial period. And while there is a growing body of scholarship that is studying present-day Afro-descendant communities in Mexico and their pasts, the bulk of this work remains in an ethnographic register and is often bound by quite specific regional markers. Christina Sue's *Land of the Cosmic Race: Race Mixture, Racism, and Blackness in Mexico* (2013) and Laura Lewis's *Chocolate and Corn Flour: History, Race, and Place in the Making of Black Mexico* (2012), with their respective focuses on the states of Veracruz and Oaxaca, are impactful examples. And there is also work, while not ethnographic, that seeks to similarly uncover and make present aspects of Mexico's cultural inheritance. Christine Arce's *México's Nobodies: The Cultural Legacy of the Soldadera and Afro-Mexican Women* (2017) is a valuable demonstration of this approach. All of this scholarship is extraordinarily beneficial for two reasons. First, it has helped to secure Afro-Mexican-based scholarship's position not only within the study of blackness in Latin American and Caribbean Studies but also, crucially, within the purview of African Diaspora Studies. Second, this body of work offers a set of coordinates without which this book would be impossible. However, very little of the scholarship circulating around Mexico and blackness significantly centers on theoretical concerns as they relate to the tenuous position blackness maintains within Mexico's dominant contemporary national imaginaries. Joshua Lund's work in *The Mestizo State: Reading Race in Modern Mexico* (2012), for example, does exist within a similar theoretical register as my own, but my work not only looks beyond the Mexican border to the United States but also brings to the fore blackness, something only briefly discussed in his notes.[11] Juliet Hooker's comparative ambitions in relation to the broader hemisphere—what she methodologically frames as juxtapositions—in *Theorizing Race in the Americas: Douglass, Sarmiento, Du Bois, and Vasconcelos* (2017) are perhaps the most aligned with my own. Grounded in an unbound and interdisciplinary understanding of political philosophy, her work discusses the largely ignored impact of the hemisphere on the four larger-than-life men who help to title her study. Most important, for her as for me, is that one must eschew simple projects of comparison, for it is precisely within the reading of these "discontinuities and resonances" that generative intellectual spaces can be discovered.[12] And while there has been substantial work managing blackness, relative visibility, and racial mixture from the standpoint of the Caribbean and the greater hemisphere, I have been particularly drawn to and informed by work grappling with sites that present a similar apparent invisibility as in Mexico. In this way, Alejandro Solomianski's early work on a secreted blackness in the Argentinian context was quite helpful as my own thoughts were coalescing while confronting aspects of the historical archive and twentieth- and twenty-first-century cultural production radiating from Mexico.[13]

Building from many of these intersections and influences, in the pages that follow I construct a framework that facilitates an examination of the aforementioned psychic vanishing in the Mexican context in order to think through how this might nurture and open up related discourses within the field of a United States–facing black studies. Approaching this comparative work cautiously but rigorously is critically important as it is becoming more common, both within and outside of the academy, to casually describe the United States as sliding, however slowly, toward a more fluid idea of race used to describe many Latin American nations. The description of this fluidity in the case of Latin America is connected to *mestizaje*. Stemming from the figure of the mestizo, mestizaje is akin to the notion of the melting pot and speaks to a racial and cultural mixture writ large. In the United States, ideas of multiracialism, multiculturalism, and (an ever-impending) postracialism dominated social discourse after the election of Barack Obama and led many to endorse the claim of a "Latin Americanization" of the racial paradigm in the United States.[14] Even with Donald Trump taking the seat of Obama and the surfacing of a somewhat legible, if tempered, black activism, this collective liberal imagination has not relinquished its desire for an eventual postracial conception of itself.

On their face, of course, these delusions run counter to the idea that from the perspective of structure the United States carries with it an incapacity to address the ontological impossibility of blackness (antiblackness) at its core. However, one needs only to look to the apparatuses that for their existence necessitate disparities in criminal justice, public education, and healthcare, among other spaces, to see the endurance of this civic foundation that remains animated by this refusal of black humanity. While these apparatuses are in many ways structured by this negation, at the heart of the collective liberal imagination of the United States there has been an ongoing erosion of what Frank Wilderson terms the "protocols of inquiry" capable of challenging these racially oriented structural imbalances.[15] Mexico's much longer trajectory concerning postraciality and the disappearance of black radical possibility gives clarity to the relation between ideas of blackness that remain legible and acceptable within the boundaries of a collective liberal imagination and those settling on the other side of this boundary that would otherwise compromise this imagination, what I understand as ideas of *radical blackness*.

Following this, I look to the center (not periphery) of several popular and canonical texts (literary, cinematic, archival, etc.) to find flashes of this nonpresence in order to sharpen an understanding of the question, *How, in this contemporary moment, can a text be read to tell the story of something that has to have no story?*[16] In approaching this unsettling presenting of the absence of protocol, my project remains distinct from those that have been drawn to the intersection of ideas of vanishing and race via theoretical frameworks grounded in haunting. Productive as these frameworks can be, I wish to move toward an unreadable fragmentation and away from the underlying assumptions of recoverability, however limited, that an idiom inflected by haunting implicitly presents. The work is thus a modeling of a practice of reading that honors and encourages the disruptive possibilities offered by a sustained, if anxious, awareness of what I understand as the *nigrescent beyond*, or that which lies, irretrievable, beyond the horizon of the process of vanishing itself. As such, nigrescence, the process of becoming dark, is mobilized to articulate the contours of a barrier at the limits of a collective liberal imagination, beyond which certain radical black matter(s) has become and is becoming unreadable even as one reads.[17]

The book is divided into five chapters and an afterword. The first chapter, "Impossible Yanga," demonstrates how Mexico has historically related to ideas of blackness in fundamentally different ways than the United States. This understanding is achieved by an investigation of how negotiations between the Spanish Crown and rebellious enslaved Africans in early New Spain have been re-membered in the historical archive. My work then points to a tendency to secret radical blackness within its psychic apparatus—a tendency influenced by Spain's previous psychic management of the Jewish and Moorish threats on the Iberian Peninsula. This brings to the surface an episteme beyond that of the Enlightenment and alongside the event of the Middle Passage as partly responsible for conditioning black subjectivity in New Spain. This is, in part, what allows for the presentation of a slightly dissimilar process in the United States, where no such negotiations with maroon communities existed. I then expose, via a reading of Miguel Hidalgo and José María Morelos's presence in the archive, that at the time of Mexico's independence from Spain a related process took place; it imagined itself as a nation free from the burden of racial distinction despite the fact that racial difference still structured much of the economic and political disparity. It was a secreting at the hands of a utopian impulse.

To understand the idea of managing secrets, and to set the stage for the theoretical maneuvers to follow, I turn to the psychoanalytic paradigm as described by Nicolas Abraham and Maria Torok. Their understanding of an intrapsychic crypt underlies the necessity for me to include ideas beyond that of dynamic repression (and the symptom of its return) when discussing blackness in the Mexican case—these ideas profoundly mark black studies, even when they are not named. Building on the intrapsychic crypt's ability to hold secrets across generations (what they put forward as the idea of "the phantom"), I theorize the existence of a *transgenerational intrapsychic gap*. I insist on the word "gap" to inaugurate the move away from an idiom tied to the idea of haunting. The remainder of the book focuses on the boundary of this intrapsychic structure, what I also refer to as the nigrescent beyond, and what emanates from it.

I explore this matter in the context of twentieth-century Mexico in chapter 2, "On Apparent Emanations." I begin by tracing the twentieth-century transcriptions and citations of Carlos de Sigüenza y Góngora's eyewitness account of the 1692 rebellion in Mexico City. I am interested in how Sigüenza's heterogenic descriptions of the racial and ethnic composition of New Spain are at times unread by, among others, Octavio Paz and Irving Leonard. This unreading affords a bridge to both Erin Graff Zivin's idea of an-archaeological thinking and Stephen Hawking's recent theorizations regarding the boundary of black holes. Graff Zivin's turn away from an "excavational mode of thought" helps to give language to the unrecoverable and unpredictable nature of what emanates from the proposed transgenerational intrapsychic gap. Hawking allows me to describe the boundary of its structure as a permeable, apparent horizon, and to understand the force that draws secrets into this gap as akin to gravity. His idea, as it applies to my theoretical architecture, is that while there is no information lost when objects fall into a black hole, the gravitational forces therein so chaotically distort the information that whatever is emitted from the apparent horizon is ultimately indecipherable.

Chapter 3, "The Gravity of Lincoln and the Matter of Black Life," encourages a broadening of the implications of my thinking beyond Mexico. As a counterpoint to Mexico's utopian forefathers discussed in the first chapter, I look to contemporary popular imaginings of Abraham Lincoln to understand how a related intrapsychic gap began to develop within the liberal psyche in the wake of the civil rights movement. While neither the certitude of Hidalgo nor the utopian grandeur of Morelos is to be found in the public rhetoric of Lincoln surrounding the issue of slavery and black equality, the collective liberal imagination has nonetheless spent much time and energy deluding itself regarding this fact. To elucidate this I am drawn, primarily, to Tony Kushner and Steven Spielberg's film *Lincoln* (2012), which was released in the buildup to the 150th anniversary of the Emancipation Proclamation, and to how its organization of the archive reads Abraham Lincoln and the boundary these readings continue to set in relation to ideas of radical blackness.

I return to Mexico in chapter 4, "The Olmecs and the Inevitability of Holeness," to build on ideas of excavation and indecipherability by way of an examination of the debates surrounding the discovery of artifacts related to the Olmec civilization in the 1940s in southern Mexico. The Olmecs, thought to be the first advanced Mesoamerican civilization, were believed by some at the time of these discoveries to have potential connections to the African continent. I analyze how this issue was addressed in archaeological circles within Mexico and beyond and how quickly the possibility that a partially Afro-descendant culture played an important role in the nation's indigenous history vanished. I begin by dissecting the active and surprising role of Miguel Covarrubias in this process. Covarrubias is the cartoonist-turned-anthropologist perhaps most famous for helping to frame the visual record of the Harlem Renaissance with his many contributions to *Vanity Fair* and the *New Yorker* and book cover designs for, among others, Zora Neale Hurston and Langston Hughes. The academic scholarship tied to and rising out of Covarrubias's work is then put into conversation with that of Ivan Van Sertima. Van Sertima, most famous for his book *They Came Before Columbus* (1976), spent much of his career refining an argument for the potential cross-pollination of African and Mesoamerican cultures. My reading of both Covarrubias and Van Sertima enables me to demonstrate how the archive as it relates to the Olmec culture deploys an archaeological mode of thought in relation to radical ideas of blackness that problematically strains for wholeness despite being presented with an irreconcilable indecipherability.

The final chapter, "2020 Visions," carries the ideas of the previous chapters to the present moment and begins with an examination of Mexico's intent to count Afro-Mexicans for the first time in its 2020 Census. The pressure for the Mexican government to take steps toward an accounting of blackness has come from local activist groups, the international humanitarian community, as well as the academy and nations in Latin America with more aggressive policies in regard to reparations for their Afro-descendant populations (Brazil, Peru, and Colombia are the most prominent examples). In 2011, in response to this prodding, the Mexican government produced the *Guía para la acción pública contra la discriminación y para la promoción de igualdad e inclusión de la población afrodescendiente en México* (*Guide for Public Action against the Discrimination and for the Promotion of Equality and Inclusion of the Afro-descendant Population in Mexico*). In the expressed mission of the *GAP*, as it is abbreviated within the document, the vestiges of what my work is pushing against are evident—words pointing to processes of recognition (*reconocidas/reconocimiento*), restitution (*restituir*), and reparation (*resarcir*) are read throughout and suggest a faith in the ability to return to a prior state, a state where things are known and an accounting for the whole of Mexican culture is possible. I argue that the results of the impending census will be at the same time limited and limiting, as without an awareness of the unthinkable nature of certain ideas of blackness—the psychic matter that lies beyond a counting—one cannot comprehend how the effects of this vanishing emanate within and throughout the entirety of the present moment.

The second half of chapter 5 describes the census project in the United States as being marked by the opposite trajectory found in Mexico. Beginning in 2000, the possibility of selecting multiple races on the census questionnaire was presented for the first time. Connected to this growing fluidity is a waning desire to track both fertility and movement in the decennial moment of self-articulation. When read in conjunction with the example of Mexico, this suggests a correlation between discrete racial categorization (and its multiracial opposite) and anxieties surrounding fertility and movement. I go on to argue that the political capital intrinsic to the sentimental conjuring of the figure of the child, once a reliable amplifier for an acknowledged politics, is diminishing. How do the historical intersections between black children and politics help us to understand the bodies most connected to the origins of the Black Lives Matter movement (Tamir Rice, Tanisha Anderson, Mya Hall, Walter Scott, Sandra Bland, and Michael Brown)?[18] To investigate this question I pay special attention to the manner in which these bodies appear and disappear in the official electronic archives of the Obama presidency.[19] I conclude by reading these dead markers, though spurring on aspects of the black radical tradition, as having found their radical nature compromised by the evolving intrapsychic borders of the collective liberal imagination of the United States.

James Baldwin begins his essay "Faulkner and Desegregation" with the insistence that "any real change implies the breakup of the world as one has always known it, the loss of all that gave one identity, the end of safety."[20] In this essay, written in 1956 for the *Partisan Review* and collected in his second book of essays in 1961, Baldwin is speaking through Faulkner to the intellectual dishonesty of white southerners in regard to the institution of slavery and the process of desegregation. How does one provoke an end of safety? While the majority of my attention here in this book is aimed at disquieting discourses that help to form and grant stability to the collective liberal imagination's seductive yet violent conjuring and delimiting of ideas of blackness, this question is perhaps now just as urgent when it is posed to the more radical elements of the discipline of black studies and toward the attendant practice they encourage. How can we continue to undiscipline ourselves in order to access a more expansive language (and thus world) to dwell in and work from?[21] With this question in mind, the afterword moves to the future and inspects how a rhetoric of recovery and wholeness has compromised central aspects of the interventions of Afrofuturism and those conversations within black studies that are reliant, consciously or not, on its patterns of thought. Through a reading of Colson Whitehead's postapocalyptic zombie novel *Zone One* (2011), I end with a discussion of how the antagonistic capacities of the nigrescent beyond can be harnessed not only in a practice of reading aimed at texts that entrap and disappear but also in a practice of writing that develops work to undermine and evade that entrapment.

Chapter 1

✦

Impossible Yanga

> A 24 del mes de septiembre pasado tuve aviso de como los negros tenían elegido un Rey, y concertado entre ellos de matar á todos los españoles, alzarse con la tierra, y que los indios eran también en ello. (On the 24th of this past September I was warned that the Negroes had chosen a King and had conspired to kill all the Spaniards, to rise up and take the land, and that the Indians were also with them.)
>
> —Viceroy Antonio de Mendoza

The epigraph comes from a missive sent by Antonio de Mendoza, the first viceroy of New Spain, to Emperor Charles V on December 10, 1537.[1] Scholars have insinuated that the reality of the rumored uprising in Mexico City, the seat of power in New Spain, ultimately may not have been substantiated. Nonetheless, the supposed conspirators were found, confessions were heard, and the leaders were drawn and quartered before any manifestation of rebellion could present itself. The anxiety in the new colony, however, remained palpable—and for good reason. Spain had already sustained significant material losses and psychic trauma due to particularly bloody rebellions on the island of Hispaniola in 1522, and in what is now Colombia in 1529, where the town of Santa Marta was destroyed. In New Spain, by the second half of the sixteenth century minor insurrections of enslaved Africans and the molestation of Spanish property owners by members of maroon communities were becoming more and more common, leading to a consolidation and rearticulation of fugitive slave laws and greater restrictions on free and enslaved blacks' access to weapons.[2]

It was within this context that in 1579 Yanga, by all existing accounts African-born, led a group of fellow enslaved persons from the African continent to escape a sugar plantation near the city of Veracruz.[3] The maroons formed a community in the mountainous region of nearby Orizaba and lived relatively undisturbed for thirty years. Shifting locations to avoid detection, they were proficient farmers and would strategically raid local haciendas for tools, weapons, food, and livestock. Several skirmishes are noted in the historical record during this time, but no large-scale military action was taken by the Spanish colonial administration. However, by the dawning of the new century, their continued presence and example were viewed as too big a threat to the surrounding haciendas and the burgeoning institution of slavery in New Spain. It appears that in 1608 or 1609 forces under the direction of Viceroy Luis de Velasco were sent to suppress the rebellious enslaved Africans. After a series of battles, a treaty was agreed to on March 8, 1609.[4] From this document, sent by the Commissary of Veracruz to the Inquisition in Mexico City, it is clear that Yanga dictated many of the terms of the eleven-point truce documented in the historical record as "Las condiciones que piden los Negros cimarrones de esta comarca" ("The Conditions for Which the Black Maroons of This Region Ask"; reproduced in full in the notes).

Among the terms, were that all enslaved persons who had fled prior to the previous September were considered free. Furthermore, Yanga and his descendants were to be the governors in perpetuity with the town selecting its own magistrates and representatives to interact with the Spanish Crown. As a part of the accord, any future enslaved person to seek refuge in their town was to be returned in exchange for compensation. To maintain this relative autonomy, they agreed to pay tribute to the king and assist in the defense of New Spain if necessary. However, and perhaps most importantly, Spaniards, with the exception of a Franciscan priest and a designated chief justice, were only allowed in the town on market days (Monday and Thursday).

Despite resistance from local owners of enslaved persons, the colonial administration accepted the offer, creating the first free black town in the Americas: San Lorenzo de los Negros.[5] Faithful to the agreement, over the following decades the interests of San Lorenzo were represented by their own *alcaldes* (magistrates), *regidores* (councilmen), and *alguaciles* (constables). Surrounding landowners did attempt to encroach on the town's borders but were held at bay by the people of San Lorenzo de los Negros and the reprimand of the Spanish authorities. An Italian traveler's account from the close of the seventeenth century reported a vibrant community, if somewhat diminished in number. However, by the second half of the eighteenth century, with continued tensions between the liberated town and neighboring haciendas and economic opportunities elsewhere drawing more and more of its inhabitants away, the surrounding haciendas were able to envelop the lands.[6] This narrative begins to push the limits of thought within the United States–centered field of black studies by not neatly aligning with scholar and political philosopher Joy James's rather representative statement from the world line of the United States that "maroon resistance failed to convince the tyrannical majority of the soundness of its reasoning, and the legitimacy of its definitions."[7] While in the case of interactions between San Lorenzo de los Negros and the architecture of the Spanish Crown it is fair to sit with the word "convince" (as the tyrannical majority were only convinced to codify a walking away), there is certainly more movement here than James's statement allows for. In order to gain the theoretical tools to confront such movement, Jared Sexton, for one, rightly demands that we "think about what makes New World slavery what it is in order to pursue that future anteriority which, being both within and irreducible to it, will have unmade it, and that anterior futurity which always already unmakes it."[8] In other words, without an understanding of how the unthinkable nature of blackness simultaneously produced and undermined the institution of slavery, it is impossible to trace how its legacies, or afterlives, are brought to bear on the present moment. I do not, however, view this unthoughtness as without slight but significant variation and thus take up (and expand on) Sexton's charge in this chapter by tracing the impossibility that San Lorenzo de los Negros presents within Mexico's national psychological apparatus. This will provide the foundation for a theoretical borrowing that will allow for, in the rest of the book, a more nuanced understanding of the role of radical blackness and its vanishing within the shifting national psychological apparatus of the United States.

Beyond the surviving treaty and the sporadic appearance of meetings or complaints contained in the Archivo General de la Nación, there are two known narratives of the founding of San Lorenzo de los Negros, both written in the generations after the formation of the town: the Jesuit missionary priest Andrés Pérez de Ribas's account within his larger *Crónica y historia religiosa de la provincia de la Compañía de Jesús de México en Nueva España* (1654); and Vicente Riva Palacios's story "Los treinta y tres negros" in *El libro rojo, 1520–1867* (1870). Pérez de Ribas is a significant figure in the record of New Spain, especially from the Jesuit perspective, and is perhaps most famous for his history of the Jesuit missions published nine years earlier, *Triunfos de la fe*.[9] Riva Palacios, one of the four politically involved members of the elite who were contributing authors to *El libro rojo*, was a liberal politician and the grandson of the partially Afro-descendant Mexican president Vicente Guerrero.[10] The oversized volume is complete with dramatic etchings that attempt to present a teleological vision of Mexican history from Moctezuma II to the execution by firing squad of Emperor Maximilian I in 1867. Because of both the temporal distance from the events and the ideological positioning of their projects, both of these documents should be considered as forms of historical fiction. Reading them as such opens up some very rich discoveries that help interpret and move beyond that which is presented in the historical record.

The account of Pérez de Ribas was written at the distance of nearly a half century, commissioned as a general history of the region by the Jesuit order. Given these origins, and given that the document had to pass through the requisite censorship of the religious superiors, it is no surprise that Yanga's narrative has been delivered in a way that clearly supports the Jesuits' ongoing mission in New Spain in the middle of the seventeenth century.[11] A large portion of Pérez de Ribas's account includes direct quotes from a letter written by the Jesuit priest Pedro Laurencio who had accompanied the Spanish soldiers on the mission to suppress Yanga's maroon community. The letter, written to a fellow Jesuit priest, served as justification of "[una] causa tan justa, contra esclavos fugitivos, salteadores que infestaban la tierra y los caminos reales de ella con tantos insultos" (such a just cause against fugitive slaves, highway robbers that infested the land and its royal roads with so many insults).[12] However, this original letter has not been recovered, so the details that are being imparted remain unverifiable. Unfortunately, much of the scholarship about the founding of San Lorenzo de los Negros uncritically relies on the detail that Pérez de Ribas is a surrogate to.

Laurencio describes the maroons as barbarians and in need of God's punishment. Early in the narrative, Pérez de Ribas's already secondhand account gives a description of a scene in which Laurencio was himself also not present. In this scene, the insolent rebels kill a nearby Spanish resident with a blow to the head for not cooperating in their ongoing guerrilla warfare: "Le acabaron de matar con tanta inhumanidad, que el que le hirió con el terciado lamía la sangre de él, y los demás bebieron también la sangre del desdichado, cogiéndola juntas las manos" (They finished killing him with such inhumanity that the one who wounded him with the sword licked his blood, and the rest joined in drinking the blood of this unlucky man, catching it in their hands).[13] In this account, the rebels go on to make a flag from the dead Spaniard's hair and escape with a Spanish prisoner and six captive indigenous women who were in the vicinity.[14]

Laurencio's notably omniscient narration then extends to the voice of Yanga himself. Speaking to the Spanish prisoner, the rebel leader declares: "'No temas, español, que has visto mi cara y así no puedes morir'; con toda esta autoridad hablaba el denegrido Yanga" ("Don't be afraid, Spaniard. Because you have seen my face, you cannot die"; the utterly blackened Yanga spoke with all of this authority).[15] This appears to be a blasphemous inversion of what the Lord says to Moses in Exodus 33:20: "You cannot see my face, for no one may see me and live." It is an inversion that can be read as casting Yanga as not just an arrogant infidel, but the devil in the flesh. And with the use of *denegrido*, I argue that the demonic barbarity of the rebel leader is tied to the extreme end of a spectrum of blackness, as the root verb (*denegrir*, "to blacken") alludes to a *process* of darkening.[16] The deployment of the past participle (*denegrido*) in this instance suggests that Yanga be understood as having been made completely black by someone or something. Owing to the evolving and complex structures of racial stratification already underway in New Spain at the beginning of the seventeenth century, Yanga's utter blackness is presented as differentiated from the blacks who were part of the Spanish expedition against him—an expedition that, according to Laurencio, also included Indians, mestizos, and *mulatos*.[17]

Against this utterly dark and barbaric force, Laurencio was not worried. This is because God was on the side of the Spaniards. Laurencio had assured as much in the days leading up to the assaults by personally taking confession for the racially heterogenic fighting force that would accompany the Spanish leadership into combat: "Muchas de las confesiones que entonces se hicieron, fueron de personas que en muchos años no habían tratado de reconciliarse con Dios, sino dar larga rienda á sus pasiones. Y así pienso, que si en aquel estado fueran á la pelea, no teníamos que esperar, sino temer el justo castigo de Dios, por mano de aquellos crueles bárbaros" (Many of the confessions that were made then were from people who had not tried to reconcile themselves with God in many years, rather giving free rein to their passions. And so I think, that if they had gone into the battle in that state, we wouldn't have had to wait, only fear the just punishment of God at the hands of those cruel barbarians).[18]

Riva Palacios's *Treinta y tres negros* is written over two hundred years after Pérez de Ribas's account and seemingly relies on it for much of its detail. Its treatment of the maroon rebels, however, can largely be read as a critical intervention with the previous account. Yanga, for example, is described as "el espíritu de aquella revolución" (the spirit of that revolution) and his soldiers as confident in "la justicia de su causa" (the justice of their cause).[19] Like Pérez de Ribas did via Laurencio, he also ventriloquizes Yanga, but in a quite different manner. While deliberating with his chief military adviser, Francisco de la Matosa, it is the bloodthirsty Spanish troops that are painted as unreasonable. Relating information received from a friend and fellow Angolan, De La Matosa says, "Los blancos quieren nuestra muerte . . . Viene una expedición contra nosotros" (The whites want our death . . . There is an expedition coming to fight us).[20] After a discussion of potential military strategies, Yanga offers that they write a letter stating "que queremos nuestra libertad, que si nos la conceden, si no nos vuelven a nuestros amos crueles, si nos dan un pueblo para nosotros, depondremos las armas" (that we want our liberty, that if they grant us this, and if they do not return us to our cruel masters, and if they give us a town of our own, we will put down our weapons).[21] By contrast, Pérez de Ribas describes this same letter as being "llena de notables arrogancias" (full of notable arrogances) and bragging about past victories in order to taunt the Spanish. Albeit with a much different tone, Riva Palacio then goes on to describe the same back-and-forth battle contained in the Laurencio segment of Pérez de Ribas's account. However, there is a significant divergence when the terms of treaty are disclosed.

In Pérez de Ribas's account, Laurencio was called back to Mexico City, and his letter ends before the conflict is resolved. Juan Pérez, another Jesuit priest, is sent to complete the mission. In the conclusion, there is a need to encircle the narrative within the terms of a process known as *reducción*, a concept described by the anthropologist William Hanks as one, associated with unassimilated indigenous communities within the context of New Spain, that "implies pacification and subordination to the new rule of law and to the hierarchical relations of colonial society."[22] Wanting to distance this term from the erroneous assumption that it necessarily speaks to a reduction of number, Hanks traces its roots to the idea of becoming convinced or persuaded.[23] In relation to the indigenous population of New Spain, the strategy of reducción was twofold. The initial task was the "relocat[ion of] the indios into centralized towns called *pueblos reducidos* (ordered towns)," followed by the shaping of the "dispositions and conduct" of the indigenous to align with a Christian doctrine.[24]

Pérez de Ribas's intent to marry this concept of reducción to the narrative of Yanga is evident in the title he gives the chapter: "Relación de la misión á que fue enviado el P. Juan Laurencio, acompañando una escuadra de soldados que salía á la reducción de negros forajidos y salteadores" (Report of the mission in which Father Juan Laurencio, accompanied by a squadron of soldiers, was sent to reduce black outlaws and highway robbers).[25] The conclusion of the narrative, specifically how the terms of the peace are represented, bears this out even more:

> Finalmente, el Virrey les concedió un partido, porque suplicaron estos morenos, y el partido fue: que las cabezas y caudillos de los forajidos entregarían á los que se hubiesen huido de sus dueños y amos, y que para que aquella serranía no sirviese más de ser madriguera de forajidos, se les concediese á los que fuesen libres de ellos, para sus mujeres é hijos, otro puesto acomodado y no muy distante de donde antes habían formado su pueblo; quedando de allí adelante obligados, á que si algún negro esclavo y huido aportarse por aquella serranía tan áspera, ellos lo recogerían y buscarían por los montes y lo entregarían á su dueño, dándoles una, aunque corta ayuda de costa por su trabajo. Y finalmente, ellos protestaron que eran cristianos y vasallos del Rey, y como á tales el Virrey les señalase el que hubiese de hacer oficio de justicia en su pueblo, y Cura para lo espiritual de sus almas, con que ellos quedarían contentos y aquella tierra gozaría de paz, y estaría libre de salteadores y ruido de guerra. Por las grandes conveniencias que en esto concurrían, hubo de conceder el Virrey lo que estos morenos pedían, y quedaron en su pueblo y puesto en que están como trescientos vecinos, que edificaron su Iglesia, y es feligresía que pertenece al beneficiado más cercano. Y con esto se dio fin á esta empresa, muy propia de los ministerios de la Compañía, y estos morenos están hoy pacíficos y en posesión de sus tierras, y muy sujetos en todo lo que por sus superiores se les manda y ordena.
>
> (Finally, the viceroy granted them a truce because they had begged for it. And the truce was: that the leaders of the outlaws would turn over those who had fled from their owners and masters and that mountainous area would no longer serve as refuge for the outlaws. He would grant to those of them that were free, for their women and children, another suitable location not very far from where they had

> formed their town before. And that they would remain from then on obligated, if any black slave who shows up in that harsh mountainous area, to track, capture and return them to their owner, and they would be given a small amount of compensation for their work. And finally, they declared that they were Christians and vassals of the King, and as such the viceroy should appoint who would officiate justice in their town and the priest for the spiritual betterment of their souls, with which they would remain content and that land would enjoy peace and be free of highway robbers and the noise of war. Because of the great advantages that were contained in this truce, the viceroy granted that which the *morenos* asked for, and that they remained in their town and location in which they are now as three hundred neighbors, and that they built their church, and it is a parish that belongs to the closest benefice. And with this the undertaking was over, very typical of the ministers of the Company. And today those *morenos* are peaceful and in possession of their lands and good subjects in all that their superiors ask and order of them.)[26]

In this conclusion, which is derived from no noted archival source, the maroons are described as outlaws and highway robbers who, thanks to the work of the Jesuits, have been now pacified and turned into proper, obedient subjects of the king. Alerting suspicion to the historical accuracy of the representation is the fact that the terms suggested above are incongruent with much of the treaty that has survived in the archive. Furthermore, this incongruence is contoured in a way that supports the reading of these events as conforming to a typical reducción. The surviving treaty makes no mention of the need to return all enslaved persons who had fled prior to the agreement, only those who had fled in the six months prior. Given that Yanga and his community had lived in the region for the last thirty years, it would be safe to assume that this number would have been a very small percentage of the population. To represent the conditions of the peace without this caveat is to avoid appearing as if the maroons had any hand, or perhaps an upper hand, in what the viceroy ultimately granted.

Along this line, since Pérez de Ribas's account maintains only that the viceroy will appoint the chief justice, there is no space to articulate that the maroons, while they agreed to pay tribute and come to the defense of the broader colony, had managed to negotiate terms that allowed them to choose their own land, as well as their own governors and representative magistrates. Even more remarkable an omission—one that, if included, would make it impossible to characterize these events as a reducción—is the fact that no Spaniards, with the exception of Franciscan friars and the designated chief justice, are allowed in the town except on market days.[27]

Riva Palacios, on the other hand, does not reference Laurencio or any other religious intermediary. Consequently, its narrative is not framed around the idea of reducción. However, his conclusion to Yanga's portion of the narrative, though more accurate in relation to the treaty, still similarly supports the idea that the maroons were the party to whom the terms were clearly dictated. In Riva Palacios's view of the events, Yanga "proponía una especie de convenio, en el que había mucho de debilidad" (proposed a kind of agreement in which there was much weakness):

> [Los esclavos] protestaban no haber tenido intención de faltar a Dios ni al rey, de quien eran leales vasallos; se comprometían a entregar en lo sucesivo todos los esclavos fugitivos a sus dueños, mediante una remuneración, y pedían un pueblo en que vivir con sus hijos y mujeres, y en el cual recibirían al cura y al justicia que se les nombrase.
>
> (The slaves declared that they had not had the intention to fail God nor the King, to whom they were loyal vassals; they committed themselves to return to their owners any new runaway slaves, in exchange for a reward, and they asked for a town in which to live with their children and women, and in which they would receive the priest and the officer of justice whom you appoint them.)[28]

Interestingly, Riva Palacios uses the Yanga narrative to highlight the culture of fear in Mexico City in relation to rebels among the enslaved in the early seventeenth century. As he tells it, in the three years that followed

> el nombre de Yanga y de Francisco de la Matosa pasaban de una a otra boca pronunciados con espanto . . . [La gente] decía que durante las frías noches de febrero, misteriosas tropas rondaban alrededor de las ciudades como ejércitos de fantasmas evocados por un conjuro, algunos afirmaban que cuando todos los habitantes de México dormían, ellos desde los terrados de sus casas habían visto en las montañas de los alrededores, hogueras que no podían menos de ser contraseñas, y habían escuchado los salvajes aullidos de los negros liberados.
>
> (the name of Yanga and Francisco de la Matosa passed from one mouth to other, pronounced with fright . . . The people said that during cold nights of February, mysterious troops prowled around the cities like armies of ghosts invoked by a spell. Some affirmed that when the people of Mexico slept, from their own rooftops they had seen fires in the surrounding mountains that could not be anything other than codes, and that they had heard the savage howls of the freed blacks.)[29]

Here Riva Palacios is deliberately connecting Yanga to the historically documented rumors of an uprising that circulated in Mexico City in 1612.[30] Similar to the instance in 1537 noted in this chapter's epigraph, the supposed conspirators were captured before any plot could be enacted. According to Rivas Palacios, "Veintinueve negros y cuatro negras fueron ejecutados en el mismo día y hora en la plaza mayor de la ciudad" (Twenty-nine black men and four black women were executed on the same day and at the same time in the city's main square).[31] Executed by way of the gallows, here are the *treinta y tres negros* of his title, sarcastically referred to within the story as an "ornato digno de la grandeza de la Audiencia gobernadora" (a worthy ornament representing the greatness of the high court).[32] As the people mulled around the square, "los verdugos comenzaron a bajar los cadáveres, y con una hacha a cortarles las cabezas, que se fijaban en escarpias . . . Se estaban castigando cadáveres y derramando la descompuesta sangre de los muertos. Aquella escena era asquerosa" (the executioners began to take down the bodies and cut off the heads with an axe, which they fixed on hooks . . . They kept punishing the dead bodies and spilling the rotten blood of the dead. That scene was disgusting.)[33] With this gruesome detail, Riva Palacios has inverted Pérez de Ribas's conceit regarding the barbarous maroons and the righteous Spanish authority and attempted to rhetorically dissociate nineteenth-century liberal Mexican thought from the colonial period.

Yanga's success, and the Spanish colonial administration's chosen route of managing the crisis of potential mass revolt, proved to be a model for the time. Though never with a documented treaty as restrictive to the colony as that of San Lorenzo de los Negros, in an effort to isolate and contain rebels, the colonial administration of New Spain would go onto allow the foundation of other former-maroon towns in New Spain: San Miguel de Soyaltepeque (1670), Mandinga (1762), Nuestra Señora de los Morenos de Amapa (1769), and Cuijla.[34]

The relationship between the blacks of the post–San Lorenzo towns and the surrounding property owners and the colonial administration was undoubtedly complicated. Patrick Carroll's archival research is a crucial component in the development of this picture of a New World in flux as related to negotiations with threats of radical blackness. The maroons who would eventually found Mandinga, then later Nuestra Señora de los Morenos de Amapa, had ongoing arrangements with the surrounding communities. He cites depositions leading up to the town's founding that spoke to good mutually beneficial relations between the maroons and a nearby blacksmith, carpenter, and farmer—all mestizos.[35] Carroll goes on to document some instances of productive relations between the maroons and the district's white elite: "The district magistrate, Don Andrés Fernández Otañes[,] . . . refrained from deploying the district militia against them, was a constant source of information, and supposedly even provided them with arms. Fernández Otañes also acted as the runaways' extra-official intermediary with the crown, drafting and forwarding their petitions to the royal audiencia in Mexico City."[36] He notes the blacks reciprocated by, among other ways, acting "as [Fernández Otañes's] agents in the local vanilla-gathering trade[,] serv[ing] as armed guards for the district's cotton warehouses [and] harass[ing] rival merchants who tried to break his monopoly of the area's vanilla trade."[37]

Speaking to the level of comfort the maroons had developed in dealing with the colonial administration, when New Spain was facing a potential military threat from the British navy in 1762, the maroons presented themselves to the viceroy and offered their military assistance in exchange for their freedom. Though the colonial administrators initially granted this arrangement, they reneged on it after the British threat had passed. The maroons, with the continued support of Fernández Otañes, would have to wait seven years before the more enduring treaty forming Nuestra Señora de los Morenos de Amapa could be agreed on.[38]

To demonstrate the rhetorical shifts that the need for the legal recognition of such communities enacted, Jane Landers reads the archive to uncover correspondence regarding a dispute about the destruction of property belonging to San Miguel de Soyaltepeque in July 1695. Of note is not only the San Miguel official's description of himself as a representative of a "República de Negros" in his letter to Viceroy Gaspar de la Cerda, but also the viceroy's reply, which addresses the leaders of San Miguel as members of said *república*.[39]

Attempting to decipher to what extent the above-noted address as a "republic" should be read as only a pragmatic tactic to neutralize an angry and threatening component of society is, for my arguments, ultimately inconsequential. Landers helps us arrive at the most important point: that by whatever means,

> for a brief historical moment in the seventeenth century, in the viceroyalty of New Spain, blacks represented themselves as a republic analogous to that of Spaniards and Indios, and the viceroy and Spain recognized them as such . . . However truncated this republican moment . . . blacks had laid successful claim to the civic values associated with a *república y común*.[40]

I would qualify Landers's use of "blacks" by adding that it was "radical blacks" who were able to represent themselves in this way. Yanga's narrative nonetheless remains especially unique within New Spain, not only for its level of recognized autonomy and sovereignty but also for its psychic and geographic distance from the colonial project. This last point is highlighted by the fact that prior to reaching an accord with the colonial administration for the founding of Nuestra Señora de los Morenos de Amapa, the maroons had to come down from their remote enclave in the hills to a more exposed and accessible location.[41]

If one is in search of an appropriate corollary in the context of the broader hemisphere, one's mind might move to the example of Haiti, commonly referred to as the first black republic in the Western Hemisphere. However, the Republic of Haiti was created as a result of an absolute military defeat in 1804 that France could not even officially (psychically) recognize until more than two decades later (1825), in a treaty that, under the threat of France's regrouped military force, was economically crippling to the young Haitian nation.[42] And while the hemisphere maintains a rich history of smaller-scale revolts and resistances, only a handful of successful maroon communities have been recorded, and even fewer have been negotiated by treaty.

The most recognized examples of such negotiated communities occurred in Guadeloupe, Brazil, Cuba, Jamaica, Ecuador, Panama, Venezuela, Suriname, and Colombia. The largest of these was Quilombo dos Palmares in Brazil.[43] It lasted for almost the entire seventeenth century and at its peak is estimated to have contained within its various compounds around ten thousand escaped enslaved persons.[44] In 1678, they signed a treaty that recognized their autonomy, only to see encroachment on their lands and the resumption of intense and bloody battles less than a year later. Factions developed among the Maroons, and in 1695, Zambi, the leader of the most radical resistance, was captured and decapitated. The public display of his head by the Portuguese marked the end of the largest-known maroon community.[45]

The other maroon population to achieve both great numbers and legal recognition, which must be considered in order to further differentiate San Lorenzo de los Negros, is the Leeward and Windward Maroons of Jamaica.[46] Ironically, this island's principal maroon communities originated when England took the island from Spain in 1655, causing many of the enslaved and their Spanish masters to flee together to the island's Blue Mountains. The majority of the Spanish died off in less than five years, and the maroons remained and flourished, albeit in a state of constant warfare with the British colonial authorities.[47] These nearly century-long hostilities are known as the First Maroon War and would end in two successive treaties in 1739 and 1740.[48] In these negotiations, the Leeward and Windward Maroons were led by the iconic rebels Cudjoe and Quao, respectively. However, unlike in the treaty that developed San Lorenzo de los Negros, the terms were largely dictated by the oppressor and, beyond a freedom to live in a state of legally recognized freedom, were far less favorable than those negotiated by Yanga. In the Jamaican treaties, both maroon groups are addressed as "rebels," and the conditions are framed not as a truce but as "submission," "surrender," and "subjection."[49] Additionally, the Jamaican Maroons had to accept that "four white men" appointed and paid by the British governor "shall constantly live and reside" in each of the maroon towns established by the agreements in order to maintain "correspondence with the inhabitants of this island."[50] These officials were paid a sum of two hundred pounds annually to perform this duty. In order to facilitate the ease of their communication it was specified in Cudjoe's treaty that "Cudjoe, with his people, shall cut, clear, and keep open, large and convenient roads from Trelawny Town to Westmoreland and St. James', and if possible to St. Elizabeth's."[51] And once Cudjoe, Quao, and a small list of other captains under their command had died, it was agreed that the colonial governor would be empowered to select the new leader of the maroon region. In other words, in the timespan of one generation, the colonial administration would gain even more control over the leadership of the maroons.

Furthermore, the granted land was selected by the governor and was of relatively poor quality.[52] In contrast, Yanga and his community, expert farmers by all accounts and extraordinarily familiar with the terrain, were able to settle where they themselves indicated.[53] To add insult to injury, the British named Cudjoe's settlement Trelawny Town to honor Edward Trelawny, the then relatively new British governor of Jamaica.[54]

Another crucial difference is the scope of the Jamaican Maroons' "runaway slave"–catching enterprise. Not only did the newly legitimized communities have to return any future runaway who fled to that community, as was the case with San Lorenzo de los Negros and most such treaties in the New World, this treaty also dictated that they "use their best endeavors to take, kill, suppress, or destroy, either by themselves, or jointly with any other number of men commanded on that service by his excellency the governor or commander in chief for the time being, all [runaways] wheresoever they be throughout this island."[55] Paid as much as ten shillings per returned enslaved person, through monetary incentivizing the region's fiercest proponents of anticolonial domination were being converted into active agents of the state policing mechanism.[56]

Most important for the direction of my argument, however, is that Yanga's narrative has no corollary to the maroon experience in the history of African slavery in the thirteen North American colonies and the United States, where no revolt led to a negotiated enclave articulated within the legal register of the oppressor.[57] This difference brings to the surface a notable incongruence with perceived notions of the formation of black subjects in the New World. The stakes for the differentiation I am offering are particularly high because the unmarked position of the enslaved remains, as it should, the foundation of the most honest and forward-thinking scholarship within black studies. However, it must be said that within the great majority of these formulations the possibility of San Lorenzo de los Negros remains impossible. Some might argue that such a sustained and legally recognized maroon community is such a rare exception that it is not worth adjusting the paradigm. This, clearly, was the view of Orlando Patterson. For while he himself had done substantial work on the maroon communities of his native Jamaica, these communities were largely ignored in his seminal book *Slavery and Social Death* (1982).[58] This gap has essentially been carried forward by all of those reliant on his work. Responding to this, my work discovers its theoretical possibility within this space between being and nonbeing that San Lorenzo de los Negros helps to articulate. In order to do so, the following question must first be addressed: What in the critical practices generated by black studies has compromised its vision of this possibility?

The answer to this question is grounded in how the discourses of black studies have come to know the hemisphere itself. In this context, the picture of an African diaspora located in the Western Hemisphere is greatly influenced by Paul Gilroy's *The Black Atlantic: Modernity and Double Consciousness* (1993), which seeks to destabilize a tendency toward essentialized ideas of ethnicity that circle around "authentic" identity as articulated in mid-1990s cultural studies. Gilroy theorizes the "black Atlantic" as fractal in its transcultural formation from the start, mobilizing the idea of the ship that transported enslaved Africans in the Middle Passage as representative, in its crew and routes (he carries this homophone throughout his work to give a different resonance to the idea of roots), of this messy, transnational ontological moment. While his work remains a valuable signpost, it nonetheless relies on a narrative of slavery that privileges the United States and the Caribbean, and thus the legacy of modernity it inherits is from a Europe that does not, in his imagination, include Spain.[59] I will not rehearse here the critiques that have been directed at Gilroy in the interest of expanding his mapping.[60] It bears repeating that my project does not point to cultural difference in order to undermine the unifying centrality of antiblackness within black studies across the hemisphere. I am drawn to the case of Mexico because the difference it helps to articulate rises to the level of forcing the adjustment of existing epistemological frameworks and, in doing so, provides new language to approach notions of hemispheric blackness. To this end, I will speak directly to Gilroy's silence regarding the role of Spain in the development of slavery in the New World.

While New Spain is not addressed in Gilroy's analysis, Columbus is briefly mentioned twice in ways that are indicative of the blindness his work produces. The mention of a prominent member of Columbus's expedition, Pedro Niño, allows Gilroy to create the umbrella for his work: "Pedro Nino [*sic*] was also an African. The history of the black Atlantic since then . . . provides a means to reexamine the problems of nationality, location, identity and historical memory."[61] In the second instance, Columbus (and the black Atlantic he opens up) appears to help argue a blindness in the "ethical and intellectual heritage of the West" to the teleological connection between the premodern "order of racial difference" and that which would structure modernity: "The figure of Columbus does not appear [from the perspective of the West] to complement the standard pairing of Luther and Copernicus that is implicitly used to mark the limits of this particular understanding of modernity."[62] The next sentence moves quickly to Locke, Descartes, and Rousseau. Then Gilroy is on, in the following paragraph, to Kant and Hegel.

With his move away from the nation, it first becomes impossible for Gilroy to dwell on Pedro Niño as having been born in Spain of African heritage. This would force a broader idea of inheritance that he is arguing for, though in a different register, in the second mention of Columbus. Gilroy thus seems equipped with a time machine that allows him to use Columbus to introduce the always intertwined relation between blackness and discourses of the Enlightenment while moving past historicities that complicate his version of a "fractal structure of the transcultural."[63]

Here it is important to remember that New Spain's participation in the enslavement of Africans peaked during the Iberian Union of 1580–1640, when it was able to take advantage of Portugal's familiarity with the African coastline and maritime expertise. By 1640 there was a rapid decline in the importation of new enslaved Africans. To put New Spain's relation to slavery in the context of England and what would become the United States, Jamestown was founded in 1607, and slavery was first codified in the North American colonies in 1642 (Massachusetts). The institution began to develop in the remaining colonies over the second half of the seventeenth century. England's investment in New World slavery beyond the thirteen North American colonies began in the 1620s with the settling of Saint Kitts (1623) and Barbados (1627). This enterprise would grow as it expanded its empire in the hemisphere with the acquisition of, among the larger territories, Antigua (1632), Bahamas (1647), and Jamaica (1655). To put this in the perspective with which Gilroy is dealing, John Locke, one of the earliest European thinkers whose ideas helped to shape the project of Enlightenment, did not publish his foundational works until 1689 (*Essay concerning Human Understanding*; *Two Treatises of Civil Government*; and *A Letter concerning Toleration*). And while I am clearly aware that the ideas that were conditioning and underwriting what would be articulated as a discourse were developing well before the work of Locke, it is nonetheless imperative to recognize that the infrastructure created by England and what would become the United States developed well after New Spain experiments with slavery, solidifies its system, expands it, and virtually completes the importation of enslaved persons. To place Yanga's rebellion within this same context, it begins one hundred years before the institution of slavery can be said to start its maturation in the United States, and more than two hundred years before Eli Whitney's invention of the cotton gin (1793) and the Haitian Revolution (1804), two events that would greatly shape the investment in and tenor of slavery in the United States.

By using slavery as a tool to reformulate ideas of modernity and the Enlightenment as he does, Gilroy encloses New World slavery within this particular discourse in a way that does not encourage the thinking of epistemological difference (or adjustment) in the case of black subjects at different moments throughout the Americas. As valuable as his coordinates are within the world lines of England (later Great Britain) and the United States, and in later iterations of Latin America, they cannot contain the idea that, at least in the case of early New Spain, what would become "the black" had been prepared for in thought from a different position and well before the ships, or routes/roots in Gilroy's parlance, entered the picture. And though some have in fact contributed to such expansion without disregarding the unifying ontological moment(s) of the Middle Passage, given the weight of Gilroy's text it is not surprising that more than twenty-five years after the work, black studies specifically, and cultural and American studies more generally, in many ways still find themselves similarly constrained.

María Elena Martínez's *Genealogical Fictions* is crucial in undoing this critical misunderstanding. She begins with the same premise sketched out above: "Spanish colonialism began long before the emergence of the politics of nationhood, liberalism, and Enlightenment-inspired universalist concepts of freedom, equality, rights, progress, and citizenship."[64] She then goes on to relate how the philosophy behind and implementation of racial stratification in early New Spain was in large part informed by Spain's practice of *limpieza de sangre*, a purity standard that sought to identify a subject's Jewish or Muslim heritage and privilege those perceived to be *cristianos viejos* (Martínez translates this term as "Old Christians"). Martínez, with the understanding that multiple historicities have played into the development of colonialism, sets about diligently untangling the unique historicity of the Spanish colonial project from uncritical inheritances of colonialism writ large.

Martínez asserts that although one cannot carry ideas of "race" from the Iberian Peninsula to the Spanish colonies in the New World, one has to recognize that a discourse that could handle the burgeoning *idea* of "race" had already begun centuries earlier—first in an attempt to rid the peninsula of the "impure" Jew and later the Muslim. In one of the many examples she offers to support this argument, Martínez notes that free and rather acculturated blacks and mulatos in New Spain were often referred to as *ladinos*, a "term having been used in Spain to refer to Muslims and Jews who mastered the Castilian language or were Hispanicized to the point that they could not be distinguished from authentic Spaniards."[65] Martínez thus prepares us to understand not only the existence of an episteme rooted in the Iberian Peninsula that played a large role in governing the creation of black subjects in the early New World, but also that within this framework of knowledge there existed a predisposition to keeping identity secrets that would transfer to the creation of a racial caste system in New Spain and how the threat of radical blackness was managed.

To help theorize a secreted radical blackness and understand its contours, I turn to the discourse of psychoanalysis—specifically, to the perspectives of Nicolas Abraham and Maria Torok. In their writing and clinical practices, they explored Freud's ideas away from what they felt was an unproductive reliance on the Oedipal complex. It is their thoughts regarding the process of incorporation that are most useful in addressing the following central question: How can we explore, in the register of theories of the mind, New Spain's and the United States' subtly distinct relationships with their openly rebellious enslaved populations?

Abraham and Torok's first task within this terrain is to separate the concept of incorporation from that of introjection. Most simply, they see incorporation as pointing to "a fantasy" and introjection to "a process."[66] This difference is most clearly articulated using the experience of death and mourning; but it is not limited to these experiences, as, for them, secrets or untellable things can evoke a similar process. Introjection, in the case of loss, is the idea of using language and/or action to substitute for the vacancy left by death. It is the idea of healthy mourning—events like wakes are designed to fill this emptiness, this loss, with a communal ritual that involves filling one's mouth (the vacant place) with words or food. Community and the idea of sharing one's thoughts about the loss are important here.

Incorporation, on the other hand, points to an incapacity to healthily mourn and to the absence of a community. This comes about when "the loss is of a type that prohibits being *commun*icated."[67] When there is such a prohibition on language, "the words that cannot be uttered, the scenes that cannot be recalled, the tears that cannot be shed—everything [is] swallowed along with the trauma that led to the loss."[68] All of this remains preserved intact inside what the authors describe as a crypt, as an intrapsychic secret or fantasy.[69] The aim of this fantasy is "to repair—in the realm of the imaginary, of course—the injury that really occurred."[70]

The crypt, for Abraham and Torok, has a secret topography where "the unspeakable words never cease their subversive action."[71] It is described as "an enclave between [the dynamic unconscious and the ego], a kind of artificial unconscious, lodged in the very midst of the ego [where] nothing at all must filter to the outside world [and where] the ego is given the task of cemetery guard."[72] Importantly, the subject who resorts to incorporation is not the hysteric despite some surface similarities. The person who has turned to incorporation is utilizing a preservative repression that protects a preexisting untellable thing, whereas the hysteric utilizes a constitutive or dynamic repression. This constitutive repression manages a desire that is the result of prohibition and manifests itself in the symbolic. This distinction takes the crypt away from oedipal-centered conversations that cannot move beyond prohibition and the return of the repressed and allows for the theorization of the secret, a valuable tool with which to distinguish New Spain's relation to its openly rebellious enslaved Africans.

Merrill Cole's arguments regarding the psychic legacy of Nat Turner—who was perhaps, alongside Denmark Vesey and Gabriel, the most notorious rebellious enslaved person in the United States—offer a typical psychoanalytic approach to the threat of radical blackness in the United States. Furthermore, they will help to launch a discussion of the ways in which psychoanalytic paradigms might be productively employed vis-à-vis the intricacies of blackness in the Mexican context. For Cole, Nat Turner's narrative, *The Confessions of Nat Turner* (1831) as told to Thomas Gray, and the insurrection that it chronicles "takes on the dimension of the Thing[,] . . . the Thing [being] a scrap of mundane existence embodying the horror of the real, which simultaneously structures and undermines the entire symbolic field."[73] Because Turner is ultimately executed, while utter disregard is displayed for his life, the law cannot "efface the marks of insurrection because they constitute its limits."[74] Thus, according to the logic of the death drive, this sets in motion an unconscious compulsion to bring to the surface the repressed thing and the reality of America living in fear of a "repeat performance" of Turner's bloodshed (272). And it is precisely Turner's refusal to compromise with the system—"Turner imagines no new home for former slaves, no reconciliation after fighting, and no pact with the whites"—that creates a doomsday perspective, an ultimate violence, which works to destabilize the system: in this case, the Enlightenment-informed master/slave dialectic.[75]

In the context of Turner's narrative, a burning desire to eradicate the rebel (literally execute him) is what leads to his reappearance as a psychological symptom. There is a fundamental insecurity launched by the prohibition of Turner. The narrative of Yanga also involves violence and insecurity, but the process, as has been made clear, is quite different, as silence, not a violent execution, is the governing principle. The colonial administration struck a deal with this unimaginable threat of blackness. It walled it in and gave it a relatively high degree of autonomy in exchange for it staying within its bounds and no longer announcing itself. The lack of Spanish houses within this territory, no stipulation to maintain the roads (as was the case in Jamaica), and the highly regulated presence of the Spanish bring to mind the rules that Abraham and Torok express for the maintenance of the crypt that restrict filtration by way of a complex, and hidden, psychological security apparatus.

This is, fundamentally, a turn away from a near-absolute reliance, in conversations of blackness that have turned to psychoanalysis in the United States, on a paradigm dominated by ideas of dynamic repression. Many of the theorists using psychoanalysis to study black subjectivity find themselves under this umbrella for good reason, given the contexts of their projects. While deployments of Abraham and Torok in conversations of race have certainly been witnessed, they have tended to be superficial engagements that do not undo ideas of dynamic repression.[76] In terms of managing racial discourses where such secreting is a constituent element, a fuller embrace of their adjustment to the psychoanalytic paradigm is necessary.[77]

I am ultimately interested in noting and responding to future manifestations of permeability emanating from the crypt-like structure I describe. And since I am positing that the evolving Mexican national imaginary can be approached with the framework of psychoanalysis inflected by the theories of Abraham and Torok, I must address a problem that persisted for them when putting their theory in practice in the clinical setting: How does one access the intrapsychic structures of previous generations? In other words: What does the transgenerational untellable thing become? However, before I move to post-Independence generations, and the theoretical problems and opportunities they present, I will dwell briefly on the generation that bridges the before and after of the independent Mexican state.

In 1753, Miguel Hidalgo, a leading figure in the struggle for Mexican independence, was born in the region that would become the state of Guanajuato. In 1771, he had already completed his preparatory education and was in the second year of his studies for a degree in philosophy in Mexico City.[78] In this same year, the Viceroy Carlos Francisco de Croix was continuing to defend the necessity of Nuestra Señora de los Morenos de Amapa, the liberated maroon enclave discussed earlier that was founded just two years before, in 1769.[79] Seven years later—in 1778, the same year Hidalgo would be ordained a priest—Viceroy Antonio María de Bucareli y Ursúa conceded to the advice of his council that "extinguishing [liberated black] towns is a serious business" and creates the anxiety that uncaptured landless blacks might return to the mountains.[80] This is evidence that the strategy of encrypting the most radical of the formerly enslaved, and the silent ex-*commun*ication it requires, persists in New Spain at the dawn of Mexico's independence, nearly two centuries after Yanga's treaty.

As is of no surprise, the mechanisms of slavery specifically (and the accouterments necessary to manage radical possibilities) and racial stratification more generally were thus by no means an afterthought in the revolutionary era. These constants of the colony were looked on with shame by a generation of revolutionaries who would become the forefathers of the new Mexican nation. Thus, a break from this past, not just the institution of slavery but also the idea of racial distinction, was a crucial aspect of their rhetorical separation from Spain. This rhetorical shift can be traced to the very beginning of the revolution when Miguel Hidalgo most famously gives the urgent call for the immediate manumission of the enslaved. This language is contained in his decree of December 6, 1810, given less than three months after his September 16 pronouncement (El Grito de Dolores), which is heralded as the symbolic beginning of the Mexican War of Independence and celebrated as Mexican Independence Day: "Que todos los dueños de esclavos deberán darles la libertad, dentro de término de diez días, so pena de muerte, la que se le aplicará por transgresión de artículo" (All slaveholders must free their slaves within a term of ten days. Failure to do so will merit capital punishment).[81] As Patrick Carroll reminds us, and as was the case in the United States, this call for emancipation had significant political advantages: "When Hidalgo issued the call for Independence, his movement received little support from the Veracruz slaves. However, as the news spread of Hidalgo's emancipation proclamation . . . slaves began to enlist in the revolutionary ranks. By the following year they were deserting their masters in droves."[82] According to Carroll, the enslaved from this region were being organized "into a single fighting force which saw action in most of the major engagements taking place along the Gulf Coast."[83]

Hidalgo was executed on July 27, 1811. José María Morelos, who would eventually succeed Hidalgo as the principal leader of the insurgency, includes a prohibition of slavery and the aforementioned sistema de castas two years later in his 1813 utopian vision of the Mexican state, "Sentimientos de la nación" ("Sentiments of the Nation"): "Que la esclavitud se proscriba para siempre y lo mismo la distinción de castas, quedando todos iguales, y sólo distinguirá a un americano de otro el vicio y la virtud" (Let slavery and the distinction of *castas* be banned forever, leaving all equal. Vice and virtue will be all that will distinguish one American from another).[84] Unlike the Hidalgo decree, which although written in a future tense demarcates clearly a fixed time period, Morelos's text is written in the subjunctive and, interestingly, uses the word *proscribir* rather than, say, *prohibir* (prohibit) or *abolir* (abolish). *Proscribir* contains the idea of prohibition but also the idea of casting away in a spatial sense, as this verb comes from the Latin *proscribere* (*pro-*, "up-front"; *scribere*, "to write") and was used in a legal sense to announce in writing those who had been outlawed.[85] Thus, the Morelos decree carries within its command a demand to both pronounce and disappear. It is rhetorically comparable to the famous words the Cuban intellectual José Martí would pen almost a full century later in *Nuestra América* (1891): "No hay odio de razas porque no hay razas" (There is no racism because there are no races). It is a utopian vanishing act that evacuates all discourse as it relates to race and blackness.[86]

In other words, Hidalgo and Morelos announce a shift in the borders that contain blackness that is read (or unread) as impossible within the national psychological apparatus. Where in the colonial period uncapitulating rebels among the enslaved marked this limit, the new Mexican state desired, albeit in a deceptively violent utopian register, for all blackness to be so contained. This maneuver is almost complete when in 1824 the first federal constitution of Mexico is produced and there is no language referring to the banishment of either slavery or the sistema de castas.[87] Though not appearing as an amendment to the constitution, slavery would have to be abolished by presidential decree two more times: first by Guadalupe Victoria in 1825 and then again in 1829 by the aforementioned Vicente Guerrero, though many of the enslaved only started to come out of seclusion after this last decree by Guerrero.[88]

A mention of slavery returns in the rewritten 1857 constitution in two instances:

> En la República todos nacen libres. Los esclavos que pisen el territorio nacional recobran, por ese solo hecho, su libertad, y tienen derecho á la protección de las leyes.
>
> (In the Republic, all citizens are born free. Slaves who enter from other nations immediately recover their liberty and have the right to the protection of the Republic's laws.)[89]

> Nunca se celebrarán tratados para la extradición de reos políticos, ni para la de aquellos delincuentes del orden común que hayan tenido en el país en donde cometieron el delito la condición de esclavos; ni convenios ó tratados en virtud de los que se alteren las garantías y derechos que esta Constitución otorga al hombre y al ciudadano.
>
> (Never will treaties for the extradition of political prisoners be honored, nor for the extradition of those delinquents of the common order that in the country where they committed the crime they had the condition of slavery; nor agreements or treaties made in which the guaranties and rights that this Constitution grants to the man and the citizen are altered.)[90]

As all other nearby nations had abolished slavery at this point, both of these references are directed principally at the United States and the New World colonies of the old Spanish Empire (Cuba and Puerto Rico). This constitutional editing process that privileges erasure over a permanent record is in stark contrast to the United States, whose original constitution can only be amended. Mexico takes full advantage of the psychic gap this allows in relation to slavery to take the moral high ground, especially in 1857, a time when there was great insecurity about the future of the Mexican state and the growing potential for hemispheric dominance by the United States.[91] This potential is thanks in large part to the institution of slavery, which the amnesic language of the first revised Mexican federal constitution conveniently delegitimizes.

Mexico's nineteenth-century constitutional documents, while disguised in a utopian embrace of liberalism, belie the very real consequences of the rhetorical violence proffered by the nation's founders. Claudio Lomnitz-Adler articulates this quite clearly:

> During the nineteenth century, Mexican elites—like their counterparts in many other Latin American countries—were in a double bind; they could not construct an image of Mexicanness that was fashioned on their own culture because that culture was European, and so the whole argument for sovereignty from European powers was undermined. On the other hand, if they reached very directly toward popular culture, they ran the risk of being excluded from the nation that they were so intricately engaged in forging.[92]

For Lomnitz-Adler, although there was a symbolic discarding of certain aspects of the colonial racial ideology, others were "simply revamped, especially those that referred to the brutishness of Indians and, generally, to the inferiority of dark skin."[93] The move away from the elaborate sistema de castas led to those formerly known as castas being "blurred into a single mass which came to be known racially as mestizos," and a continued "discrimination against Indians and a particularly flagrant valorization of whiteness."[94]

In the nineteenth century, blackness is located beyond the borders of the contemporary Mexican state, whether in a geographic beyond, in the case of the United States, or a temporal beyond, as is seen even in Riva Palacio's liberal retelling of Yanga's narrative in *Treinta y tres negros*, which nonetheless contains blackness and racial distinction in the colonial past. For the nascent state's fragile imagination of itself, the idea of a present-day reality being structured by supposedly outmoded racial distinctions was an embarrassment. The presence of blackness, the most extreme point of this register, is experienced as particularly shameful.

It is Esther Rashkin, in her deployment of Abraham and Torok, who reminds us that "it was not the concept per se of an event but the fact that an individual lived it intrapsychically as shameful, humiliating and thus potentially annihilating that made the event 'traumatic' and that compelled the individual, consciously or more often unconsciously, to envelop it in silence and render it 'unspeakable.' "[95] Per this line of thought, it is the utopian declarations, first of Hidalgo then of Morelos, which produce an impossible black subject. Where in the colonial period the threat of radical blackness helped to structure this gap in the psyche, the birth of the new nation sees this gap envelop the entire spectrum of blackness.

To address the idea of what these untellable things become when carried across generations, Abraham and Torok mobilize the idea of the transgenerational phantom as "a formation of the unconscious that has never been conscious [that] passes—in a way yet to be determined—from the parent's unconscious into the child's."[96] Following their logic of the individual crypt, "the phantom's periodic and compulsive return lies beyond the scope of symptom formation in the sense of a return of the repressed [and] indicates the effects, on the descendants, of something that had inflicted narcissistic injury or even catastrophe on the parents."[97] Freud had attempted to think through the idea of an "archaic heritage" in his work and had lightly entertained the idea of subconscious communication between two people.[98] This is, of course, advanced significantly in Jung's notion of the collective unconscious, which Frantz Fanon would further expand on in his arguments for a racialized, sociogenic unconscious in *Black Skin, White Masks* (1952). However, Abraham and Torok's notion of the secret, which they explored both clinically and theoretically, is unique in its ability to theorize the particular psychic gap being discussed here.

As Rashkin points out, the key to Abraham and Torok's investigations is the fact that the child who inherits such secret psychic matter is "unaware that she or he carries another's secret, and that there is even someone else with a secret."[99] More importantly, "the child is also unaware that she or he functions as a guardian who stands vigil, intrapsychically, to insure the absolute inviolability of the secret and hence the integrity of the parent and the family, who would otherwise be assailed by the secret's exposure."[100] In Abraham and Torok's clinical experience, it is precisely this "horror at violating a parent's or family's secret" that makes for the most difficult approach when a transgenerational phantom is involved.[101] This is especially true when such an intrapsychic uncovering runs "the risk of undermining the fictitious yet necessary integrity of the parental figure in question."[102]

In Abraham and Torok's push toward "curing" an imbalanced psychic state caused by a transgenerational phantom in their clinical environment, they turn toward an idiom of exorcism. The process of bringing this haunting element out centers on laying bare, for the patient, the absolute distinction between the investments of the phantom and the investments of the host. Nicholas Abraham, in his early work on this subject, theorizes that "the phantom will vanish only when its radically heterogeneous nature with respect to the subject is recognized, a subject to whom it *at no time has any direct reference*."[103] He underlines this point as his argument continues: "In no way can the subject relate to the phantom as his or her own repressed experience."[104] Only when the patient feels that this presence does not "endanger their own topography" are they able to "eject [this] bizarre stranger."[105] Maria Torok echoes this sentiment in her own work, claiming that "the phantom is alien to the subject who harbors it."[106]

However, in aligning the transgenerational phantom with the Mexican national psychological apparatus, and other national psychological apparatuses that depend on similar secrets more generally, a slight revision in this distinction between the bizarre stranger of a supposedly bygone period and the psychic typography of the contemporary moment must be forced. In the case of Mexico, there is no simple ejection without great harm to the subject (the imagined nation), because with each passing generation this phantom becomes at the same time more unknowable and more imbricated in the topography of the imagined nation's psyche. In other words, the contemporary generation who unknowingly keeps secret this relationship to blackness is in fact invested in the maintenance of this secrecy in a similar way to previous generations. Undermining this secreting would not only undermine a parent or ancestor but would also upend the idea of the nation that gives the present-day subject meaning. Thus, the unconscious investment in the secrecy crucial to this intrapsychic construction is maintained across generations.

My embrace of the idea of a transgenerational crypt-like structure within a national psychological apparatus has been provisional. This is because the field of language deployed by Abraham and Torok to describe the term on which it rests is itself plagued by what I feel is an impeding reliance on the metaphor of the cemetery and the attending metaphors that such a reliance demands. In this context, while there remains, underground, the possibility of decay and decomposition, these processes can themselves be mapped and understood, and an idea of wholeness reproduced. And even the more ephemeral metaphors (the phantom, haunting) still gesture toward embodiment.

Though not in the register of Freudian repression, theirs ultimately remains an idiom of discoverability. And many of the recent conversations on the presence of blacks within the bounds of the Mexican nation are structured by a similar language. For a popular example, the episode from Henry Louis Gates's 2011 series of documentaries (Black in Latin America) about Mexico comes with the subtitle "The Black Grandma in the Closet"; and Christine Arce's important academic contribution, *México's Nobodies: The Cultural Legacy of the Soldadera and Afro-Mexican Women* (2017), organizes the second half of her book around "The Blacks in the Closet."[107] In other words, there is an alignment with Abraham and Torok's practice grounded in the possibility of the discovery of, or at least an awareness of, the existence of once-whole objects.

Abraham and Torok are themselves helpful in effecting a separation from a description of their crypt in the terms of a metapsychological concept of Reality: "that which *is*, all the more so since it must not be known; in short, Reality is defined as a *secret* . . . and the metapsychological concept of Reality refers to the place, in the psychic apparatus, where the secret is."[108] Thus, before the metaphor of the cemetery is attached, this "place" can be understood as a gap within the psychic apparatus—and for the purposes of my work, as a transgenerational intrapsychic gap. Because, as discussed above, Abraham and Torok understand their phantom and the subject it haunts as utterly distinct, and because they are working within a clinical setting grounded in helping the subject, their approach is oriented toward a cure: "How can the phantom be weakened so as to make it restore the unhappy subjects' own speech . . . that had been victimized by the haunting?"[109] However, because of my acknowledgment of the irrevocably interwoven nature of hegemonic culture,[110] and my understanding in the context of national psychological apparatuses of the shared investment of the phantom and the subject articulated in this chapter, as my argument continues I will work to address the following question: How can what emanates or escapes from this transgenerational intrapsychic gap be made visible in order to activate anxieties that give a slight sense of the contours of the unthinkable intrapsychic gap itself? To begin an answer, I must first characterize the nature of what I contend are incoherent emanations. To do so, I will next examine such emanations in the context of twentieth-century Mexican culture.

Chapter 2

✦

On Apparent Emanations

> What emanates are not the dead, but the indecipherable matter from gaps left within us by the secrets of others.
>
> —Author unknown

> Debo a la conjunción de un espejo y de una enciclopedia el descubrimiento de Uqbar.
>
> —Jorge Luis Borges, "Tlön, Uqbar, Orbis Tertius"

In chapter 1, a reading of the formation of San Lorenzo de los Negros in New Spain led to the proposal of the existence of a transgenerational gap within Mexico's national psychological apparatus where, among other secrets, the depth and intricate nature of its Afro-descendant heritage, a structuring element of its collective psyche, has been vanished. Here I turn to the twentieth century to examine how portions of the archive have been read and assembled in relation to this now radical blackness. My analysis is framed initially by readings of Carlos de Sigüenza y Góngora's eyewitness account of the 1692 rebellion in Mexico City. I am interested in how emanations of a secreted blackness permeate the barrier of this intrapsychic gap—or, more precisely, the manner in which they compromise it.

The reorganization of the Mexican state at the turn of the twentieth century forced a psychic adjustment that endangered the barrier of this gap in relation to an idea of blackness. Despite the relatively stable national economy that lasted for all but four years between 1877 and 1911 and thus largely characterized the extended rule of Porfirio Díaz, reaction to great societal imbalance and disproportionate economic hardship in certain regions threatened the viability of the state. In the course of the Mexican Revolution of the early twentieth century, the creole political elites adopted a pragmatic strategy aimed at more successfully incorporating the masses in their political agenda in order to create a more socially stable state.[1] To this end, the Mexican Revolution would settle on the mestizo as the nation's symbolic figurehead in a move that, as Claudio Lomnitz-Adler writes, "resolved many of the old nationalism's problems, identified the political elite with 'the people,' and provided an ideological platform for a protectionist economy and strong state."[2]

Like the previous symbolism announcing the disappearance of racial distinction, this new mestizo face is visualized in the new federal constitution of 1917. Both symbols are understood here as being generated and supported by the same utopianism described in chapter 1. The language used to evoke these symbols, however, differs greatly. While in the 1824 and 1857 constitutions there are no uses of the words *raza* (race), *cultura* (culture), or *indígena* (indigenous), the 1917 document has evolved over the course of the last hundred years to be peppered with all of these terms. Most importantly, there are special provisions to protect and sustain indigenous elements of society. In the first article of the first chapter of the constitution, the new Mexico is announced as a nation that "tiene una composición pluricultural" (has a pluricultural composition). In the public embrace of the mixed nature of this new identity, there is an urgent need to contain the potential emergence of the black portion of Mexico's heterogenic identity, those formerly banished remnants from a century before.

José Vasconcelos addresses this directly in his 1925 essay *La raza cósmica*. Though Vasconcelos has fallen out of favor within the imagined pantheon of significant figures of the twentieth century, and is seen almost as an embarrassment by some, he was extraordinarily influential as Mexico began the delicate psychic process of reimagining itself after the Mexican Revolution. As minister of public education in the administration of Álvaro Obregón, for example, Vasconcelos put a great deal of focus and capital into the rediscovery of the beauty of Mexico's indigenous population. He famously sent Diego Rivera to the south of Mexico, a trip that fundamentally shaped Rivera as an artist, and, more importantly, encouraged what would become a large aspect of the visual record of Mexico's new self.[3] Although his run for the presidency in 1929 was unsuccessful, he ended up serving in various prominent roles in Mexico's state-sponsored cultural and educational sectors.

According to Vasconcelos, strength was to be found in Mexico's history of racial mixing, and this placed the nation's citizens as central agents, the avant-garde, in the coming of a quite mystical aesthetic revolution. How the various racial elements were to be blended into this new race—*la raza final*—is expressed in its clearest language here:

> Los tipos bajos de la especie serán absorbidos por el tipo superior. De esta suerte podría redimirse, por ejemplo, el negro, y poco a poco, por extinción voluntaria, las estirpes más feas irán cediendo el paso a las más hermosas. Las razas inferiores, al educarse, se harían menos prolíficas, y las [*sic*] mejores especímenes irán ascendiendo en una escala de mejoramiento étnico, cuyo tipo máximo no es precisamente el blanco, sino esa nueva raza a la que el mismo blanco tendrá que aspirar con el objeto de conquistar la síntesis. El indio, por medio

> del injerto en la raza afín, daría el salto de los millares de años que median de la Atlántida a nuestra época, y en unas cuantas décadas de eugenesia estética podría desaparecer el negro.
>
> (The lower types of the species will be absorbed by the superior type. In this manner, for example, the Black could be redeemed, and step by step, by voluntary extinction, the uglier stocks will give way to the more handsome. Inferior races, upon being educated, would become less prolific, and the better specimens would go on ascending a scale of ethnic improvement, whose maximum type is not precisely the White, but that new race to which the White himself will have to aspire with the object of conquering the synthesis. The Indian, by grafting onto the related race, would take the jump of millions of years that separate Atlantis from our times, and in a few decades of aesthetic eugenics, the Black may disappear.)[4]

In this oft-quoted passage, absorption, voluntary extinction, aesthetic eugenics, and a disappearing blackness all bespeak the relation between Vasconcelos's symbolic embrace of a mestizo cosmic race and discourses of whitening. Within this matrix, blackness is nevertheless something to be managed in 1925. However, the language of Vasconcelos, which predicts the disappearance of this remaining trace, this problem, "en unas cuantas décadas," is more than prophetic: it was only twenty-five years later that Octavio Paz confirmed the apparent absence of Afro-descendant elements from conversations of Mexican identity.

Octavio Paz's 1950 collection of essays *El laberinto de la soledad* is a seminal work in the discourse of *mexicanidad* (Mexicanness) that would help to solidify the cosmic musings of Vasconcelos into what Carrie Chorba describes as "a new coherent, and cohesive discourse that would effectively cement its populace as citizens of a modern nation."[5] In its second essay, "Máscaras mexicanas," Paz opens with the following sentence: "Viejo o adolescente, criollo o mestizo, general, obrero o licenciado, el mexicano se me aparece como un ser que se encierra y se preserva" (The Mexican, whether young or old, *criollo* or mestizo, general or laborer or lawyer, seems to me to be a person who shuts himself away to protect himself).[6] The vulnerable barrier that Vasconcelos drew attention to has been reinforced: to be included as Mexican, you must be either of pure Spanish blood or a mix of indigenous and Spanish blood.

Paz's intellectual endeavor in regard to the articulation of the elusive contours of Mexican identity, the labyrinth, was revisited twenty years later in his 1970 *Posdata* (translated as *The Other Mexico* in 1972). In large part, this essay responds to the events of 1968 in Mexico, which culminated with the gunning down and imprisonment of student and other protestors by government forces just before the country was to host the Olympic Games. In light of the fractures exposed by this violent suppression of a popular movement, he sees a need to add further nuance to the idea of *mexicanidad*:

> La mexicanidad no es sino otro ejemplar, una variación más, de esa cambiante idéntica criatura plural una que cada uno es todos somos ninguno. El hombre/los hombres: perpetua oscilación . . . En aquella época [de *El laberinto*] no me interesaba la definición de lo mexicano sino, *como ahora*, la crítica: esa actividad que consiste, tanto o más que en conocernos, en liberarnos. La crítica despliega una posibilidad de libertad y así es una invitación a la acción.[7]
>
> (Mexican-ness is no more than another example, another variety, of that changing, identical, single, plural creature that each is, all are, none is. Man/men: perpetual oscillation . . . But while we live we can escape neither masks nor nouns and pronouns: we are inseparable from our fictions, our features. We are condemned to invent a mask and to discover afterward that the mask is our true visage . . . In those days [of *El laberinto*] I was not interested in a definition of Mexican-ness but rather, *as now*, in criticism: the activity which consists not only in knowing ourselves but, just as much or more, in freeing ourselves. Criticism unfolds the possibility of freedom and is thus an invitation to action.)[8]

The idea of an "other Mexico" encourages Paz, and his readers, to be aware of this heterogenic excess, this other that is both within and without, in order to be prepared for a generative (and necessary) criticism and self-reflection. When pressed to define such an imprecise idea, he does so by describing it as a "realidad gaseosa que forman las creencias, fragmentos de creencias, imágenes y conceptos que la historia deposita en el subsuelo de la psiquis social, esa cueva o sótano en continua somnolencia y, asimismo, en perpetua fermentación" (gaseous reality formed by the beliefs, fragments of beliefs, images, and concepts which history deposits in the subsoil of the social psyche, that cave or cellar in continuous somnolence and likewise in perpetual fermentation).[9]

Here Paz is admittedly relying on Freud's ideas of the subconscious in order to explain this "pasado [que] reaparece porque es un presente oculto" (past [that] reappears because it is a hidden present).[10] While his description of hidden elements does leave room for the gaseous appearance of fragments that might align with the articulation of Mexico's transgenerational intrapsychic gap I have put forward, his turn to the subsoil is primarily framed as an archaeological expedition: "El mexicano no es una esencia sino una historia" (The Mexican is not an essence but a history).[11] Furthermore, a great irony lies in the fact that in this tract seeking to uncover Mexico's repressed "invisible history" there is no conscious recognition of Paz's replicating this disappearing maneuver in relation to Afro-descendant elements deposited in that "subsoil" of the Mexican psyche.[12] Instead, in the final paragraphs of *Posdata* we see a familiar and restrictive cementing: "Los verdaderos herederos de los asesinos del mundo prehispánico no son los peninsulares sino nosotros, los mexicanos que hablamos castellano, seamos criollos, mestizos o indios" (The true heirs of the pre-Columbian world are not the peninsular Spaniards but ourselves, we Mexicans who speak Spanish, whether we are Creoles, mestizos, or Indians).[13]

Remaking Paz's own concept of the labyrinth, Lomnitz-Adler clearly articulates how by remaining within a discourse of the nation, Paz and others have managed to trap themselves:

> In short, most of the writers who have meditated on and criticized Mexican national culture have done so without resolving the theoretical obstacles that block our comprehension of the very nature of "national culture." The political importance of national culture and the difficulty in describing national culture in any terms other than the terms of nationalism has generated a circular dialect, a vicious circle that is built on the tensions that occur between the maze of social relations that exist within the national space and the ideologies regarding a common identity, a shared sense of the past, and a unified gaze toward the future. I call this complex of issues the labyrinth.[14]

Roger Bartra, in *The Cage of Melancholy: Identity and Metamorphosis in the Mexican Culture*, similarly identifies the hegemonic culture as an accumulation of "mythological expressions" that produce a metadiscourse that has become "the common drinking trough in which the thirst for identity is quenched; it is the source of the myths that not only give *unity* to the nation, but also render it different from any other."[15] Bartra thus claims that "studies on Mexicanness constitute an expression of the dominant culture [and, as such,] this hegemonic political culture is *bound* by the set of imaginary power-networks that define socially accepted forms of subjectivity and that are customarily considered as the fullest expression of national culture."[16] In other words, both Lomnitz-Adler and Bartra identify the hegemonic project as particularly brilliant in its ability to enlist not only its primary stakeholders (the creole elite) to carry the project forward, but more importantly those with nothing to gain and often much to lose who nonetheless desire to imagine themselves as articulated within the matrix of a Mexican identity.

Thus, we can see how Paz's meditations, regardless of their progressive intent, were doomed to be bracketed by and in service of the very hegemonic political culture they seek to disrupt. Whether using the metaphor of the labyrinth or the cage, these thoughts trace the barrier or limit of the hegemonic political culture, the reverse side of which limits the transgenerational intrapsychic gap. Thus, "the definition of the 'Mexican'" is an articulation of this barrier, "a description of how he or she is dominated and, above all, how exploitation is legitimized."[17] But this domination is not total. There are gaps through which evidence of the underlying heterogeneity, however incomplete and fleeting, emerge. We get an example of such an emergence in Paz's own work. In 1971, Elena Poniatowska published *La noche de Tlateloco*, which grapples with the aforementioned events of 1968 that Paz's *Posdata* attempted to speak to. Poniatowska's effort is essentially a collection of interviews, slogans, and photos organized and edited to leave a record of the events that, like those in France and other locales around the world in the same year, lasted months and were extraordinarily complex in their manifestations and reasons for being. In 1975, Poniatowska's work was published in English as *Massacre in Mexico*, and Octavio Paz was charged with introducing an English-reading public to the nuances of this crisis.

Paz contends in this introduction that he "has always considered it necessary to look back to our colonial history in order to have even a partial understanding of the Mexico of today."[18] He continues: "By so doing, we will not, of course, find the answer to all of our questions. But since the world of New Spain is the immediate antecedent of the world we live in today, our colonial past enables us to establish certain parallels with our present."[19] Immediately following this particular quote, he specifically notes the similarities between the events of 1968 and those of June 8, 1692, when a rebellion shook the ruling elite in Mexico City. In this comparison, Paz relies heavily on the eyewitness account of Carlos de Sigüenza y Góngora, a scientist, historian, and member of the creole elite. From Paz's perspective, this work of Sigüenza, which comes in the form of an extensive letter written to the Spanish Admiral Don Andrés de Pez, is as "impressive as Elena Poniatowska's."[20]

While the 1692 rebellion is most often attributed to a corn shortage, the constellation of causes has been long discussed within the colonial record and the academic scholarship interested in interpreting that record. Tracing both the wheat and maize harvests, Douglas Cope does an excellent job of asserting that despite whatever else was likely to have been going on socially, food shortage was palpable and definitely among the pressures. Nonetheless, how much of this can be laid at the feet of poor yield resulting from the previous year's floods and market manipulation remains undetermined. Firsthand accounts paint contradicting perspectives regarding culpability for the rebellion, as do the court proceedings held by the viceroy in the months that followed. The testimonies of the elite tend toward a conspiracy led by the city's indigenous population, but this has been challenged by those who claim this perspective was only developed as pretense to change the physical structure of the city to further contain this same population. Some blame the network of bars serving *pulque*, the intoxicating drink made from fermented agave. Still others blame the blacks and mulatos who live among the indigenous for compromising their natural morals.[21] Nonetheless, this significant event energizes the populace and forces self-reflection among the elite, making it an appropriate corollary to the events of 1968.

As is to be expected, the great majority of the surviving archive related to the events of June 8, 1692, is dominated by the creole elite. In all of this discourse, Carlos de Sigüenza y Góngora certainly looms larger than the rest. Anna More's *Baroque Sovereignty: Carlos de Sigüenza y Góngora and the Creole Archive of Colonial Mexico* puts his letter and the rest of his known life's work in proper perspective. She adeptly uses Sigüenza's output to connect to and trace the development of a cohesive creole political discourse that relied on a selective incorporation and refashioning of the existing pre-Columbian archive that allowed creoles to "invent a deep history extending beyond the Spanish conquest."[22] This "turn to history [was] as an archive rather than a chronological narrative" and had nothing to do with establishing "esoteric dissent" but rather "a local authority and tradition following the fragmentation of indigenous communities and the demise of evangelical utopianism."[23] For More, Sigüenza's letter aligns with this evolving creole project, which seeks to dominate the present while recalling an essentially fictionalized and self-serving past.

More emphasizes that this discourse should not be viewed merely as part of the smooth teleology leading from seventeenth-century creole life to the battles for Mexican independence that would take place over a century later. Alternatively, More describes the archive produced in the second half of the seventeenth century not as concerned with hatching the visions that would undermine Spanish authority, but as quite narrowly focused on responding to the local insecurity felt because of the developing crisis of Spanish imperial rule in Europe. This decline in influence and power began with the restoration of self-rule by Portugal in 1640 and was punctuated by the death of heirless Charles II in 1700, which ended the Hapsburg dynasty in Spain and marked the clear beginning of a new geopolitical reality. Sigüenza's life span (1645–1700) almost exactly traces this decline. This fact, combined with his intimate relationship with the Crown in both official and unofficial capacities, make him the perfect centerpiece to More's project, and yet an awkward ally to Paz's work that seeks to extend his ideas regarding an "other Mexico."

In other words, even though it does not signal a rebellion from Spain just yet, this evolving discourse is the foundation of a creole ideology of crisis management in relation to its racial others that would evolve through the eighteenth century only to be cast away to serve as part of the invisible structuring force of Mexico's national psychological apparatus. I will quote at length the most substantial portion of the Sigüenza letter that Paz invokes, as it is central to this inheritance. It is a description of the rebellion and its participants as hostilities are just beginning to erupt. Prior to this quotation in Sigüenza's account, an indigenous woman demanding answers from the Spanish authorities regarding the corn shortage has been killed. She is then carried through the streets by the protestors. For those who blame a premeditated indigenous conspiracy, this woman is alive and only playing dead to incite the rebellion. In either case,

> hordes of men came rushing down the street where I was standing (and down all the others that led into the public squares). The Spaniards had unsheathed their swords, but they stopped in their tracks for the same reason that kept me standing there as though rooted to the spot: because the blacks, the mulattos, and all the raggle-taggle plebes were shouting: "Death to the Viceroy and all his henchman!" And the Indians: "Death to the Spaniards who are eating up our corn!" And exhorting each other to bravely enter the fray, since there was no Cortez [*sic*] on the scene this time to conquer them, they stormed into the plaza to join the others and throw rocks.[24]

Though not quoted in Paz, Sigüenza would again refer to the commoners' diversity in similar language throughout the document. These accountings of the gathered crowds are by no means unusual. Though the records tracking punishments doled out by the court and those tracking deaths during the rebellion show an indigenous majority, the racial diversity that Sigüenza describes is present in numbers too significant to ignore.[25] However, despite these accounts encouraging a racially diverse view of the uprising and of New Spain, Paz, in the same paragraph that contains the above noted quotation, chooses to summarize the events as follows: "In 1692 a shortage of corn caused an uprising among the common people—Indians, mestizos, and even impoverished creoles—and for the first time in its colonial history Mexico City was the scene of serious disturbances as the poorer classes rioted in the streets."[26] The blacks and mulatos of Sigüenza's description who emerge in Paz's text go unnoticed in relation to his larger project which uses this colonial history to help articulate Mexico's "other half, its hidden face: an Indian, mestizo face, an angry blood-spattered face."[27]

Sigüenza's work, and this letter in particular, arrive to the twentieth century, and to Paz, through the same imaginative archival work that Sigüenza himself obsessed over. The American literary historian Irving Leonard's participation in this process is crucial. His interest in the seventeenth-century creole intellectual began with his work as a graduate student at the University of California, Berkeley, which culminated in the book *Don Carlos de Sigüenza y Góngora: A Mexican Savant of the Seventeenth Century* (1929) and continued throughout his career with scholarly texts that highlight the Mexican figure's interest in, among other things, fiction, philosophy, astronomy, and geography. The aforementioned letter to the Admiral Andrés de Pez was excavated from the archive by Leonard's dissertation adviser and published (in English) as an appendix to Leonard's 1929 book.

Given Leonard's significant role in raising the profile of Sigüenza both in Mexico and abroad, it is no surprise that he was given the task of introducing

Seis obras (1984), an offering that includes the author's essential writings. Leonard chooses to begin the publication with an epigraph quoting none other than Octavio Paz: "Siempre lo he dado por imprescindible echar un vistazo a nuestra herencia colonial para conseguir siquiera una comprensión parcial del México de hoy" (I have always considered it necessary to look back to our colonial history in order to have even a partial understanding of the Mexico of today).[28] Although Leonard does not clarify which Paz text this quote comes from, it is itself, in an odd symmetry, a translation of a portion of Paz's work in the foreword to Elena Poniatowska's book that I quoted earlier.

Interestingly, the evolution of the baring of racially diverse conversations as they are related to discussions of Mexican identity in the twentieth century is echoed in the publication and citation history of the Sigüenza letter that Paz's work both relies on and negates. As was mentioned above, the letter was originally included in the appendix to Leonard's 1929 volume on Sigüenza and titled "Letter of Don Carlos de Sigüenza y Góngora to Admiral Pez Recounting the Incidents of the Corn Riot in Mexico City, June 8, 1692." In 1932 Leonard published this letter separately and in the original Spanish as *Alboroto y motín de México, del 8 de junio 1692: Relación de Don Carlos de Sigüenza y Góngora en una carta dirigida al Almirante Don Andrés de Pez*. Then, in 1940, the letter was published in a modernized Spanish in *Relaciones históricas*, a collection edited by Manuel Romero de Terreros. Here it bore the abbreviated title "Alboroto y motín de México, del 8 de junio 1692." Leonard, in a review of another Sigüenza collection for the *Hispanic American Historical Review* in 1946, references the 1932 publication of this letter by the same abbreviated title used by Romero de Terreros.

However, in both a note and in the bibliography of Leonard's 1959 *Baroque Times in Old Mexico: Seventeenth-Century Persons, Places, and Practices*, his own 1932 publication of the letter was retroactively retitled adding the descriptor "de los indios" (of the Indians): *Alboroto y motín de los indios de México del 8 de Junio de 1692*.[29] And in 1984, when Sigüenza's work was collected in the volume *Seis obras*, the letter abbreviated this title in a way that further solidified the event as an indigenous uprising: "Alboroto y motín de los indios de México."[30] In that same year, a Spanish translation of Leonard's 1929 book was published in Mexico, and the letter was again given this new title. In an interview with Leonard in 1983, as the manuscripts for these two projects were being completed, he was asked how he chose Sigüenza for his dissertation work, and he responded: "[My adviser] put me on to that. He had an original manuscript that I published later as *Alboroto y motín de los indios de México*."[31] In much of the contemporary scholarship that manages Sigüenza in very productive ways, this re-membering is carried forward and solidified, as bibliographic references to the 1932 publication often include the incorrect title.[32] And while the original letter was not titled for publication by Sigüenza, it is nonetheless telling to trace the evolution of its naming as its present form works to foreclose the much richer racial makeup of the events it describes.

An examination of the reproduction of another portion of the original letter presents the meanderings of a similar foreclosure. In the following segment, Sigüenza is describing for the admiral the nature of the gathering mob. Leonard's original 1929 version (an English translation) is vastly different than the standalone version of the letter in the original Spanish that he published in 1932:

> It is composed of Indians, Creoles, *bozales* from various nations, *chinos*, mulattos, *moriscos*, mestizos, *zambaigos* (Indian and *chinos* half-breeds), lobos (half-breeds), and Spaniards as well who, in declaring themselves "saramullos" (which is the same as knaves, rascals, and cape-snatchers) and in falling away from their allegience, are the worst of them all in such a vile rabble.[33]

> Componerse de Indios, de negros Criollos y Vosales de diferentes Naciones, de Chinos, de Mulattos, de moriscos, de mestissos, de Sambaigos, de lobos y tambien de españoles que, en declarandosse Saramullos (que es lo mismo que pícaros, Chulos y arreuata Capas) y degenerando de sus obligaciones, Son los peores entre tan Ruin Canalla.[34]

Leonard's 1929 translation comes with no glossary, so *bozales* and *moriscos*, not clarified parenthetically, go unregistered. *Bozales* refers to African-born blacks and *moriscos* to light-skinned mulatos.[35] *Chinos*, named for the appearance of curly hair, demarcate a mixture of mulato and indigenous. In his parenthetical clarification of *zambaigos*, Leonard seems to define *chinos* as half-breeds, but it is unclear because an opportunity is missed to provide that definition earlier in the paragraph. Nonetheless, *zambaigos* (also known as *zambos*) were a mixture of indigenous and black, as were *lobos*.[36] What is clear from all of these omissions and misrepresentations is an inability to register blackness as such in Mexico, even when it is being pointed to by Sigüenza.

What is most interesting, however, is how he works against Sigüenza. While Sigüenza does demonstrate to the admiral that some Spaniards have "degenerando de sus obligaciones" (fall[en] away from their allegience), the creole elite maintain their fealty to the Crown. However, Leonard cannot read Sigüenza's description of blacks ("de negros Criollos y Vosales de diferentes Naciones") for what it suggests, as Anna More has: "creole and bozal blacks of different nations."[37] Leonard's 1932 more faithful reproduction of the Spanish original shows a striking fluidity in the idea of a creole, as here it is an adjective that was not always as firmly attached to Spanish blood. But in failing to read this in his first English version, he has perhaps given what the original author of the letter might have felt as a greater insult by inserting creoles into the rabble.

This passage regarding the native and foreign-born blacks has been remarkably unstable throughout its rewritings. Romero de Terreros's 1974 edition in *Relaciones históricas* and both 1984 editions credited to Leonard's editorial hand (*Un sabio mexicano* and *Seis obras*) use the following phrasing: "componerse de indios, de negros, criollos y bozales de diferentes naciones."[38] Sigüenza's original intent seems to be maintained, but to achieve this there is a need to insert a comma to separate *negro* from *criollos*.

Though this remains the most common contemporary reproduction of this portion of the quote, José Rabasa contributed a "new" edition in his aforementioned *Without History*. In a portion of his work where he is critiquing the Spanish "impulse to classify races," he quotes Leonard's 1932 Spanish version and then immediately translates it via Leonard's 1929 English version.[39] While representing the English, he erroneously substitutes "Chinese" for *chinos*. However, what is more revealing is that when the two quotes are placed side by side, as they were above, there is no notation of the vast difference between them. This re-presents Leonard's original act of unreading in an even more dramatic manner. There is, seemingly, some sort of gravitational force at work here.

These twentieth-century disappearances made manifest in the work of Paz and the transcription and citation of Sigüenza run counter to the prominent Afro-Mexican scholar Ben Vinson's understanding that "the period stretching from 1821–1940 can be described as one of a conscious 'historical forgetting' of the black population."[40] Vinson is singling out the 1940s as the beginning of an academic renaissance in the study of Mexico's Afro-descendant heritage. This is a clear and appropriate acknowledgment of Gonzalo Aguirre Beltrán, the famous Mexican anthropologist trained at Northwestern University by Melville Herskovits.[41] Aguirre Beltrán's 1946 *La población negra de México* deals with the presence of an Afro-descendant population in New Spain, and largely sparked the development of Afro-Mexican studies. Nonetheless, whatever progress has been made within certain corners of the academic community, the middle decades of the twentieth century saw the broader zeitgeist embrace a disappeared blackness.

Aguire Beltrán's own work, to a certain and perhaps for some unexpected extent, mirrors this disappearance. It is not a new criticism that in *La población negra de México* absolutely no time is spent on the present-day Afro-descendant populations. However, in 1971 Aguire Beltrán would go as far as to release a "corrected and augmented" edition that added a short final chapter, "Integración del negro," and a prologue. He included this final chapter because, in his own words from the prologue (his rereading of his original project), "era necesaria para cerrar el panorama total del transcurrir del negro desde sus lejanos orígenes en el África hasta su completa integración en el Estado mexicano" (it was necessary to close the panorama of the black's journey from his distant origins in Africa to his complete integration into the Mexican state).[42] Beltrán's deployment of the verb *cerrar* (to close) is valuable as it makes visible within the discourse of Afro-Mexican studies itself this barrier that disappears the Afro-descendant elements that lie beyond it and helps give shape to Mexican culture.

Erin Graff Zivin has identified a similar dangerous tendency, what she accurately terms a reliance on an "excavational mode of thought," within not only the context of decolonial and subaltern studies but, of greater concern to her, contemporary Latin Americanist political thought. Building on Alberto Moreiras's engagement with *marranismo*, or that which escapes the "conversion to hegemonic submission," Graff Zivin argues for an an-archaeological critical practice that exposes the instability of a logic dependent on "an unburied truth, a once forgotten truth brought to light . . . that betrays a compatibility, or complicity, with the logic of archaeology."[43] More precisely, this excavational mode of thought *reads* "that which hides beneath it [as] an identifiable and revealable truth."[44] My italics mimic those by Graff Zivin, which underline what she sees as the incapacity of this particular mode of thought to know "the limits of its own thinking or theorizing, the inability to call reading *reading*."[45] This limit is analogous to the barrier I have articulated here.

Such an an-archaeological imagination, one that embraces reading as such, offers a distinct challenge to those working within the study of blackness in Mexico. The truth can be, and must be, dug out. This mantra has essentially framed the academic study of Afro-descendant populations in Mexico. This is why the bulk of the scholarly output can be characterized as either ethnographic or anthropologic in nature, with very little concerned primarily with a more philosophical register. In the push to decipher and uncover whole narratives, for one example, Pérez de Ribas's account of the founding of San Lorenzo de los Negros discussed in chapter 1 has been relied on, not as much for its transparent ideological position, but, of greater danger, for the set of coordinates that has allowed it to be mapped in time and space without a recognition of the fictive nature of this mapping.

This is not to say that the exposed artifacts are not without great value. My project, for one, would be impossible to articulate without them. However, these artifacts simultaneously create a discourse tripped up, or trapped, by their discovery. In other words, this mode of thought has helped to create a discourse founded, primarily, on ideas of phenotype and the accompanying notions of authenticity and its trace. These require not only the pointing to fragments of found objects and cultural expression but to their mapping and reconstruction, while, by and large, avoiding the more central and pressing meditation on the ways in which this disavowal of blackness, an aspect of the transgenerational intrapsychic gap, helps to structure contemporary Mexican culture and the nature of what radiates through it.

But how can the permeability of this barrier be approached—the falling out of or being drawn into its state of disappearance? On many registers, especially from many of the world lines emanating from Mexico, material that makes it into or comes out of this part of the apparatus is effectively no longer read, even while we read. The void of scholarship addressing such an emergence in the work of a Mexican thinker as prominent as Paz testifies to this, as do the ever-disappearing citations in the case of Sigüenza. At the very least, we know these instances of permeability are not read as violent repressions or their return, which an oedipal-centered orientation would force. At most, they might be felt as incomplete, almost benign, interruptions within an otherwise stable world line.

The idea of black holes and the recent debates surrounding their boundaries offer a tentative interstellar analogy to help give language to this gap within the Mexican national psychic apparatus and the nature of the permeability of its border. This analogy is particularly appropriate here given Mexico's cosmic relation to discourses of racial mixture and the natural correlation to the field of black studies stemming from the fact that, from the perspective of astrophysics, a black hole is a near-perfect black body that is both the antithesis of light and can emit and sustain a galaxy-forming energy. Despite the complicated nature of the scientific discourses that have attempted to more fully understand black holes, they have retained a position within a global imagination as the region of the unthought par excellence.

A black hole is defined as "an object with such a strong gravitational field that its escape velocity exceeds the velocity of light."[46] In its classical theorization, the radius of such an object is described as an event horizon, an absolute boundary that obliterates the possibility of any remnant escaping and the complete loss of information beyond its border. However, Stephen Hawking recently proposed a new theory regarding the permeability of its horizon. Though Hawking himself had helped to articulate our traditional understanding of black holes that included the event horizon, the discovery of their potential emission of particles forced him to reevaluate over the course of decades the assumption that black holes were true black bodies—"regimes from which light can't escape to infinity."[47] Consideration of this emission of particles—what is sometimes termed Hawking Radiation—ultimately led to his new postulation wherein in some cases the relevant boundary is an apparent horizon rather than an event horizon. With the apparent horizon, some information will pass through, but it will be chaotically mutated in such a way that it "will effectively be lost."[48] While direct observation of a black hole eludes astrophysicists, its contours are perceptible in this emitted matter, as well as in the effects it has on nearby objects falling toward it.[49] I intend to use this idea of an apparent horizon as a border to the transgenerational intrapsychic gap within which the remnants of the unthought are contained.[50]

Unless one embraces the fact that these remnants are ultimately indecipherable (an-archaeologic) radiation that emerges from this apparent horizon, the discoveries owed to an excavational mode of thought will remain in service of contemporary iterations of the hegemonic culture that demand their marginalization, if not disappearance. This is either by remaining fictionally stagnated in the past—evidenced in Beltrán's closure of the panorama—or on the very margins of thought—evidenced in the surge of ethnographic studies of present-day Afro-descendant populations in the remote coastal regions of Oaxaca and Guerrero, which nonetheless remain largely isolated from central conversations about the nature of Mexican identity.

For an insight into how this restriction has been carried through to contemporary Mexican public discourse, one need only look to the nation's imagination of itself as it prepared to celebrate its bicentennial in 2010. To commemorate the milestone, the Mexican government, in conjunction with the Instituto Nacional de Antropología e Historia (INAH) and the Consejo Nacional para la Cultura y las Artes (Conaculta), commissioned the book *Viaje por la historia de México*. Intended to document Mexico's diverse and impressive history, the book uses text from the Mexican historian Luis González y González's *Álbum de la historia de México* and features reproductions of photographs and paintings and descriptions of important Mexican figures and moments. Although intended for a mass audience, including children, it aims to present a quite complete historical overview from Mexico's pre-Columbian era to the present. Twenty-five million copies of the full-color, glossy booklet were printed and freely distributed to commemorate the nation's diverse history.[51]

In President Felipe Calderón's introductory statement to the volume, we see the same coordinates we have come to expect to bind Mexican identity: "A través de los siglos, México ha sido hogar de grandes historiadores. Los ha habido indígenas, españoles, criollos y mestizos" (Across the centuries, Mexico has been home to great historians. They have been indigenous, Spaniards, creoles, and mestizos).[52] In the final words of his introduction, Calderón prepares the reader for a vision of Mexican history that is "generosa, plural, abierta, y constructiva" (generous, plural, open, and constructive).[53] As one might expect, the narrative that follows, including the gaps it presents, contains an extraordinarily bracketed plurality, especially in regard to Mexico's Afro-descendant elements. There are two brief mentions of slavery being abolished, first in 1810 by Hidalgo and later in the biography of Guadalupe Victoria. No reference is made to the subsequent 1829 abolition by Vicente Guerrero. Furthermore, the idea of African slavery is never specifically presented, and neither the benefits to the state nor the large population it produced are discussed.

In the book, there are two explicit references to the presence of Afro-descendant people in what would become modern-day Mexico: Juan de Oñate, an explorer in early New Spain, is described as bringing an expedition that included "130 soldados, algunos frailes franciscanos, negros e indios" (130 soldiers, some Franciscan friars, blacks, and Indians) in order to claim

Figs. 1–2. Attributed to Manuel Arellano (Spanish, ca. 1663–1722). *Transfer of the Image and Inauguration of the Sanctuary of the Virgin of Guadalupe*, ca. 1709 (bottom, detail). Oil on canvas. Private collection, Spain.

New Mexico for New Spain at the end of the sixteenth century;[54] and the former president Vicente Guerrero is described as being an "agricultor y arriero mulato" (a mulato farmer and mule driver) prior to his ascension through the military to the presidency in 1829.[55] When describing the concept of mestizaje, González y González's text does contend that it was both biological and cultural and that within this mix were "ideas prehispánicas, europeas y africanas" (25). But this reads as out of place, given that outside the one adjective used to describe Guerrero and the mention of the blacks who traveled with Oñate, there is no other reference to a Mexican Afro-descent. If one is reading this document to educate oneself about the history of Mexico, which is how it is intended, one might be quite confused as to the origin of these otherwise invisible "ideas africanas."

This is no more evident than in the section of the book dedicated to the height of the baroque period in Mexican history, the seventeenth century. The highlight of this section is a discussion of la Virgen de Guadalupe, whose symbolic importance was cemented during this time.[56] Above the text referencing la Virgen there is a detail from *Transfer of the Image and Inauguration of the Sanctuary of the Virgin of Guadalupe* (figs. 1–2), painted around 1709 and attributed to Manuel Arellano of the Arellano family, which was commissioned by Viceroy Francisco Fernández de la Cueva to commemorate the completion of the new basilica in honor of la Virgen in Mexico City. The Arellano family contributed greatly to the genre of *casta* paintings, the predominantly eighteenth-century style of painting in colonial Mexico that sought to categorize and classify the racial and social makeup of New Spain. So although this particular painting was intended to recognize the completion of the new basilica, the painter's interest in classification and representation of the various strata of Mexican culture is evident. The editors of *Viaje por la historia de México* have chosen a close-up that highlights the image of la Virgen that miraculously appeared on the garment of Juan Diego in 1531 as proof of her existence. Just above this image, the artist has placed a black man and a black woman who are dressed in somewhat regal garments standing on a balcony. There is nothing in the text that prepares a reader for the emergence of these figures; from the world lines of contemporary Mexico, I would argue, they remain illegible.

Chapter 3

The Gravity of Lincoln and the Matter of Black Life

> That ground has been fully occupied and completely covered both here and elsewhere.
>
> —Frederick Douglass, 1876

Since my work is a comparative project that flows, hemispherically speaking, from south to north and moves against many of the currents related to legibility and ideas of blackness, it is now time to turn more squarely to the United States. In chapters 1 and 2, I describe the existence of an intrapsychic gap within Mexico's collective imagination that carries within it intergenerational secrets too harmful to the limits this imagination has set for itself. I have theorized that this gap, conterminously understood as the nigrescent beyond, is bordered by a horizon that is not absolute but permeable—an apparent horizon. However, as the gap has matured across these generations, grown in its destructive gravitational force, much of the matter that now manages to escape this horizon is ultimately indecipherable. This chapter will use this foundation to better explore how the collective liberal imagination of the United States' understanding of and inquiries into the matter of black life can and should be read as simultaneously effecting a vanishing of radical blackness similar to what has been experienced in Mexico. Central to this idea are the violent repercussions, both rhetorical and physical, that are supported by the link between utopian discourses of racial egalitarianism and the shameful secret of remaining structural imbalances tied to and dependent on these same vanishing ideas of race. To make this plain, I will examine the contemporary collective liberal imagination's interactions with Abraham Lincoln and the ideas of slavery that gravitate toward him. And while an undressing of the moral gymnastics surrounding Abraham Lincoln and his "liberation" of the enslaved is not particularly difficult, the details herein speak, especially given the existence of a particularly coherent archive in relation to the man, to the disfiguring capacity of this nascent (relative to Mexico) gap. This examination aligns with Lindon Barrett's reading of

Saidiya Hartman's understanding of a collective desire within the United States to read emancipation—of which Lincoln has become the symbol—as a "discrete historical event" rather than the "structural exposure" of the state's ongoing reorganization of its "regulatory mechanism."[1]

Academics who have dealt with the topic of emancipation in the United States can be arranged on a spectrum stretching from those who see Lincoln as "the Great Emancipator" to those who record a process of self-emancipation through efforts of the enslaved and free blacks. The collective liberal imagination, on the other hand, can be read as wanting to imagine Lincoln's words as having the impact of a clear utopian declaration similar to those discussed in chapter 1 by Miguel Hidalgo and José María Morelos that surrounded slavery, racial castes, and the formation of the Mexican state. We of course know not to search for a parallel in the two principal documents produced in the American Revolution (the Articles of the Confederacy and the U.S. Constitution) while slavery in the United States was at its apex. However, given the stature that Abraham Lincoln now seems to maintain in the historical imaginary of the United States, it may be surprising to some that equivalence cannot be sought here either. Putting aside the extent to which Hidalgo's rhetoric was or was not employed to gain a military advantage, or any evaluation of its sincerity, it delivers a clear directive (that all slaveholders release their slaves), time frame (ten days), and punishment (death). Morelos's "Sentimientos de la nación" replaces authoritative specificity with a grand utopian embrace that is worth quoting again here: "Let slavery and the distinction of *castas* be banished forever, leaving all equal. Vice and virtue will be all that will distinguish one American from another."[2] Neither the certitude of Hidalgo nor the utopian grandeur of Morelos is to be found in the public rhetoric of Lincoln surrounding the issue of slavery and black equality. Yet the developing collective liberal imagination has nonetheless spent much time and energy deluding itself to this fact. This delusion is my focus here.

Lincoln's Preliminary Emancipation Proclamation was delivered on September 22, 1862, and, on its face, serves to warn Confederate slave states that if they remained "in rebellion" at the start of the following year, their enslaved population would be freed. It is a calculated political strategy, and no clear immediate judgment is included on the institution of slavery or the current social hierarchy in the document itself. In fact, the threat of mass rebellion can be read as being held up against the carrot of southern states potentially keeping their status as slave states if they join the Union. Alongside the proposed emancipation, the document formally announces the idea of compensating slaveholders and slave states for such emancipation, as well as a continued commitment to the "effort to colonize persons of African descent, with their consent, upon this continent, or elsewhere, with the previously obtained consent of the Governments existing there."[3] Though the final Emancipation Proclamation signed on January 1, 1863, does not contain mention of consensual colonization or compensated emancipation, it does refer to and uphold the original document.[4]

The idea of consensual colonization, ongoing with both whites and free blacks in the North since the beginning of the nineteenth century, was a great psychic comfort to a nation that, though divided on the issue of slavery, was far more united on the idea of social segregation. It was long supported by Lincoln and thus has become a major sticking point in the narratives wishing to insulate his image from this gray area. Lincoln rose to the presidency as the nation was coming to grips with the question of what to do with the soon-to-be-freed blacks. In Lincoln's first set of debates with Stephen Douglas for the U.S. Senate in 1854, for example, he spoke of his strong preference to return enslaved persons to Liberia.[5] Lincoln would again address the issue prominently as president in his first two State of the Union addresses. In 1861, he outlined the fact that such a colonization, which could include portions of the already free black population, would need the financial support of the federal government and the acquisition of new territories. One year later, and just weeks before he would announce and sign the final Emancipation Proclamation, Lincoln again addressed Congress on the issue and clearly spelled out the advantages to white citizens:

> I cannot make it better known than it already is that I strongly favor colonization . . . With deportation, even to a limited extent, enhanced wages to white labor is mathematically certain. Labor is like any other commodity in the market—increase the demand for it and you increase the price of it. Reduce the supply of black labor by colonizing the black laborer out of the country, and by precisely so much you increase the demand for and wages of white labor.[6]

In December 1862, this plan had already advanced far enough to where Lincoln could announce in the speech that "the Spanish American Republics have protested against the sending of such colonies to their respective territories."[7] In this same address, he would go on to propose three detailed constitutional amendments that would (1) ensure the compensation of states for lost labor if they were to agree to abolish slavery by the first day of the coming year; (2) ensure similar compensation for individual slaveholders who were able to prove their loyalty; and (3) earmark federal funds for the deportation and colonization of significant portions of the black population in the United States.

Most historians concerned with this aspect of Lincoln's political legacy acknowledge that the United States' government-led project of colonization was ongoing while Lincoln was imagining, drafting, and declaring the emancipation of the enslaved in rebellious territories. By July 1862, while Lincoln was contemplating the idea of a proclamation, Congress had already appropriated $600,000 at the direction of Lincoln to support the deportation and colonization of blacks.[8] The two most famous and documented colonization projects were located off the coast of Haiti on the Île à Vache and in the Chiriquí region of Panama. While the effort in Panama would fail in October 1862, the push for the settlement of Île à Vache would continue well after January 1, 1863, which has become somewhat of a psychic boundary marking the end of colonizing efforts in the Lincoln administration.[9] In fact, on the eve of his signing the Emancipation Proclamation (December 31, 1862), Lincoln signed an agreement relating to the Île à Vache settlement. He is said to have developed concerns regarding the trustworthiness of the contractor for the project, Bernard Kock, and canceled the agreement by way of a presidential proclamation on the technicality that the signature had not yet been paired with the seal of the United States.[10] But this did not derail the project. Under a new agreement, Kock remained involved on the ground in Haiti, but the transportation of 453 blacks was arranged by Charles Tuckerman and Paul Forbes. Months later, the colony, under the misdirection of Kock, was found to be an abject failure. And in February 1864, Lincoln would send a U.S. Navy ship to recover the 368 colonists who had managed to survive a smallpox outbreak and disastrous living conditions.[11]

The common narrative for most scholars who deal with Lincoln's interest in deportation and colonization is that the failures of Île à Vache punctuated the colonization experiment. However, recent work on the subject, particularly that of Phillip Magness and Sebastian Page, uncovers a great deal of archival material detailing Lincoln's significant commitments to the project of colonization after this date. Though Lincoln's comments regarding colonization evaporate, their study follows the development of colonization schemes in British Honduras, Guyana, and Suriname under the direction of Lincoln's director of the U.S. Emigration Office, James Mitchell. These three projects represent a change in the United States' strategy "to negotiate an agreement with established European powers to designate specified northern port cities as points of emigration and, from each, induce a voluntary mass migration of the freedman."[12] Henry Highland Garnet, the noted black abolitionist and key supporter of colonization within the black community, was to be a crucial piece in this design.[13] His influential African Civilization Society was to help encourage blacks to emigrate to the new colonies. Ultimately, the challenge of convincing large numbers of black settlers to emigrate contributed to the project's waning in the early months of 1864 and the ultimate discontinuation of the Emigration Office in July 1864. For Magness and Page, the two most common narratives of Lincoln's interest in colonization—either as a mere "ruse to 'defuse' white backlash" or something he let go of when his personal beliefs on race shifted—are complicated by the fact these colonization projects would be vigorously pursued throughout 1863.[14]

Even historians who allow for Lincoln's expressed prepresidential misgivings on racial equality often do so by tying them into a narrative of gradual but ultimate arrival to a firm moral ground on the issues of slavery and equality.[15]

The above-noted developing archive forces the concession that if one is going to include an eventual moral enlightenment as a cause for Lincoln's gradual disconnection from his oft-proposed and partially implemented colonization project, it must be alongside the lack of feasibility of the projects themselves and the perceived growing political risk. However, my concerns here are ultimately elsewhere. Lincoln's ambition to deport significant numbers of black American citizens—even if it is just as he is proclaiming emancipation, or if it is argued as a "necessary" aspect of an involved political strategy—merely underlines that we are quite far from anything resembling a utopian declaration regarding the value of black life and the dream of a unified and integrated nation. Yet the enduring image of Lincoln in the American imagination as the founding father of our contemporary utopian desire seems to have not suffered for any of this.

Former president Barack Obama, for an example of perhaps the most visible investor in this symbolism, firmly tied his presidential brand to this idea of Lincoln ever since he announced his candidacy on the steps of the Old State Capital in Springfield, Illinois, where the sixteenth president gave his famous "House Divided" speech in 1858. Even Donald Trump seems to be governed by the gravitational force of Lincoln as a psychic object: in a rally in Youngstown, Ohio, he proclaimed that "with the exception of the late great Abraham Lincoln I can be more presidential than any president that has ever held this office."[16] Returning to Obama, in the months prior to his inauguration, he would note the impact of Doris Kearns Goodwin's best-selling book *Team of Rivals: The Political Genius of Abraham Lincoln* on his own potential strategy in regard to his impending cabinet selections.[17] Obama would go on to be sworn in for his first term with his hand on the same Bible that Lincoln had used for his 1861 inauguration—of note, the same inauguration which saw Lincoln state that he had "no purpose, directly or indirectly, to interfere with the institution of slavery in the States where it exists. I believe I have no lawful right to do so, and I have no inclination to do so."[18] Adding to this symbolism and creating a direct link from Lincoln to the civil rights movement's most visible icon, Obama would be sworn in for his second term with his hand on the same Lincoln Bible stacked above one used by Martin Luther King Jr.[19]

It was in this spirit, three weeks before Obama's second inauguration, that the Emancipation Proclamation itself received a makeover by the president on its 150th anniversary. In a proclamation of his own ("Presidential Proclamation—150th Anniversary of the Emancipation Proclamation"), Obama summarized the original document, papering over the language that had once been described by Richard Hofstadter as having "all the moral grandeur of a bill of lading" with a decidedly grandiose, if not utopian, prose:[20]

> On December 31, 1862, our Nation marked the end of another year of civil war. At Shiloh and Seven Pines, Harpers Ferry and Antietam, brother had fought against brother. Sister had fought against

sister. Blood and bitterness had deepened the divide that separated North from South, eroding the bonds of affection that once united 34 States under a single flag. Slavery still suspended the possibility of an America where life and liberty were the birthright of all, not the province of some.

Yet, even in those dark days, light persisted. Hope endured. As the weariness of an old year gave way to the promise of a new one, President Abraham Lincoln issued the Emancipation Proclamation—courageously declaring that on January 1, 1863, "all persons held as slaves" in rebellious areas "shall be then, thenceforward, and forever free." He opened the Union Army and Navy to African Americans, giving new strength to liberty's cause. And with that document, President Lincoln lent new moral force to the war by making it a fight not just to preserve, but also to empower. He sought to reunite our people not only in government, but also in freedom that knew no bounds of color or creed. Every battle became a battle for liberty itself. Every struggle became a struggle for equality.

Our 16th President also understood that while each of us is entitled to our individual rights and responsibilities, there are certain things we cannot accomplish on our own. Only a Union could serve the hopes of every citizen, knocking down the barriers to opportunity and giving each of us the chance to pursue our highest aspirations. He knew that in these United States, no dream could ever be beyond our reach when we affirm that individual liberty is served, not negated, by seeking the common good.

It is that spirit that made emancipation possible and codified it in our Constitution. It is that belief in what we can do together that moved millions to march for justice in the years that followed. And today, it is a legacy we choose not only to remember, but also to make our own. Let us begin this new year by renewing our bonds to one another and reinvesting in the work that lies ahead, confident that we can keep driving freedom's progress in our time.

NOW, THEREFORE, I, BARACK OBAMA, President of the United States of America, by virtue of the authority vested in me by the Constitution and the laws of the United States, do hereby proclaim January 1, 2013, as the 150th Anniversary of the Emancipation Proclamation. I call upon all Americans to observe this day with appropriate programs, ceremonies, and activities that celebrate the Emancipation Proclamation and reaffirm the timeless principles it upheld.

IN WITNESS WHEREOF, I have hereunto set my hand this thirty-first day of December, in the year of our Lord two thousand twelve, and of the Independence of the United States of America the two hundred and thirty-seventh.[21]

Obama's proclamation is, all told, a five-hundred-word document that retains only twelve words from the original: *All persons held as slaves . . . shall be then, thenceforward, and forever free.*[22] Gone entirely is the reference to the preliminary act, enacting a further distancing of compensated emancipation and colonization. With no mention of the states that were in rebellion, gone as well is the uncomfortably long list of parishes and counties in Louisiana and Virginia that, due to their loyalty to the Union, were entitled to keep their enslaved persons "as if this proclamation were not issued."

It has become, in this re-envisioning, a utopian declaration.

Immense investment along this line stretches well beyond the political arena and can be observed in Steven Spielberg's Golden Globe– and Oscar-nominated biopic *Lincoln*, which came to the theaters amid the buildup to the proclamation's 150th anniversary in 2012. The screenplay, also nominated for the two major United States–based cinematic award competitions, is written by Tony Kushner and based, in part, on a portion of Goodwin's best-selling book.

In Goodwin's foreword to Kushner's published screenplay, she notes how Kushner had openly struggled to frame for the screen a project that was potentially so large. Ultimately, the final story's arc begins with a brief prologue that takes place around the brutal Battle of Jenkins' Ferry (Arkansas) in 1864, showing white and black soldiers fighting side by side. The narrative ends with a series of scenes depicting the Thirteenth Amendment's passage in the House of Representatives on January 31, 1865, General Robert E. Lee's subsequent surrender on April 9, and Lincoln's assassination six days later. The remaining body of the two-and-a-half-hour film circles around Lincoln's leadership role in the process of passing the amendment.

This narrow temporal frame aids the moral vigor of its dramatic arc. By remaining in 1865, Spielberg and Kushner are able to avoid the awkward subjects of colonization and deportation all together and construct a narrative that attempts to forcefully demonstrate Lincoln as the principal architect of black freedom to the diminishment of those around him (or off-screen). Thaddeus Stevens, played by Tommy Lee Jones, and James Mitchell Ashley are the two Republican members of the House given the most screen time. However, as the film centers on the passage of the bill in the House, there is no great focus on the Republican senators who had worked alongside Stevens and Ashley to develop the language for the amendment and pass it in the Senate eleven months prior.

Chief among these absences are the Massachusetts senators, Charles Sumner and Henry Wilson. Wilson is not in the film, while Sumner makes two very brief appearances.[23] Sumner, in particular, would work to craft an unused but nonetheless recorded version of the amendment that is an absolute contrast to the final version. Drawing from France's Declaration of the Rights of Man, Sumner proposed the following language: "All persons are equal before the law, so that no person can hold another as a slave; and the Congress shall have power to make all laws necessary and proper to carry this declaration into effect everywhere in the United States."[24] This constituted, in his mind, not only a universal declaration of human rights that extended "the idea of human rights which is enunciated in our Declaration of Independence," it presented the radical legal foundation for equal protection that would have to wait until the Fourteenth Amendment's ratification in 1868.[25] Sumner's proposal was rejected for a variety of reasons. Many Democrats and conservative Republicans rejected it outright on ideological grounds, while others simply decried the audacity of evoking the French document.[26] Some Republicans like Jacob Howard of Michigan, however, while in support of its ambition, felt that its language, "in a legal and technical sense[, was] utterly insignificant and meaningless."[27] Though Sumner would eventually relent, his remarks in the Senate would attempt to underscore the "transcendent importance" of language in that particular moment: "In placing a new and important text into our Constitution, it seems to me we cannot be too careful in the language we adopt . . . Universal emancipation, which is at hand, can only be won by complete emancipation of the Constitution itself, which has been degraded to wear chains so long."[28]

The fact that the gravitational pull of this coalition of Republican congressmen worked both independently of and in alignment with Lincoln is evidenced by the presidential election that took place in the months prior to the passing of the Thirteenth Amendment in the House. Thaddeus Stevens and Senator Ben Wade, among others, initially supported Benjamin Butler in Lincoln's own National Union Party.[29] And in a more dramatic pressuring of Lincoln, a group of disheartened Republicans would form the Radical Democracy Party and nominate in a separate convention John Frémont in 1864, the major-general and former senator who had famously been forced by Lincoln to rescind his emancipation decree in the border state of Missouri in August 1861.[30] Though Frémont would step out of the race in September 1864, the party's convention had received public support from Frederick Douglass and the abolitionist community.

Returning to the film, it is enough to state that much of the work of those devoted to the possibility of a Thirteenth Amendment remains beyond the frame of the film. How these characters, devoid of this past to ground them in, are translated to the screen is summed up well by Joshua Zeitz in his review of the film for the *Atlantic*:

> With the exception of Secretary of State William Seward (played convincingly by David Strathairn), *Lincoln* presents almost every public figure as either comical, quirky, weak-kneed or pathetically self-interested. Only the president is able to rise above the moment and see the end game. This treatment does injustice to men like Rep. James Ashley, Sen. Charles Sumner, and Sen. Ben Wade . . . These men were serious, committed legislators who fought a lonely fight for black freedom before the war, and a difficult struggle for black equality after it.[31]

However, if Kushner and Spielberg were to spend valuable screen time fleshing out the characters of this coalition, it would have diminished Lincoln's stature as an unadulterated "master among men"—this moniker being one of the alternative titles considered by Goodwin for her book on Lincoln before she suddenly realized the unfortunate resonance with slavery.[32]

And though Stevens is drawn as the most well-rounded of the Republicans presented, even he is cast as the foil Lincoln must rein in so that Stevens may learn to more effectively channel his own assertive political will. This perspective belittles the political savvy and accomplishments of a man who began his career in local Pennsylvania politics in 1833 and rose to the national level in the House of Representatives in 1849 at the age of fifty-eight. In his legal practice, he was known to defend fugitive enslaved persons pro bono and had offered up his offices as a stop along what has come to be known as the Underground Railroad.[33] In the film, Stevens exits the screen on the evening of January 31. He has taken the official bill home for the evening to share with Lydia Smith, his supposed "colored" mistress who maintains the public role of his housekeeper. It is in this private moment that Stevens delivers one of the film's most important lines: "The greatest measure of the nineteenth century. Passed by corruption, aided and abetted by the purest man in America."

This is one of several lines in the film that comes "straight from the archive," boosting the film's reputation as a historical resource. However, this line is deployed in a disingenuous fashion. While the line is attributed to Stevens, Michael Vorenberg shows that it might in fact have been said to Senator James Scovel. Scovel mentioned the remark more than thirty years afterward in a reminiscence for *Lippincott's Monthly Magazine*, claiming that a deal had been struck between Charles Sumner and the Senate Commerce Committee to oppose a railway in New Jersey that Sumner was originally a strong proponent of. In exchange for not pushing the railway project, Lincoln and Sumner were able to gain the support of certain influential lobbyists to procure votes for the Thirteenth Amendment. Vorenberg even doubts the veracity of this delayed secondhand reminiscence because it seems to contradict an immediate firsthand report by another senator.[34]

In either case, the line was not recorded as having been said to Lydia Smith. But for Kushner and Spielberg, this moment is a particularly poetic cosigning of Lincoln's moral purity by a grateful but silent colored woman and a once rival who had in the months prior initially opposed his nomination for his second term in favor of Benjamin Butler. And though the romantic nature of Smith's relationship with Stevens remains unconfirmed, Smith herself is not an unknown character in both Washington, D.C., and Pennsylvania.[35] Smith was a successful businessperson with several properties in both states.[36] However, beyond the exploitation of the rumor of their romantic relationship, none of her character's complexity comes to the screen; her tenuous legibility is only tied to a white masculinity. In a certain light, the last-minute portrayal of their relationship serves to provide a motivation for Stevens's uncommon passion on behalf of blacks that is displayed throughout the film. But as Michael Shank notes, this reading dismisses the fact that his "relationship with Smith was an outgrowth of his conviction, not the cause of it." Speaking to Stevens's long-held beliefs, historian Edward J. Blum is similarly disappointed that the film does not portray "the deep biblical commitment of radicals like Thaddeus Stevens who saw his plans for massive redistribution of wealth and property as fitting within the Exodus narrative."[37] Blum sees this evasion as diminishing how, in that time and in relation to the issue of slavery, "religion—on its own—generated authority or power."[38] If such a perspective were present, it would compete with and perhaps put into a less heroic perspective Lincoln's measured political approach.

However, because of this large collection of omissions, there is little to steer the absolute grandeur of the film's climax in any direction away from Lincoln. Instead the man, like his proclamation in the hands of Obama, is refashioned as the point of origin for our utopian discourse on race and equality. One of the film's official trailers prepares viewers for such a reading of the film by reaching well beyond the temporal scope of Lincoln's life to emotionally connect the film's rather focused time frame to an imagined teleology of twentieth-century battles (and wars) for civil and human rights. With a nod to this unbroken line, this trailer, appropriately titled "Unite," debuted during the first presidential debates between Mitt Romney and Barack Obama, and the film was released days after the election.[39] The first forty seconds of the trailer, with their complex interaction of sound and image, are crucial to this encouraged reading.

The viewer first sees an aerial color view of the present-day U.S. Capitol looking onto the Washington Monument. It is the only color image in the trailer that does not come from the film. This image quickly becomes sepia-toned. Then the screen fades to black: "FOR EVERY DREAM" appears against the now-black screen. This phrase crossfades into an image of Martin Luther King Jr. walking arm in arm with other civil rights leaders in the march from Selma to Montgomery as the word "DREAM" lingers over the photo.[40] This image transitions to an aerial photo of the March on Washington, then a shot of soldiers in the United States' war in Afghanistan (a.k.a. Operation Enduring Freedom). Fade to black: "FOR EVERY BELIEF." As all but "BELIEF" fades away, the viewer is presented with the image of Nelson Mandela, then a march for women's suffrage, then Mohandas Gandhi. Fade to black: "FOR EVERY FREEDOM." The iconic photo of soldiers raising the flag on Iwo Jima comes to the screen before bleeding into soldiers exiting a naval landing craft on D-Day. Finally, the viewer is offered a night cityscape of Manhattan with the 9/11 Memorial's two beams of light and the Statue of Liberty. Fade to black: "THERE ARE THOSE WHO UNITE US ALL." This segment ends with a profile view of Lincoln as played by Daniel Day-Lewis.

The position of the women suffragists is perhaps the most deceptively anachronistic. The picture comes from a march in Brooklyn in 1920 just before the Nineteenth Amendment was ratified by three-fourths of the states.[41] And while Lincoln was a noted early supporter of women's suffrage, it was the Women's National Loyal League, then headed by Susan B. Anthony, that worked with abolitionists to present a petition with over 400,000 signatures asking for a constitutional amendment abolishing slavery.[42] The initial 100,000 signatures were presented to the League's ally in Congress, Charles Sumner, on February 24, 1864, providing the more progressive Republicans with a mandate to begin work pressuring the Lincoln administration, which up to that point had held the position that state-enacted emancipation was the way forward.[43]

The trailer also extends emancipation's morally justified use of force to the twentieth and twenty-first centuries. The above-described images from the European and Asian fronts of World War II (the "Good War"), the United States' war in Afghanistan, and the 9/11 Memorial are immediately followed by a clip from the film's depiction of the Battle of Jenkins' Ferry. The gesture here is double. The images encourage a prioritization of the just and moral cause of slavery over the pragmatic objective of preserving the Union. If this is understood and accepted, then the war to "free the enslaved" can be deployed to extend our already collectively understood battle against Hitler's pure evil in World War II to the justification of the United States' contemporary global reach with the ongoing war in Afghanistan and the "War on Terror" in general.

All of the anachronistic images of this first segment and the passionate moments of the film that are presented in the remainder of the trailer are further sutured by two consistent sonic elements. The first is Veigar Margeirsson's *Dawn of the Titans*, an orchestral composition originally created to score several prominent dramatic elements of the first-person-shooter video game franchise *Halo*. The highly emotive piece underscores the entire trailer and, though darker, evokes the European tradition of musical nationalism. The second binding sonic element is Lincoln's dialogue from the film. In the first segment discussed above it plays ominously off screen, first heard as we see the image of King: "Can we choose to be born? Are we fitted to the times we're born into? We begin with equality. That's the origin, isn't it? That's justice. Say we've shown that people can endure awful sacrifice and yet cohere? Shall we stop this bleeding?" This last question comes as the trailer transitions from the black-and-white historical images to color scenes from the film. Through this suturing, the trailer sets the stage for a film that will depict a clear, Lincoln-directed moral triumph, punctuated by an assassination that further solidifies his image as one of the United States', and the world's, moral martyrs—the origin of democratic liberation that the United States has bravely carried through the twentieth century and beyond. As such, Abraham Lincoln might be thought of as a gravimeter attuned to the pull of the United States' maturing postracial impulse.

Beyond the film's content, *Lincoln* very much understands itself within a larger utopian discourse. It is produced by Participant Media, the self-described "global entertainment company" whose stated mission is to produce "feature film, television, publishing and digital content that inspires social change."[44] Through its various platforms, "Participant seeks to entertain, encourage and empower every individual to take action."[45] The first major release that propelled the company, which was founded in 2004, was Al Gore's *An Inconvenient Truth*, and it has gone on to produce over sixty films, including, to name just a few, *Citizenfour*, *Darfur Now*, *The Help*, *The Kite Runner*, *The Soloist*, *The Square*, and *Food Inc.*

In a review of Participant Media's ambitions for the *Washington Post*, Ann Hornaday focuses on their 2012 documentary film *Last Call at the Oasis*, which treats the subject of water shortage and contamination. Near the film's end, the environmental scientist and social activist Peter Gleick speaks the following words: "The more we know, the more likely we are to do the right things."[46] For Hornaday, these remarks accurately speak not only to the film, but to the "driving artistic ethos" of the company that produced it. In a remark that aligns with what Frank Wilderson understands as the mendacity of liberally oriented cinema's embrace of conflict and resolution over unresolved antagonism, Hornaday describes an ethos that desires to "first plunge viewers into panic, then bring them to the surface, convincing them that they can stem the tide of disaster if they act decisively and quickly."[47] Hornaday identifies the danger in "soothing [the] audience with false optimism" and producing an exaggerated sense of their own participation by alluding to a scene in which moviegoers are asked to participate by texting "water" to register a complaint. For Hornaday, this moment of "bourgeois art-house liberalism" is made both more appealing and more appalling by the fact that the emotional singing of R.E.M. front man Michael Stipe undergirds it.[48]

This commercially packaged utopian ethos is seen in the trailer for *Lincoln* that was examined earlier. Participant Media is a content producer that has positioned itself as capable of providing the truth that, once known, can lead to "right" action. Such an exchange might be expected in the realm of documentary filmmaking. However, stretching this exchange to narrative filmmaking is particularly dangerous for what it works to disappear under the umbrella of an ethos of an emotionally engaging "truth." (And those responsible for the production of the film found shelter [and capital] in this blurred zone by simultaneously distributing the coffee-table book *Lincoln: A Cinematic and Historical Companion*.)[49] The trailer's reliance on the presence of King and Mandela, for example, is particularly troubling when one considers the absolute omission of radical black thought in Kushner and Spielberg's cinematic archival project. For even more pronounced than the diminished role of other white political figures discussed above, is the fact that not one black abolitionist is presented or directly referred to on screen. Because Frederick Douglass has become, in the American imaginary, the go-to black abolitionist to eclipse so many others doing similar work, most notably the enslaved themselves, it is a particular surprise that he is among the absent. But there is no room.

Several movie reviewers have pointed to the irony of a film that opens with the scene of blacks in battle alongside whites making vanish the man who most vocally challenged Lincoln to grant blacks the right to fight and die for the Union and who later worked with him to recruit black soldiers and defend their rights when Lincoln belatedly and desperately understood their necessity.[50] This omission is even more telling given that Douglass's public urgings of the Lincoln administration and ongoing frustration pepper the entire recorded landscape from Lincoln's first inauguration to well beyond the Emancipation Proclamation. When Charles Sumner pressed the president to reconsecrate Independence Day by issuing an emancipation decree on July 4, 1862, the president responded that it was "too big a lick" and would force "half the army [to] lay down its arms."[51] Frederick Douglass compounded this pressure with a speech on the same day directing pointed criticism at Lincoln and announcing the need for a proclamation:

> I do not hesitate to say, that whatever may have been his intentions, the action of President Lincoln has been calculated in a marked and decided way to shield and protect slavery . . . He has steadily refused to proclaim, as he had the constitutional and moral right to proclaim, complete emancipation to all the slaves of rebels who should make their way into the lines of our army . . . He has assigned to the most important positions, generals who are notoriously proslavery, and hostile to the party and principles which raised him to power . . . To my mind [the policy of the administration] is simply and solely to reconstruct the union on the cold and corrupting basis of compromise.[52]

Eleven days later Lincoln tells his Secretary of State Seward and Secretary of the Navy Gideon Welles in a private carriage ride that he is going to issue a decree against slavery in the rebel states; on July 22, he produces a draft of the proclamation for his cabinet to review.[53] It is impossible to know the exact role this rising pressure from Douglass and other particularly vocal abolitionists played, but their absolute nonpresence is indicative of the requisite secreting that helps to structure the collective liberal imagination of the United States.

While Douglass is a missing character in *Lincoln*, he is present throughout Goodwin's *Team of Rivals*. But, as Michael Vorenberg points out in one of the more complete scholarly articles on the film, Goodwin's book "has little sympathy for radicalism and minimal coverage of race and Reconstruction."[54] And this extends to Douglass. Goodwin paints the Douglass-Lincoln relationship as it evolved in the broadest possible strokes. She notes, among others, Douglass's criticisms of Lincoln's first inauguration speech and the pace at which Lincoln moved toward emancipation and the eventual enlistment of black soldiers. She also includes his harsh description of Lincoln's decision to rescind Frémont's emancipation decree as the largest "blunder" of Lincoln up to that point.[55] All of this to say, Douglass can in no way be characterized as absent in Goodwin's account. However, he is certainly used in a manner to support the mastery of Lincoln. Though she in one instance puts forward the caveat that "there is no way to penetrate Lincoln's personal feelings about race," she is able to see into his brain enough to judge that in his "initial approach" to colonization "Lincoln's remarkable empathy had singularly failed him."[56] For Goodwin, "Though he had tried to put himself in the place of blacks and suggest what he thought was best for them, his lack of contact with the black community left him unaware of their deep attachment to their country and sense of outrage at the thought of removal."[57]

For Goodwin, Lincoln would shift his consciousness entirely, and Douglass's feelings for the president would soften as their relationship developed. She then turns, as many historians have, to Douglass's 1886 reminiscence of Lincoln where he described the president as the "first great man that I talked with in the United States freely, who in no single instance reminded me of the difference between himself and myself, of the difference of color."[58] And with this Goodwin ties a bow on the relationship, imagining a smooth trajectory from misplaced good intentions to enlightenment on the question of equality.

But it is Douglass's treatment in Goodwin's introduction that most strikingly belies her overly simple characterization of this relationship and portends Douglass's vanishing in Kushner and Spielberg's film. The book's first words are nearly his as he helps to frame her project:

> In 1876, the celebrated orator Frederick Douglass dedicated a monument in Washington, D.C., erected by black Americans to honor Abraham Lincoln. The former slave told his audience that "there is little necessity on this occasion to speak at length and critically of this great and good man, and of his high mission in the world. That ground has been fully occupied . . . The whole field of fact and fancy has been gleaned and garnered. Any man can say things that are true of Abraham Lincoln, but no man can say anything that is new of Abraham Lincoln."[59]

The ellipsis in the above quote is Goodwin's and leads to a rereading of Douglass that contains a mild judgment on his capacity to say, in that moment, anything of great "new" consequence. Goodwin goes on to note that Douglass, at the distance of only eleven years, was too close to uncover such insights. The implication is that Goodwin, armed with an archive that has matured since Douglass's speech, regards her book, which draws on the stories of Lincoln's four rivals for the Republican presidential nomination, as poised to bring such "illumination."[60]

But what has been omitted by Goodwin's ellipsis? The italicized section of the following quote highlights what has vanished: "That ground has been fully occupied *and completely covered both here and elsewhere*. The whole field . . ."[61] In other words, Douglass feels compelled to say no more in that moment because he, in his almost-five-thousand-word portrait of the sixteenth president, had himself done his part to occupy "that ground." Fully cognizant that the occasion of free black citizens dedicating a monument to Lincoln would be "an act which is to go into history," Douglass is especially sure throughout his speech to contribute a complicated, nuanced, and emotionally stirring portrait of the man.

Douglass delivered the speech with President Ulysses S. Grant and members of his cabinet, as well as Supreme Court justices and members of Congress seated behind him. It was not lost on him that such a mass gathering would not have not have been possible just years prior. Though he would later express displeasure that the monument "showed the Negro on his knees," on that day he chose to laud the "monument of enduring granite and bronze, in every line, feature, and figure of which the men of this generation may read, and those of aftercoming generations may read, something of the exalted character and great works of Abraham Lincoln, the first martyr President of the United States."[62] But for Douglass, this was not the only part of the legacy that demanded remembrance: "It must be admitted, truth compels me to admit, even here in the presence of the monument we have erected to his memory, Abraham Lincoln was not, in the fullest sense of the word, either our man or our model. In his interests, in his associations, in his habits of thought, and in his prejudices, he was a white man."[63] He continued with his delicate portrait: "He was preeminently the white man's President, entirely devoted to the welfare of white men. He was ready and willing at any time during the first years of his administration to deny, postpone, and sacrifice the rights of humanity in the colored people to promote the welfare of the white people of this country."[64]

In Douglass's view, America's white citizens were "the children of Abraham Lincoln," while the blacks were "at best only his step-children; children by adoption, children by forces of circumstances and necessity."[65] All of this, and much more, precedes the statement that Goodwin quotes, and this is the principal reason it is no longer necessary for Douglass to speak critically of Lincoln. Douglass turns his oration toward guarded yet compassionate praise:

> Despite the mist and haze that surrounded him; despite the tumult, the hurry, and confusion of the hour, we were able to take a comprehensive view of Abraham Lincoln, and to make reasonable allowance for the circumstances of his position . . . Though he loved Caesar less than Rome, though the Union was more to him than our freedom or our future, under his wise and beneficent rule we saw ourselves gradually lifted from the depths of slavery to the heights of liberty and manhood.[66]

In presenting this speech in *Frederick Douglass: Selected Speeches and Writings*, Phillip Foner expresses disappointment that Douglass did not go further and make it known that "everything Lincoln had achieved for the Negro was being wiped out in state after state in the South."[67] Eleven years later, after a trip to South Carolina and Georgia, he would do so in a speech entitled "I Denounce the So-Called Emancipation as a Stupendous Fraud" given on the twenty-sixth anniversary of slavery's abolition in Washington, D.C. (April 16, 1888):

> I here and now denounce his so-called emancipation as a stupendous fraud—a fraud upon him, a fraud upon the world. It was not so meant by Abraham Lincoln; it was not so meant by the Republican party; but whether so meant or not, it is practically a lie, keeping the word of promise to the ear and breaking it to the heart.[68]

Goodwin acknowledges neither of these more radical moments from Douglass. Their absence preserves the narrative that caution and deliberate pace was part and parcel of Lincoln's political genius to create a foundation for an enduring emancipation. If Douglass's judgment that very little had changed more than twenty years later were to be made present, though not in any way Lincoln's "fault," this narrative would still lose a portion of its imagined continuity.

Goodwin is not alone in this project responding to a need to lay claim to the topography of Lincoln's mind. Richard Striner's *Father Abraham: Lincoln's Relentless Struggle to End Slavery* (2006), for example, attempts to restore Lincoln as the "Great Emancipator" in the face of what he feels are attempts to diminish this reputation. Like Goodwin, an uncomplicated and manipulated Douglass is instrumental:

> Another clue to Lincoln's feelings on race can be found in the memoirs of blacks who encountered him in person. They, above all, were in an excellent position to sense and to feel his racial attitudes. Frederick Douglass, the black abolitionist, was in such a position.
>
> Though Douglass concluded in a speech before a largely black audience in 1876 (*presumably on the basis of Lincoln's public statements in the 1850s*) that Lincoln "was a white man and shared toward the colored race the prejudices common to his countrymen," he reached a very different conclusion in the summer of 1865—*when the memory of Lincoln was vivid*. Douglass stated that Lincoln was "emphatically the black man's President: the first to show any respect for their rights as men."
>
> . . . Historian David Grimsted has argued that Lincoln was struggling with a "self-admitted racism." In the course of this struggle, he would not allow his prejudice to "cloud his sense of blacks' full humanity." If

> such a theory is correct, then Lincoln's struggle, as Grimsted suggests, "has something of the transcending dignity of Huck Finn's."
>
> *But there remains the possibility that no real prejudice existed in the mind of Lincoln.* It is possible that Lincoln, under pressure and confronting a militantly white supremacist electorate, pretended to feelings he did not really have on the subject of race. Whatever his innermost feelings on race, Lincoln's overall intention in the 1850s was apparent to all: to make whites disgusted with slavery, as much for its oppression of blacks as for its ancillary menace to themselves.[69]

Goodwin's and Striner's efforts are reminiscent of what Anna More describes as Sigüenza's and the other creole elite's need to "invent a deep history extending beyond the Spanish conquest"—it is a turn to the archive to organize new histories of greater psychic comfort.[70] But note how now the terms of such discussions revolve around Douglass without even registering the recognized black abolitionists beyond him, none of which are mentioned in the projects by Goodwin or Kushner and Spielberg. This, in itself, is indicative of the gravitational pull of the developing intrapsychic gap I am proposing.

But it is the figure of the enslaved person—after all, the most committed abolitionist and the reason for *Lincoln*'s narrative—who is the most conspicuously absent in the film. Tad, Lincoln's youngest son, at two points in the film is examining glass-framed photographs depicting the horrors of slavery while his father is in the room. These images were then widely circulated and published. On this first occasion, a couple of the photographs show young boys around Tad's age and list their monetary value. From the conversation that follows, the viewer is to understand that the photos also remind Tad of the loss of his brother Willie, who had died at the age of eleven three years prior. Lincoln carefully takes the photographs away from his son and proceeds to lie next to him and offer comfort. This and another brief appearance of Tad studying other photographs are the only moments in which any enslaved person is represented on screen.

The tender moment with Tad in particular highlights both Lincoln's empathy toward the figure of the enslaved person and his support of his son's color-blind association with the photographs. However, it also serves to distance the Lincolns from the institution of slavery, as these physical reminders are necessary to connect them to that institution and feed their (and the moviegoers') empathy. This aligns with Goodwin's characterization of Lincoln's desire to colonize blacks as due principally to his "lack of contact with the black community."[71] Here Lincoln, having learned his lesson, is shown diligently refining this empathy in his son. But this distancing is a fairy tale. Slavery was not abolished in Washington, D.C. until more than a year after Lincoln took office, making the argument of proximity invalid. More than this, however, the appearance of only these "distant images" works to vanish the active role that the enslaved played in securing their own freedom. As

Lincoln scholar Eric Foner points out in his op-ed in the *New York Times*, during the January 1865 deliberations on the Thirteenth Amendment that Kushner and Spielberg's project is dedicated to, "Sherman's army was marching into South Carolina, and slaves were sacking plantation homes and seizing land. Slavery died on the ground, not just in the White House and the House of Representatives."[72]

Foner's thinking simultaneously illuminates the film's central flaw and, unintentionally, makes clear the need for Hartman and others to continue to insist on understanding the always-present after*life* rather than after*math* of slavery.[73] However, for the sake of the present discussion, the fact that such rebels remain unthinkable in a film that firmly embraces "radical" ideas of equality tells of the rapid expansion of a transgenerational intrapsychic gap in the United States and the attendant gravitational forces marking the limit beyond which black matters are simply becoming indecipherably unthought. And this incoherence, these visibly invisible black bodies that speak to those on the balcony of the painting discussed at the end of chapter 2, brings us back to my interaction with Hawking, and the radiation that first brought him to examine the border of a black hole more closely. Hawking, intent on explaining what happens to the information lost in a black hole, relies on the metaphor of the encyclopedia: "If you jump into a black hole, your mass energy will be returned to our universe but in a mangled form which contains the information about what you were like but in a state where it cannot be easily recognized. It is like burning an encyclopedia. Information is not lost, if one keeps the smoke and the ashes, but it is difficult to read."[74] I remain steadfastly uninterested in excavating a quantity of fragments to approximate a "truth"; rather, I gather these fragments to present a new way of exposing the dependence on the fostering of a nonknowledge of the gaps which generation after generation give the collective liberal imagination structure.

If, as the rereading of Nicholas Abraham in chapter 2 suggests, "what [emanates] are not the dead, but the gaps left within us by the secrets of others," I am calling for an embrace of a critical practice, buoyed by anarchaeological notions, that honors a sustained awareness of these gaps and the valuable uncertainty they contain.[75] As such, what better tool than archaeology itself to further demonstrate, and therefore continue to refine an approach to unsettle, the thickness of an excavational mode of thought that structures a so-very-real imaginary as it relates to ideas of blackness? With this in mind, the following chapter moves to the south of Mexico in the decades following the Mexican Revolution as the nation remained in the process of archaeologically disrupting ground to solidify an understanding of itself. I am ultimately interested in how a practice of archaeology that is unable to allow for the possibility of blackness has endured from these beginnings to the present day.

Chapter 4

The Olmecs and the Inevitability of Holeness

> When he had secured the boat and settled onto the sloping meadow, he sat, to wet his throat with water from his winesack, and orient himself, and rest. Only then did he look back.
>
> —John Keene, "Mannahatta"

In 1939, Mathew Stirling, an archaeologist from the United States, began to unearth a site in the Mexican state of Tabasco known as La Venta. Stirling was building on information gained in a previous archaeological effort organized by Tulane University in 1925, which was sparked by a passage from the Spanish chronicler Bernal Díaz del Castillo that spoke of a ruined town along the Gulf Coast.[1] It was Stirling's work, however, that led to the "discovery" of the Olmec culture, which predated both the Mayan and the Aztec culture in Mexico and for this reason launched a brief but vigorous debate about the nature of Mexico's indigenous identity. By 1940, photographs of Stirling's findings were splashed on the pages of *National Geographic.* The most striking of his initial discoveries were the colossal heads (fig. 3) taller than a human being carved out of basalt that were, in Stirling's mind, Negroid in appearance. And while many smaller artifacts were unearthed that had no visible Negroid features, the possible implications of Stirling's discovery were enormous: a new culture was now to replace the Mayan and Aztec as the fountainhead of Mesoamerican culture, one with the possibility of an African ancestral presence. This possibility, no matter how small, disrupted two things. First, the racial composition of the Mexican identity grounded in its negation of blackness was no longer acceptable. Second, if outsiders (Africans, in this case) played a role in the construction of the first American, an argument described as diffusionist, it would compromise the idea of an entirely "new" culture that when combined with the blood of the European offered the theoretical separation so necessary in defining New Spain's difference relative to Europe.

Stirling was not the first to unearth a colossal head. That distinction belongs to José Melgar y Serrano. In an article published in 1869, Melgar makes the following observation of his discoveries in a remote agricultural

Fig. 3. Olmec. San Lorenzo Colossal Head I, ca. 1200–900 B.C.E. Basalt; 8.53 × 6.76 × 5.09 in. Museo de Antropología de Xalapa, 10958. Reproduced with permission from the Museo de Antropología de Xalapa, Catálogo digital/MAX Universidad Veracruzana.

area in southern Mexico: "Lo que más me impresionó fue el tipo etiópico que representa: reflexioné que indudablemente había habido negros en este país, y esto había sido en los primeros tiempos del mundo, aquella cabeza no solo era importante para la arqueología mexicana, sino también podía serlo para la del mundo en general" (What most stood out to me was the fact that it represents an African: I thought that there had undoubtedly been blacks in this country, and that this had been in the early ages of the world, that head wasn't only important for Mexican archaeology, but it could also be important for the archaeology of the world in general).[2] And unlike Stirling, Melgar does not merely stop at this observation. Archaeological evidence of an African presence in Mesoamerica is a crucial aspect of his article. In particular, he focuses on a quotation attributed to Francisco Núñez de la Vega, bishop of Chiapas in the late 1600s, in which the bishop reports: "Tienen los indios gran miedo al negro, porque dura la memoria de uno de sus primitivos ascendientes de color etiópico, que fue gran guerreador y cruelísimo, que los de Ochuc y de otros pueblos de los llanos veneraban mucho, al que llaman Yalahau, que quiere decir negro principal, ó Señor de negros" (The indigenous are very afraid of the blacks because the memory of one of their primitive ancestors that had the same coloring endures. He was such a great warrior, and cruel, that those from Ochuc and other towns of the plains venerated him a lot. They called him Yalahau, which means the first black or Lord of the blacks).[3]

Melgar points out that two other historians have referenced this quotation but have not taken it at face value; instead, they have argued that it was a custom for indigenous priests to paint their faces this color.[4] For Melgar, it is important to consider that these scholars were not themselves confronted by the overwhelming evidence of a colossal statue of a warrior with a helmet and Negroid features. Melgar is not trying to claim Africa as the origin of Latin American culture; rather, he is exploring what in his mind is an undeniable connection. This point of a relationship with Africa dovetails with his other explorations—principally connections with the Ancient Phoenician and Icelandic cultures—that suggest that a distinct separation between the so-called New World and regions on the other side of the Atlantic is a fallacy.

I am not concerned with whether or not this assertion that both Melgar and Stirling make is correct. What interests me is how the assertion was handled and rejected in the years immediately following Stirling's popularizing of the discovery and before the archaeological evidence had accumulated—if it ever has—to the point that its dismissal was deemed warranted by the archaeological community. The fact is, two archaeologists very familiar with the region and with seemingly no political motivations had described the colossal heads independently. However, within six years and without rigorous cross-examination these assertions within the archaeological community, in Mexico and beyond, evaporated.

An unexpected yet very influential character in this disappearance is Miguel Covarrubias. Covarrubias was a self-trained caricature artist who, as his career developed, became increasingly interested in anthropology and archaeology and used his artistic skill to produce, among other things, a visual and textual record of faraway places. He traveled to the United States as a young artist and was quickly embraced by the New York publishing industry. His exaggerated portraits of prominent public figures were featured in both *Vanity Fair* and the *New Yorker*. While in the United States, Covarrubias was accepted within the community of Harlem. He developed close relationships with many of the black artists and white benefactors, and his artwork was on the covers of, among others, works by Langston Hughes (fig. 4) and Zora Neale Hurston. He would also design the set for Josephine Baker's famous *La revue nègre* (1925) in France and provide images for the 1938 reprint of Harriet Beecher Stowe's *Uncle Tom's Cabin*.[5] Covarrubias enjoyed an audience

Fig. 4. Miguel Covarrubias (Mexican, 1904–1957). Cover of Langston Hughes's *The Weary Blues* (1926). Reproduced with the permission of María Elena Rico Covarrubias.

both in Mexico and the United States, much like his friend and contemporary Diego Rivera. Among his most famous early books were *Negro Drawings* (1927) and *Island of Bali* (1937). *Negro Drawings* collected many of the submissions he had made to *Vanity Fair* and other drawings inspired by Harlem nightlife (figs. 5–6). In many ways, the exotic nature of his drawings of black life would help to frame the visual record of the Harlem Renaissance.[6]

Island of Bali, the result of several trips to the island, combined drawings with a similar exotic flair and texts that described customs, dress, and rituals with a great eye for detail. It was in 1946, however, that Covarrubias turned his formally untrained anthropological eye to Mexico and the exotic within. He had been fascinated by the culture that was in the heart of its rediscovery in the south of Mexico at the Isthmus of Tehuantepec. Adriana Williams, in her biography of Covarrubias, describes the artist as greatly influenced by Vasconcelos's call to rediscover and bolster the indigenous component

Figs. 5–6. Miguel Covarrubias (Mexican, 1904–1957). *Comedian*, no. 26 (left) and *Dancing Waiter*, no. 45 (right) from *Negro Drawings*. Copyright © 1927 by Alfred A. Knopf, a division of Penguin Random House LLC, copyright renewed 1955 by Miguel Covarrubias. Used by permission of Alfred A. Knopf, an imprint of the Knopf Doubleday Publishing Group, a division of Penguin Random House LLC. All rights reserved.

of Mexican culture.[7] Long before he would write about the region, he was hired by Vasconcelos, then minister of education, to teach in the open-air art schools of Mexico City the value of certain elements (color, line, etc.) of indigenous Mexican art to contemporary artists. The famous Mexican painter Rufino Tamayo was also among this group of artistic missionaries.[8] However, Covarrubias's participation in the Mexican dialogue regarding identity would move way beyond the open-air schools with the publication of *Mexico South: The Isthmus of Tehuantepec* (1946). With this book, he played a fundamental part in the formation of Mexican anthropological thinking surrounding the Olmec culture. In *Indian Art of Mexico and Central America* (1957), Covarrubias would deepen his connection to the narrative of the Olmec culture by publishing a chart that "graphically illustrated the derivation of all later Mesoamerican rain deities from an Olmec progenitor."[9] This was the first attempt to connect the Olmec civilization to what had been previously put forward as the "Continuity Hypothesis." Before the discovery and placement of the Olmec civilization, it had been suggested that the Mayan creation myth (Popol Vuh) connected to the Aztec, Mixtec, and Zapotec cultures that followed.[10] Covarrubias's suggestion, which has since been endorsed by much of the archaeological community, solves the Olmec problem by creating a psychically comforting continuity between the first Americans and the contemporary Mexican state that had then just recently been reorganized around an Aztec/Mayan indigenous paradigm.

As a member of the Sociedad Mexicana de Antropología (Mexican Society of Anthropology), Covarrubias was a participant at the 1942 conference on the Olmecs in Tuxtla Gutiérrez, Chiapas, and his 1946 book was central in disconnecting blackness from what was the Olmec culture's largest sign, the colossal head. The conference hosted a significant contingent of influential figures from the anthropological and archeological communities within Mexico and beyond. Here Stirling and Melgar's observation of the Negroid quality of the heads was mentioned, but the implications of such an observation went unexplored.[11] By the time Covarrubias published *Mexico South*, the specific racial referent that had been used to discuss the colossal heads vanished. He mentions racial types (Mongoloid and Semitic) when discussing smaller figurines common to Olmec archaeological sites but leaves out a racial description of the colossal heads, instead listing characteristics as follows: "The first monument we saw was the seven-foot-high colossal head, the masterpiece of La Venta. It represents a chubby youth with a flat nose, heavy lids, and a full, sensual mouth."[12] Over seventy years later, this interpretation has held fast. Richard Diehl, who authored one of the most comprehensive books on the Olmecs in 2004, carries forward Covarrubias's observation and sums up the contemporary debate as follows:

> When José Melgar y Serrano published his pioneering description of Tres Zapotes Colossal Head 1 in 1869 he proposed that it depicted an "Ethiopian." This fiction recently resurfaced in the writings of Ivan van Sertima and others as part of an Afrocentric rewriting of world history. Melgar may be excused for his mistake, but today there can be no doubt that the heads depict the American Indian physical type still commonly seen on the streets of Sotepan, Acayucan, and other towns in the region.[13]

Diehl's remark brings one squarely to the work of Ivan Van Sertima, a footprint that cannot be avoided when tackling the issue of a potential black element associated with the Olmec culture. In 1976, Van Sertima published the controversial *They Came Before Columbus: The African Presence in Ancient America*. This book presents traditional scholarship combined with a narrative akin to historical fiction to plant the seed of the possibility of pre-Columbian contact between Africa and what would become the Americas.

Van Sertima's genre-bending project was, and continues to be, perceived by the great majority of the archaeological establishment as adhering to a blinding and inappropriate Afrocentricity. Certainly, the element of historical fiction played a role in this immediate and often virulent condemnation. The first chapter, for example, begins as follows: "On Saturday evening, March 9th, 1493, a week after Columbus had been driven by a storm into Lisbon, following his first voyage to the Indies, he sat down to dinner with the Portuguese king [John II] at his court in the valley of Paraiso. Don Juan seemed to be in an extremely good mood."[14] The meeting with the king is supported in the endnotes with citations attesting to this historical fact. The emotions, however, are the invention of Van Sertima. The employment of this dual strategy throughout the book appears to be, in part, an attempt to write blacks into the imagined narrative of an idea of America. When seen in this light, and in view of the backlash his work has received, it has been a largely successful pressuring on traditional narratives, one that takes archaeology beyond the realm of how the discipline understands and articulates itself. However, the albatross of Van Sertima's historical fiction tends to obscure some potentially cogent and traditionally archaeological ideas that present the possibility of an African component in the construction of America.

In 1991, Van Sertima delivered an address defending his work at the Smithsonian Institution. Stripped of any fictional element, this traditional academic address was later reproduced with minimal edits as the book chapter "African Presence in Early America" and published in the Smithsonian's collected volume *Race, Discourse, and the Origin of the Americas* (1995). He covers much of the terrain of the 1976 book: the connection between a black Egypt and the artistic, architectural, and spiritual elements of the Olmec culture; botanical and linguistic traces that suggest pre-Columbian contact between the African continent and the Americas; the historical fact of ocean currents and the development of watercraft that speak to the plausibility of such contact. In this restatement of the foundations of his previous work, Van Sertima is careful to foreground the fact that his strategy, especially when dealing with the suggested contact in the pre-Christian era, is to open up the "possible influence of [African] contact on an early American civilization."[15] Pressing on this idea of possibility, he opposes the school of thought holding that the civilizations inhabiting the Americas before the conquest developed in complete isolation. America, in his opinion, "is no laboratory for the study of virginal culture. It shows not only traces of an alien presence but of alien penetration."[16] In doing so, he makes sure to distance himself from the more extreme Afrocentric discourse that has dogged his work, claiming that he cannot, and should not, be boxed in by the reputation of "wild diffusionists," which he claims are "making absolute fools of themselves, claiming everything to be African."[17] Instead, Van Sertima frames his mission as a search for fragments of the "shattered worlds" of ancient America and Africa.[18]

David Kelley, an archaeologist with a lifelong commitment to the region, responds to Van Sertima's article in the same Smithsonian volume. It is one of the more level-headed critiques coming from what Kelley admits is the largely white archaeological establishment. He likens the resistance Van Sertima has faced to that of Carl Christian Rafn, who in 1837 proposed the then-radical idea that there had been Norse contacts in pre-Columbian America.[19] That archaeological record had to accumulate for over 120 years before the archaeological community could accept this idea. From the perspective of the Americas, Kelley highlights an intellectual bias in the training of archaeologists that necessitates the same virginal space Van Sertima disrupts in order to allow the discipline to make suppositions about human behavior.[20] Warfare, Kelley offers as an example, can be considered a natural behavior if it happens in this pure zone, and so forth. Thus, Kelley concedes that this purity is difficult to let go of and admits that evidence that could support Van Sertima's claims remains potentially buried and possibly irrecoverable. With respect to disease, his interest is piqued, and he pushes Van Sertima to go further with this aspect of his argument. His largest disagreements surround the link to Egypt and the reliance on botany that can be easily transported without a human subject. Nevertheless, Kelley comes to grips with the fact that the "archaeological record is still very incomplete" and that, especially in relation to the focus of my work—the potential African features of some of the Olmec heads—the possibility of significant African contact with the Americas "should be treated as a reasonable hypothesis, not dismissed to the crackpot fringes where it has been placed."[21] Going a step further, Kelley argues that in addition

> to the general likeness, the specific fact that several of the Olmec heads are represented with clearly sculptured lip seams. As far as I know, this is a genetic characteristic limited to African blacks, (not found in Melanesians, for example). Moreover, Van Sertima's discovery of the seven braids on the back of one of the Olmec heads is strong support for a hair type that is characteristic of African blacks.[22]

Kelley's premise "is that if a realistic model is available, one should not assume conventionalization of a less realistic model, unless there is very direct evidence it occurred."[23]

This call for reason has not been heeded by much of the archaeological mainstream. A trio of critics (Bernard Ortiz de Montellano, Gabriel Haslip-Viera, and Warren Barbour) came together just two years after Kelley's essay to pen an article in *Current Anthropology* addressing what it viewed as Van Sertima's Afrocentric pseudoscience.[24] Framed as an "attempt to address the issues articulated by students and concerned educators with regard to the validity of Van Sertima's hypotheses and the failure of the academic establishment to confront them in a systematic way," the collective project's title

("Robbing Native American Cultures: Van Sertima's Afrocentricity and the Olmecs") announces from the start an emotionality that belies the "systematic" approach it imagines attempting.[25] To accomplish the assigned task, the authors set up a straw man which ignores the more recent body of work and makes the exaggerated claim that Van Sertima presupposes that "the Nubian rulers of ancient Egypt . . . created, inspired, or influenced the creation of the Olmec civilization, which in turn influenced Monte Albán, Teotihuacan, the Classic Maya, and all other Mesoamerican civilizations that followed."[26] Ironically, the article maintains that "because relatively little information is available about the Olmecs, Van Sertima is able to make iconographic claims."[27] This relative lack of information, however, does not translate to a flexibility in their own positions and the realization that moving against the version of Van Sertima they have created does not necessarily suggest that there was no significant contact between Africa and the New World. The article ends with the near-absolute statement that "hardly a claim in any of Van Sertima's writings . . . can be supported by evidence found in the archaeological, botanical, linguistic, or historical record."[28] This negation is duplicated by the comments from renowned archaeologists assembled after the main article. Michael Coe, a pre-Columbian Mesoamerican specialist, announces that he has "spent three field seasons excavating the great Olmec center of San Lorenzo" and "would like to state unequivocally that there is nothing in these Olmec sites that *looks* African, Chinese, European or Near Eastern. The Olmec culture was created and maintained by American Indian peoples with a completely Mesoamerican way of life."[29]

In the spirit of David Kelley, Martin Bernal responded in the same journal a year later. Like Kelley, Bernal offers texture to the barrier that refuses the ideas of even slightly diffusionist conceptions of America. He articulates that such barriers would be "painful to surrender" but nevertheless calls for a "measured response" to what he believes is a "serious challenge to the academic disciplines concerned with ancient America."[30] In his view, "there is nothing inherently impossible in there having been contacts between Africa and America at any time in the past 5,000 years."[31] Whatever one may say about the validity of Van Sertima's claims, he has triggered a latent anxiety. Both Kelley and Bernal point to the improbability of significant pre-Columbian ocean crossings as "an important factor in 'establishment' rejection of international contacts" even though such logic ignores what is known of ocean currents and the development of watercraft.[32] The Canary Current and its relation to the North Atlantic Gyre is a large part of Van Sertima's 1976 book, as it connects the Senegambian region (where the majority of American enslaved Africans came from) to the Americas. Anthropologic and oceanographic studies of such currents have undoubtedly sparked some controversy, but not nearly as much when those conversations are connected to the protection of a virginal America from African contamination. Richard Callaghan, a scholar interested in water transport working in the disciplines of anthropology and archaeology, wrote "Drift Voyages across the Mid-Atlantic" in 2013 in an attempt to quantify the inevitability of such pre-Columbian crossings. His argument begins with the discovery of the Dufuna canoe in 1987 in the modern-day nation of Nigeria. This boat has been accepted within the traditional archaeological and anthropological communities to be at least eight thousand years old and of a style of which, being made of water-resistant mahogany, make it "the most probable, but not exclusive, candidate for a crossing [of the mid-Atlantic] anytime over the last 8,000 years."[33] These potential crossings could reflect intentional voyages, shipwrecks, and mariners lost at sea with cargo both human (arriving dead or alive) and nonhuman. To support this inevitability, he points to the twentieth-century crossings of Alain Bombard (1952) and Hannes Lindemann (1958), both of whom traveled in watercraft similar to the Dufuna.

Callaghan then turns to computer simulations that take into consideration current and wind data from the U.S. Navy's *Marine Climactic Atlas V.1.1*, and "these forces are then allowed to operate on [a variety of small open boats similar to the Dufuna] for a 24-hour period before a new selection is made."[34] The maximum duration with potential survivors was set at two hundred days, and the simulation launched one hundred watercraft each month just off the coast of the Canary Islands. The results are staggering, especially when contrasted with the obstinacy of the archaeological community working around ideas of blackness and the barrier of the ocean in Mexico. In the month of January, for example, 100 percent of the virtual watercraft made landfall in the Americas; the mean number of days was ninety-six, clearly within the bounds of possible human survival. Ten of the boats came ashore in Central America, and the great majority did so in the Antilles. The percentage of drifting watercraft making landfall only dips below 80 percent twice (July and August) with the months of June, September, October, November, and December maintaining a success rate at or above 90 percent. In Callaghan's entire simulation, "about 82% of vessels made landfall in the Americas, with most landing in the Antilles or Brazil, yet in some months as many as 21% of vessels landed on the Central American or Mexican coasts."[35] And even with the great majority of landfall occurring in the Antilles, Callaghan makes the reasonable assertion that "if ships were not severely disabled during the voyage, survivors may have opted to continue westward with the winds and currents rather than stay on small, unoccupied islands."[36] Callaghan is by no means a lone voice with such peer-reviewed work in the disciplines of geography and oceanography, and the existence of such research brings to the fore the authors who patently reject all of Van Sertima's claims under the banner of an Afrocentric pseudoscience.[37]

Van Sertima's largest pitfall, in the eyes of Haslip-Viera, Ortiz de Montellano, and Barbour, is an unhealthy reliance on "outdated secondary sources [and the] pseudoscientific writing of others."[38] This claim calls into question Van Sertima's training and academic integrity. Van Sertima received his

BA from the University of London's School of Oriental and African Studies, and an MA in anthropology from Rutgers. Importantly, he began his teaching career at Rutgers in 1972 and retired as an associate professor of Africana Studies at the same institution in 2005, all without earning a doctoral degree.[39] The criticism of Van Sertima's lack of a doctorate, perhaps surprisingly, beats a path back to Miguel Covarrubias. The Mexican artist would earn his high school degree at the age of fourteen, the last formal education he would receive, and proudly claim that "part of his success was a result of his lack of academic training, which left him free to develop his own style rather than be compressed into someone else's."[40] He moved to New York at the age of nineteen as a talented artist, and his rise from that point was mercurial. Despite lacking traditional academic paths, both Van Sertima and Covarrubias would have remarkable influences on the academic aspects of the cultural movements relating to their specific concerns. For example, Covarrubias had a significant relationship with Mexico's National Museum of Anthropology in its infancy,[41] while Van Sertima was the founding editor of the *Journal of African Civilizations*. However, Van Sertima's *They Came Before Columbus* is often derided on the basis of being published by Random House, a nonacademic press. Covarrubias's influential *Mexico South*, on the other hand, was published in English by Knopf, a similarly popular publisher that Covarrubias had established a relationship with through his links to the patrons of the Harlem Renaissance and his previous Knopf-published books (*Negro Drawings* and *Island of Bali*) and illustrations for books from the same imprint.[42] But despite the lack of formal training and publishing record with exclusively nonacademic presses, Covarrubias's standing is not called into question by the archaeological and anthropological establishment that relies on him. In fact, the response to his work is quite the opposite. Where, as noted above, Diehl accuses Van Sertima of "rewriting history," he lauds Covarrubias as "the great Mexican artist and pioneering historian of pre-Columbian art."[43] Diehl continues, stating that "despite the many discoveries in the past fifty years, Covarrubias's words remain as valid today as when he first penned them."[44] He announces himself as an adherent to the idea initially supported by Covarrubias in the 1942 summit of the Olmecs as the "Mother Culture" of Mesoamerican indigenous society.[45] This is done without reference to, or a discussion of, his qualifications to assert such a claim. And Diehl is not alone in this awkward yet invisible reliance on Covarrubias as a scholar. Michael Coe puts forward that "the best analyses of Amerindian art styles have thus come not from anthropologists, but from art historians, and artists like Miguel Covarrubias" and calls him "the great expert on the pre-Spanish art of Mexico."[46] In *Olmec: Colossal Masterworks of Ancient Mexico*, an edited volume produced by the Fine Arts Museums of San Francisco and the Los Angeles County Museum of Art in conjunction with Yale University Press, Covarrubias is, without hesitation or qualification, introduced and relied on as a "scholar" in the same breath as

Fig. 7. Self-caricature of Miguel Covarrubias as an Olmec, date unknown. Pen on paper. Reproduced with the permission of María Elena Rico Covarrubias.

trained archaeologists.[47] For example, it is noted that the work of Covarrubias and Beatriz del la Fuente, who earned her doctorate in art history from the National Autonomous University of Mexico, has "made it possible to recognize that some of the basic premises of Olmec sculpture have spread through space and time."[48] But how is that space and time imagined and governed?

Along with maintaining a similar professional trajectory, both Van Sertima and Covarrubias rely heavily on a phenotypic rhetoric when making the case for or against a black presence at the perceived fountainhead of Mexican culture. In *They Came Before Columbus*, Van Sertima includes two photos of Nuba chiefs from Africa alongside a collection of Olmec heads in order to further articulate his belief in the incontestable similarities between the Olmecs and populations on the continent of Africa.[49] Covarrubias's most lasting visual argument comes in *Mexico South*, where he places a photo of a young man, presumably indigenous, sitting beside a colossal head interpreting the countenance of the statue. On the same page is a photo of the face of a Totanac woman of the nearby city of Papantla with a similarly shaped mouth.[50] Given Covarrubias's presence during the debates regarding the origins of the Olmec culture, both of these images certainly helped to put a different face on features that had theretofore been described as Negroid and helped to condition the unreading that Van Sertima understands himself as working against. Though lighter in tone, Covarrubias's undated caricature of himself as an Olmec statue (fig. 7) chases this continuity.

Beyond the bounds of archaeology as this and other gestures may be, they have had remarkable staying power. Ignacio Bernal, author of one of the more significant academic texts related the Olmecs, *El mundo Olmeca* (1968), would introduce this work with the following epigraph: "A la memoria de Miguel Covarrubias, el ultimo Olmeca" (In memory of Miguel Covarrubias, the last Olmec). And Haslip-Viera and colleagues carry this forward: "[The] people represented in the Olmec sculptures had short, round, flat faces with thick lips, flat noses, and epicanthic folds; that is, they resemble people who still live in the tropical lowlands of Mexico."[51]

While the collection of academics growing out of Covarrubias is correct to point out similarities between the statues and the current native population of the region, to wholeheartedly reject any possible connection to Africa appears not to be driven by archaeological and anthropological inquiry alone. Negations such as these are double and speak to the strength of the gravitational forces beyond an apparent horizon that work to make unreadable Mexico's potential Afro-descendant elements. First, the very populations that are being compared to the colossal heads are in fact the most likely to have mixed with the colonial population of enslaved persons, as Veracruz (where the majority of the heads were found) maintained the largest population of enslaved Africans in Mexico. Second, there remains the possibility that the local indigenous population is in part descended from an Olmec population that was mixed with African blood. In a related irony, another site containing significant Olmec ruins was discovered in 1945 and given the name San Lorenzo Tenochtitlán.[52] This site, believed to be Mesoamerica's earliest city, is located less than 150 miles from what was San Lorenzo de los Negros, the first free black town in the Americas, which I discussed in chapter 1.[53]

And the archaeological community is open, to a certain extent, to question the ground they are quite literally walking on. Coe, for example, admits that "so few Olmec sites have been excavated—and even fewer published—that it remains difficult to be very precise about the nature of the Olmec presence beyond the Gulf Coast."[54] And in terms of the idea of found objects in excavations related to the Olmecs, Diehl relents that "virtually their entire output, save for objects made of clay and stone, has perished in the humid tropical environment."[55] In other words, the quality of the soil itself has so disfigured any archaeological approach to "truth" that it becomes about what truths are possible and who is allowed imagination. It is seemingly a healthy hole within the field of excavation itself, but the ideas of Van Sertima nonetheless find no space here. The discourse that conditioned this erasure is by no means cordoned off from our present thought processes. Two of the more important texts referenced above that solidify this vanishing, *The Olmecs: America's First Civilization* and *Olmec: Colossal Masterworks of Ancient Mexico*, were published in 2004 and 2010, respectively. And while Coe's words above come from a book originally published in 1994, this work has been carried forward as a standard-bearer in a 2013 updated seventh edition. Given this sustained presence, in following chapter I contend that one of the present-day consequences of a mind-set so blinded by an archaeological orientation rears its head in the accounting for the renewed visibility of black bodies in the upcoming Mexican Census. Moreover, I articulate how an understanding of such a consequence helps to read related ideas of archives, counting, and black bodies in the United States.

Chapter 5

✦

2020 Visions

> It is impossible to pretend that you are not heir to, and, therefore, however inadequately or unwillingly, responsible to, and for, the time and place that give you life—without becoming, at very best, a dangerously disoriented human being.
>
> —James Baldwin, *The Evidence of Things Not Seen*

Nearly one hundred years after José Vasconcelos presciently imagined the process of a cosmic erasure of blackness within the bounds of the nation, Mexico, it might appear, is prepared to reverse course. In 2020, after more than twenty years of pressure from Afro-descendant communities within Mexico and throughout Latin America and the world, Mexico's National Institute of Statistics (Instituto Nacional de Estadística y Geografía [INEGI]) will conduct a census giving the populace an opportunity to irrevocably, for now, become *negro* in the eyes of the federal apparatus. This step puts Mexico on par with every other Latin American nation, with the exception of Chile, in the tabulation of a statistical representation of blackness. While in Mexico *negros* will appear on the national register, there will be no more Negroes to the north: this descriptor has fallen off the 2020 U.S. Census. This shifting merely underlines the fact that, while embracing imperfection, census projects nonetheless orient themselves toward a full accounting and appear unaware of the science-fictional nature of the documents they produce. As such, they are most clearly aligned with ideas of recording and retrieval that my work unsettles. What follows caps the efforts of the preceding chapters by demonstrating that, despite this re-cognition, the psychic borders that make illegible ideas of blackness remain intact in the case of Mexico and are ever solidifying in the case of the collective liberal imagination of the United States.

It is important to lay alongside a census project that understands itself as scientific a perspective grounded in an understanding of reading as reading, as has been articulated throughout this book, to perpetually and productively mystify this work. As such, my intention is to read the census projects of Mexico and the United States (and the documents that revolve around them) as they relate to Afro-descendants as part of the fabric of a national literature.

The 2015 Encuesta Intercensal (Intercensal Survey) granted members of approximately 6 million of Mexico's 30 million households the opportunity to answer the question "De acuerdo con su cultura, historia y tradiciones, ¿se considera negra(o), es decir, afromexicana(o) o afrodescendiente?" (According to your culture, history, and traditions, do you consider yourself black, that is to say, Afro-Mexican, or Afro-descendant?).[1] The respondents were given four options: (1) yes; (2) yes, partially; (3) no; (4) I don't know. The results showed that Mexico as a whole had a 1.2 percent black population; Guerrero (3.3 percent), Oaxaca (4.9 percent), and Veracruz (6.5 percent) were the only states with a self-articulated black population higher than 2 percent.[2] Seventy-eight municipalities throughout the nation were found to have an Afro-descendant population between 10 percent and 29.9 percent, with twenty-two coming in over this mark, and six of the twenty-two, all in Oaxaca, having a population above 49 percent.[3] In the entire nation, 64.9 percent of the self-articulated Afro-descendant population consider themselves indigenous.[4]

This desire for an accounting of blackness has been present since planning for the 2020 Census began to formally take shape at the beginning of this decade. In 2011, Ricardo Bucio Mújica, then president of Mexico's Consejo Nacional para Prevenir la Discriminación (National Council to Prevent Discrimination), addressed the potential of the unprecedented acknowledgment, reminding readers of a *New York Times* article of the importance of counting to any neoliberal project of inclusion: "If it is not known how many there are, their conditions, there can't be an agreement on the part of the government for their inclusion at large."[5] The timing is not coincidental, as the United Nations (UN) High Commissioner for Human Rights declared 2011 the Year for People of African Descent and strongly encouraged UN member nations to participate in the effort to "fight against racism, racial discrimination, xenophobia and related intolerance that affect people of African descent everywhere."[6] Only after this declaration did the Mexican government, under Bucio's direction, produce its *Guía para la acción pública contra la discriminación y para la promoción de igualdad e inclusión de la población afrodescendiente en México* (*Guide for Public Action against the Discrimination and for the Promotion of Equality and Inclusion of the Afro-descendant Population in Mexico*) in 2011. To put this in context, just two years before this the Mexican government, in conjunction with a common sponsoring government agency (Consejo Nacional para la Cultura y las Artes), produced the book *Viaje por la historia de México* to celebrate Mexico's coming bicentennial. As I discussed in chapter 2, this document, designed to give both children and adults an understanding of Mexico's rich history, visualized the continued nonpresence of blackness at the center of the Mexican imaginary, offering a rare legibly illegible glance of an emanation from the nigrescent beyond. Yet a principal objective of the *GAP*, as it is, ironically, abbreviated within the document, was to change the national census to be inclusive of Afro-descendants in Mexico in order to diagnose the scope of the problems related to their invisibility.[7] Leading academics were consulted throughout the development of the document, and the distinguished María Elisa Velázquez was recognized as one of the authors. The *GAP* also highlighted organizations within Mexico and abroad that are working in various capacities to support the nation's Afro-descendant populations.[8] Its self-described goals are as follows:

> Ofrecer información sobre la importancia de las poblaciones afrodescendientes en el pasado y presente de nuestro país y datos para entender por qué no han sido reconocidas oficialmente en México.
>
> (To offer information about the importance of Afro-descendant populations in the past and present of our nation and information in order to understand why these populations have not been officially recognized in Mexico.)
>
> Presentar los principales ámbitos en que las poblaciones afrodescendientes han sido invisibilizadas, las acciones y actividades que se han hecho para resarcir esta situación y las recomendaciones para la realización de políticas públicas.
>
> (To present the principal areas in which Afro-descendant populations have been made invisible, the actions and activities that have been made in order to repair this situation, and recommendations for the enactment of public policies.)
>
> Proponer acciones encaminadas a restituir el derecho a la identidad de las personas afrodescendientes, invisibilizadas por la historia oficial, por acciones y omisiones, así como estrategias para promover el respeto, protección y garantía de sus derechos.
>
> (To propose actions aimed at restoring the right to identity of Afro-descendants who have been made invisible by the official history, by actions or omissions, as well as strategies to promote the respect, protection, and guarantee of their rights.)
>
> Proponer estrategias y acciones para el reconocimiento e inclusión de las personas afrodescendientes en los distintos ámbitos de la vida pública y de sus derechos económicos, sociales, culturales, civiles y políticos.

> (To propose strategies and actions for the acknowledgment and inclusion of Afro-descendants in the distinct areas of public life and of their economic, social, cultural, civil, and political rights.)[9]

The imprint of what my work is addressing is evident in all four goals of the *GAP*'s mission. Words outlining a processes of recognition (*reconocidas/reconocimiento*), restitution (*restiuir*), and reparation (*resarcir*) all point to a confidence in an ability to return to a prior state, a state where things are known and an accounting for the whole of Mexican culture is possible. Bucio offers a brief introduction to the *GAP* that mirrors this ability to "emprender esfuerzos que reviertan acciones y omisiones que se han infligido en contra de las personas afrodescendientes durante toda su historia" (undertake efforts that may reverse actions and omissions that have been inflicted against Afro-descendants throughout their history).[10] Later in the document, the proposed work is framed as a project of spreading awareness (*sensibilización social*) in which it is possible "recuperar la historia" (to recuperate the history) of people who have been rendered invisible.[11]

Given the faith in the possibility of reproduction, it is of no surprise that ethnographic-oriented academic forums and photographic expositions are the privileged tools of the action plan to enact such a reversion.[12] At one point, the text nevertheless acknowledges the failure of these methods to have the "repercusión necesaria para la valoración social de las culturas de origen africano en México" (necessary impact on the social valorization of the cultures of African origin in Mexico).[13] However, rather than call for an investigation of the methods themselves and their attendant reproductive blindness (or gaps), the *GAP* instead expresses the need for increased governmental support of the same methods in order to achieve a comprehensive analysis that will lead to a more permanent recognition.[14] It is a hyper-archaeological strategy that suggests an incapacity, or refusal, to understand the pull of what I have articulated as the national psychological apparatus's intrapsychic gap that has enacted Mexico's vanishing of blackness across generations. And, as I have argued in the previous chapters, without paying attention to the unthinkable nature of certain ideas of blackness, one cannot trace how the effects of this vanishing emanate within and throughout the entirety of the present moment.

Complicating a collective insensitivity to this unstable yet productive awareness is the fact that the focus of the entire document is to address present-day Afro-descendant persons and communities in Mexico. It is a fixation on ideas of blackness that are only embodied and thus more easily presented as set apart. No attention is paid to the idea that racial mixture has spread ideas of blackness beyond the confines of the marginal peoples and communities whose rescue is being attempted. With this limited perspective, the *GAP* is able to understand itself as benevolently calling for a redoubled effort to identify this distinct community so that the powers that be—implicitly unmixed with the Afro-descendant population—may diagnose and more fully redress centuries of vanishing. Tianna Paschel's scholarship on blackness and Colombia's 2005 Census persuasively suggests that such counting strategies in the hemisphere predate and stretch beyond Mexico. Focused on the resulting effects on land rights, Paschel sees this limiting or imaginative banishing of blackness to such rural, coastal areas as removing the threat of encroachment on more valuable central lands if and when ideas of recompense connected to land titling come to the table.[15] However, if one is for a moment able to shed this cynicism that an encounter with the Mexican state apparatus deserves, one could argue that such a counting is an appropriate first step in the recognition of a long-forgotten community. And, depending on the amount and integration of these investments, one could imagine the achievement of some identifiable positive results—especially given the number of grassroots organizations and academics connected to such investments.

One such individual is Emiko Saldívar Tanaka, a United States–based anthropologist drawn to interethnic relations in Mexico. She has taken aim at this idea of counting in relation to indigeneity and, since the 2015 survey, Afro-descent. Much of her work is dedicated to unpacking the dangerous implications of Mexico's neoliberal postracial understanding of its own mixture, even in its recent turn toward a more pluricultural model in the wake of the challenge to the Mexican state offered by the Zapatista movement in 1994. She examines how the federal apparatus's approach toward indigenous communities, even after this shift from a magical idea of assimilation to an awareness of difference, remains incapable of redressing the scourge of poverty which continues to mark indigeneity in the idea of the Mexican nation.[16] For Saldívar Tanaka and her cowriter, Casey Walsh, this is largely because the adjustment in statistical recognition has "not changed the way the state conceives of the dominant majority."[17] The current process, in her opinion, stems from "the erroneous assumption that conflict in interethnic relations is due to an ignorance of the 'other.' This reproduces the official assumption that culture is the axis of differences and the source for change in the dynamics of interethnic relations. It assumes that there is an essential 'other' that has a cultural matrix that is different from 'ours.' "[18]

Saldívar Tanaka astutely points out that this separation is reinforced by the counting of only blacks and indigenous in Mexico's census, creating the sense that "the only ones that we need to count are the ones that are vulnerable" and highlighting the problematic presentation of vulnerability as a condition of indigeneity or Afro-descent.[19] Staying within the bounds of an ethnographic approach, Saldívar Tanaka is working with INEGI to address this discrepancy as the census is being sharpened. At a 2017 UNAM-sponsored colloquium on the 2020 Census, Saldívar Tanaka situated herself within a community that nevertheless views census statistics, in great measure, as "central in solving the problem of the invisibilization" of these communities.[20] Saldívar Tanaka desires a statistical nuance that respects the fluctuation of regional imbalances, as different racial dynamics lead to different structures of support and/or oppression to be addressed through federal, state, and local resources. Hers is a welcome and necessary voice to have in the room. As a scholar who has done great work laying bare the project of mestizaje as a postracial ideology that disavows structural racism, her intent is to steer the ongoing census project away from such a neoliberal embrace of racial difference and toward resource allocation, general recognition, and the humanity that comes along with it.[21]

However, despite this insistence on nuance, and in part because of it, within this approach there too remains, as was the case with the architects of the *GAP*, a faith in the possibility of counting that undermines the goal, as it relies on a logic of excavation I have been working against. The vision of excavation is perhaps most noted in the phenotypic rhetoric that was discussed in chapter 4 in the context of Covarrubias and Van Sertima. This rhetoric, and discourses speaking to visibility more generally, is understandably necessary for those attempting to account for Afro-descent and in some way make reparation to physical communities. For this reason, Saldívar Tanaka and others fighting for the recognition and rights of Afro-descendants are critical of the hypocrisy of a UN that discourages linking phenotype to conversations of Afro-descent, all the while covering their website with images of black faces that have long been the staple of international intervention in communities of color.

To combat this, there is an obvious determination to present images of Afro-Mexicans to the greater public. This is clear in almost every article dedicated to covering the advancements in the movement and much of the government-sponsored documents that similarly push toward a greater awareness of what is now more and more legibly discussed as *la tercera raíz*, or third root, of Mexican culture. The federally sponsored Instituto Veracruzano de la Cultura and the Centro Nacional de Investigación y Difusión del Danzón, for example, sponsor many events that revolve around such rediscovery and the sonic and visual components of *son jarocho* and *danzón*, the music of the region that, like its Caribbean counterparts, contains a fusion of African, indigenous, and Spanish elements.[22] While some ethnomusicologists have connected to this current to articulate what they see as music's capacity to demonstrate Afro-Mexican resistance,[23] Hettie Malcomson, echoing my work, questions the imagined solid ground of such "cultural rescue" being promoted by what she labels as Veracruz's various culture industries.[24] In her ethnographic research on the region, Christina Sue astutely points out that the exotic nature of these musical discourses have, in fact, allowed citizens of the region uncomfortable with this growing connection to blackness to place such blackness beyond Mexico's border.[25] Laura Lewis's ethnographic research on the Costa Chica region of Oaxaca identifies what she calls "culture workers" as coming from both outside the region and the nation imposing rigid Afro-centric racial categorizations. For Lewis, this forecloses more nuanced articulations of identity and thus disrupts the processes of understanding community needs in order to improve social conditions on the ground. And, like Saldívar Tanaka, she takes issue with the need to name Afro-Mexicans while the perceived homogeneous population assumes no such descriptor.[26] Whatever the position, there is an unquestionable pressure on the idea of making black bodies and voices visible and heard in this push for both recognition and distance.

This legibility, however, both depends on and deepens the fortification of a separation between an "us" and "them" that Saldívar Tanaka's necessary work aims to deconstruct. From the perspective of the dominant majority, such a sterile sequestering works to create the comfortable and necessary distance to launch humanitarian efforts. In other words, and in the context of Mexico, such a project of recognition simultaneously allows for the lack of a re-cognition of a central blackness and the elusive apparent horizon that governs it. It is clear that the results will be severely limited and limiting, as the Mexican collective psyche is simply in the process of inventing a new legible darkness. However progressive this may appear, it is an idea of blackness that can only be registered if it identifies itself without laying claim to the radical possibility that trapped within the benevolent gesture between "us" and "them" is a failure of cognition that has always remained, however vanished, at the center of and not apart from the collective psyche of the nation. Without an attempted engagement with this vanishing force itself—the nigrescent beyond or that which structures how one reads without itself being read—a central idea of blackness will remain beyond awareness. The fact that such a process escapes awareness in the *GAP* and the ensuing 2015 Intercensal Survey, projects that so directly trumpet awareness, only further reifies what I have identified as the apparent horizon within the liberal imagination, beyond which ideas of blackness are not only unthought but irrevocably indecipherable.

Given the *GAP*'s connection to the aforementioned culture industry, it is of no surprise that the document uses a distinctly phenotypically black face to introduce each section of the document. With four of these eight images being of children, this phenotypic rhetoric seems to require some investment in the figure of the child. In this way, it might be understood within the genre of protest literature and the all-too-common reliance on the trope of sentimentality. Gleaning from the poet Claudia Rankine and Beth Loffreda's conversation with the spirit of James Baldwin on the subject of such literature, sentimentality can be both a "common language for race" and because of the rigid borders of such tropes can represent "the signal of [a] secret and violent inhumanity."[27] Further betraying the link of the vision of 2020 to this idea of the child is the census project's historical connection to an insistence on ideas of fertility.

Table 1
Mexican Census Questions, 1895–1930

Census date	Questions regarding indigeneity and Afro-descent	Questions regarding fertility
1895	Is your native tongue Spanish or an indigenous language (examples given: Mexicano or Náhuatl, Zapoteco, Otomí; Tarasco, Maya, Huscateco, and Totonaco)?	None
1900	Is your native tongue Spanish, French, English, etc., or an indigenous language? (examples given: Mexicana, Zapoteco, Otomí, and Maya)	None
1910[1]	Based on collected responses, citizens were asked if they spoke Spanish or another language or dialect.	None
1921	Do you speak Spanish? What other language or dialect do you speak?	None
1930	Do you speak Spanish? What other language or dialect do you speak?	None

Data on Mexican censuses in this and the following tables come from "Population and Housing Census and Countings: Census and Intercensal Historical Series," Instituto Nacional de Estadística y Geografía, https://en.www.inegi.org.mx/programas/ccpv/cpvsh/default.html.

[1] No record of the original questionnaire has been found, so the specific framing of the questions is not known.

In both the first census in 1895 and the subsequent counting five years later, there is an apparent, and easeful, flexibility in identity as it relates to one's native language (table 1). In the instructions attached to the 1895 document, however, there is a note that speaks to the process of the solidification of the Mexican identity around that of a position of Spanish: "La persona que hable el castellano y un idioma indígena como el otomí ó mexicano, se le apuntará de preferencia el castellano" (The person who may speak Spanish and an indigenous language, like Otomí or Mexicano, would mark Spanish).[28] In conjunction with this push toward a Spanish homogenization, there is no tracking of fertility. The 1910 Census precedes the Mexican Revolution, which would fight in the name of indigenous rights, and it maintains a similar framing. It is under Álvaro Obregón's rise to power in 1921 that a relative stability exists and the the revolution is declared to be over. The following year contains the first census since the revolution. Indigeneity becomes somewhat less legible: respondents are asked whether they speak Spanish or another dialect, with no reference within the question or the form's instructions speaking directly to indigeneity. However, unlike in 1895 and 1900, in 1922 the respondents are allowed to mark both Spanish and another language or dialect. (José Vasconcelos was the secretary of public education under President Álvaro Obregón [1921–24], so one might conclude that this census represents an aspiration toward the cosmic hetero-homogeneity he represented.) The 1930 Census follows the Partido Nacional Revolucionario's (PNR) consolidation of power in 1929. In this census, there is a continued pause in linguistic questions relating to indigeneity.

Table 2
Mexican Census Questions, 1940–90

Census date	Questions regarding indigeneity and Afro-descent	Questions regarding fertility
1940	Do you speak Spanish? What other language or dialect do you speak (examples given: English, French, Otomí, Náhuatl)?	How many live births have you had? How many are still living?
1950	Do you speak Spanish? Do you speak an indigenous language or dialect (examples given: Náhuatl, Otomí, Zapoteco)?	How many live births have you had?
1960	Do you speak Spanish? Is an indigenous language your mother tongue (examples given: Náhuatl, Otomí, and Zapoteco)?	Same as 1950
1970	Do you speak an indigenous language (specify)? Do you also speak Spanish?	Same as 1950 and 1960
1980	Do you speak an indigenous language (specify)? Do you also speak Spanish?	How many live births have you had? How many are still living? When was your last child born alive?
1990	Do you speak an indigenous language (specify)? Do you also speak Spanish?	How many live births have you had? How many are still living?

However, with the 1940 Census, conducted two years after the populist president Lázaro Cárdenas came to power and recast the PNR as the Partido de la Revolución Mexicana (PRM), there was a move to present, for the first time since prior to the Mexican Revolution, a linguistic choice that explicitly names on the form itself the possibility of indigeneity: Otomí and Náhuatl (table 2). Along with the return of an explicit indigeneity, this census begins the process of self-reporting fertility that remains a part of the Mexican census project to this day. The 1950 and 1960 censuses baldly placed these questions under the heading of *fecundidad* (fertility). In relation to indigeneity, the 1950 Census was conditioned by the same moment, discussed in chapter 2, that produced, in the same year, Octavio Paz's backward glance to

Mexico's buried yet psyche-shaping pre-Columbian cultural past in *El laberinto de la soledad* (*The Labyrinth of Solitude*). Like no previous census, the instructions further underline what is at stake: "Uno de los fines más importantes del censo de población en México es obtener el número de habitantes que hablan exclusivamente lenguas indígenas o bien español y una lengua o dialecto indígena" (One of the more important objectives of the Mexican Census is to obtain the number of inhabitants who exclusively speak indigenous languages, as well as those who speak Spanish and an indigenous language or dialect). The 1960 Census shapes questions around indigeneity and language in a similar manner, though the extended clarification in the instructions is no longer present. The censuses from 1970 to 1990 all ask whether the respondent speaks an indigenous language, with no specific example given.

Table 3
Mexican Census Questions, 2000–2015

Census date	Questions regarding indigeneity and Afro-descent	Questions regarding fertility
2000	Do you speak an indigenous dialect or language (specify)? Do you also speak Spanish? Are you Náhuatl, Mayan, Zapoteco, Mixteco, or of another indigenous group (select yes or no without specifying an indigenous group)?	How many live births have you had? How many of these children have died? How many are still living? When was your last child born alive? Is this last child still alive? If not, how old was this last child when he or she died?
2010	Do you speak an indigenous dialect or language (specify)? Do you also speak Spanish? Do you understand an indigenous language? According to your culture, do you consider yourself indigenous (select yes or no without specifying an indigenous group)?	Same as 2000
2015	According to your culture, history, and traditions, do you consider yourself black, that is to say Afro-Mexican or Afro-descendant (choose yes, in part, no, or I don't know without specifying an indigenous group)? According to your culture, do you consider yourself indigenous (choices: yes, in part, no, I don't know)? Do you speak an indigenous dialect or language (specify)? Do you also speak Spanish? Do you understand an indigenous language?	Same as 2000 and 2010

The 2000 Census—collected five months prior to the first federal-level defeat of the Partido Revolucionario Institucional (PRI, a recasting of the PNR), which ended a political reign stretching from 1929 to 2000—represents the most significant refashioning since 1950 (table 3). The first since the Zapatista uprising's demand for indigenous autonomy, it offers an illuminating expansion. Beyond language, this is the first time in the history of the Mexican Census that, in conjunction with identifying fluency in an indigenous language, respondents are given the choice to identify, culturally speaking, as part of an indigenous group. This new articulation of belonging comes with an expansion of questions relating to fertility from three to six. These changes are sustained in the 2010 Census and the 2015 Intercensal Survey, with this last document adding the question relating to Afro-descent. With this exposure and recognition of a distinct cultural difference comes a heightened scrutiny in relation to movement. Since the debut of a category of linguistic indigeneity in the modern Mexican state in 1950, there has been an increased tracking of domestic movement.[29] The 1950 Census followed all of its antecedents in simply asking for the respondent's place of birth. In 1960, and all of the censuses to follow, a question regarding one's prior residence is included. However, until the year 2000, respondents were only asked, in varying language, to include the name of the Mexican state or territory, or foreign nation. In 2000, and all subsequent counting where there is a distinct shift in indigeneity and fertility, the tracking of respondents' movements is refined with the specificity of municipality.

In the context of self-articulated identity in the eyes of the federal apparatus, the United States has charted an opposite course to that of Mexico. Reflective of the increasing gravity of its psychic ambitions regarding racial identification, a large portion of the liberal national psychic apparatus in the United States is imagining, despite resistance from an emboldened right, a march toward the postracial. The long view from Mexico is helpful in thinking through and giving language to this faint sense of an emerging texture of its apparent horizon and the consequences of what I understand as a growing gravitational singularity. Barack Obama, both symbol and catalyst for much of this ambition, made this explicit link between Mexico and the United States in remarks during his 2008 election campaign at the National Council of La Raza's annual meeting:

> That's how we'll make the system work for everyone. By living up to the ideals of NCLR. Living up to the ideals reflected in your name—La Raza, the people. I'm told that the original phrase was "La raza cósmica"—the cosmic people. That's big. A term big enough to embrace the rich tapestry of cultures and colors and faiths that make up the Hispanic community. Big enough to embrace the notion that we are all part of a greater community—that we all have a stake in

> each other; that I am my brother's keeper, I am my sister's keeper; and we rise and fall together as one people.[30]

While Obama is clearly missing the context that renders this a strange statement for a black man to make, analysis of census questionnaires not only aligns with a liberal United States' burgeoning racial understanding of itself but supports the suspicion put forth by the analysis in the Mexican case: anxiety of racial or cultural infection may be in part correlated to the federal apparatus' decennial questioning of fertility and movement.

As was noted in the introduction to this chapter, the racial descriptor "Negro," present in the 2000 and 2010 U.S. censuses, disappears in 2020. This belated abandonment is due in large part to the fact that in the late 1990s the Census Bureau conducted research that showed over fifty-six thousand people self-identifying as "Negro" when given the option to input "some other race."[31] As former Census Bureau director Robert Groves maintained in defending the decision, "Full inclusiveness was the goal."[32] It was thus, ironically, neoliberalism's mantra of inclusion, and a correlative anxiety born out of the desire for full awareness, that maintained the antiquated descriptor for fear that older generations not yet accustomed to identifying as black or African American would go uncounted. The combination of a growing tide of news outlets lambasting the continued use of the outdated descriptor and the drop in self-identifying "Negroes" in 2010 led the Census Bureau to conduct more research and make the decision to hereafter banish "Negroes" from the official record of the United States.[33]

Since 1930, blackness has been solidified under a single categorical choice: Negro (through 1960), Black or Negro (1970–90), and Black, African American, or Negro (2000 and 2010).[34] This view of blackness is reflective of a return to the one-drop rule of hypodescent that separates any contagion of blackness from the figuration of imagined whiteness. Following this, from 1930 to 1960 respondents were, through the parameters given in the enumerator's instructions, expected to select one race. Interestingly, in the census after the Supreme Court's 1967 decision to deem antimiscegenation laws unconstitutional, a check box appears for the first time alongside the question relating to race with an explicit instruction to "fill one." This is consistent with Jared Sexton's conclusion that

> when faced with the specter of violent black sexuality or sexualized black violence, white supremacy in the United States has consistently conflated blacks and mulattos through retrenched enforcement of the one drop rule. That is to say, when blacks move against the structures of white supremacy, "mixed race" is revoked as a viable social identity and racial blackness is again understood as a broad spectrum.[35]

The sequestering seen in the 1970 Census was continued in 1980 and 1990, as it was not until the 2000 Census that respondents were allowed to check as many racial categories as they desired. Further tracing this development of a federally recognized multiracialism and connecting it to the revelations gleaned from the Mexican context, while fertility and intercensal movement had been tracked without interruption since the 1940 Census, the 2000 Census, with its embrace of the multiracial subject, saw the disappearance of the category of fertility. The 2010 Census inquired neither about fertility nor about movement. And as of March 2018, the planned subjects for the 2020 Census remain consistent in this regard.[36]

Statistics of fertility and movement are still tracked by the American Community Survey (ACS), a survey sent to approximately 3.5 million households each year.[37] While decisions in terms of the allocation of resources come from this count, they are not presented in this seminal moment of self-articulation for the individual citizen and the nation's imagination of itself. Thus, the example of the United States, especially when contrasted with that of Mexico, suggests a correlation between discrete racial categorization designed to articulate cultural diversity within an "us/them" framework (and its multiracial opposite), and questions of fertility and movement. This appears to interact with Lee Edelman's reminder that the child "remains the perpetual horizon of every acknowledged politics, the fantasmic beneficiary of every political intervention."[38] The key here is an *acknowledged politics*. Radical black politics, as opposed to neoliberal politics of multiracialism, remain unacknowledgeable, or, at the very least, drifting quickly toward a developing nigrescent beyond. Consequently, as ideas of blackness have begun to vanish in this march toward the cosmic in the United States, so have acknowledged liberal politics circulating around the figure of the black child.

There is a historical trajectory to be accounted for here that, for the sake of this conversation, will "start" with the significant moment in the traction of the civil rights movement when, in 1951, the NAACP filed the class action suit on behalf of parents attempting to enroll their children in segregated public schools. Olivia Brown, whose name would famously be attached to the landmark 1954 ruling in *Brown v. Board of Education of Topeka, Kansas*, was in third grade at the time. This effort led to the ruling that overturned *Plessy v. Ferguson*'s 1896 doctrine of "separate but equal." While other public facilities similarly affected by the 1896 ruling would have to wait, the legible starting point was the education of children. Three years later, when many states maintained an independence from the demands of the ruling of the Supreme Court, it was the image of the nine students with armed escorts walking into Little Rock Central High School that would help to exert a pressure on the American conscience that led to a strengthening of the Supreme Court's 1954 decision by declaring unconstitutional the enactment of state laws to maintain segregated schools.[39] However, perhaps the most demonstrative support of this connection between the child and political legibility is the probability that the civil rights movement as we have come to view it would have had an entirely different trajectory had it not been for the role of children in protests in Birmingham, Alabama, in May 1963.

After John F. Kennedy refused to speak publicly at an event organized for the hundredth anniversary of the Preliminary Emancipation Proclamation for fear of turning away southern Democrats in advance of the next election cycle, Martin Luther King Jr. would send many unheeded requests for Kennedy to announce, alongside the proclamation's anniversary, a "Second Emancipation Proclamation" more directly connected to the ongoing battle for black equality.[40] This stonewalling by the powers that be in Washington was a motivating factor in King's post-1962 more radical turn, during which he went to Birmingham and personally approved the enlistment of women and children marchers (known as the "Children's Crusade"). The photographs of these children's mistreatment went a long way in returning the issue of civil rights to the front of the nation's consciousness and back to Kennedy's desk.[41] The bombing of the Sixteenth Street Baptist Street Church, which killed "four little girls" (Addie Mae Collins, Cynthia Wesley, Carole Robertson, and Carol Denise McNair), and the images it produced, came just four months after Birmingham. Less than a year later (July 2, 1964), and more than seven months after the assassination of Kennedy, Lyndon Johnson would step into Kennedy's void and under the pressure of a building social crisis not only sign the Civil Rights Act into law but also stand in front of the American people and broadcast, with an implicit apology for the delay, a presidential declaration of the value of black life that approaches the utopian grandeur of Morelos's "Sentimientos de la nación."[42] In this speech, Johnson reflected on the U.S. Constitution in an attempt to grant blacks legibility, claiming it declares that "the only limit to a man's hope for happiness, and for the future of his children, shall be his own ability."[43] On March 15, 1965, Johnson followed this up by convincing Congress to sign the Voting Rights Act with the use of a tenuous equivalence between the value of white and black children: "Negroes are not the only victims. How many white children have gone uneducated?"[44] Building on this, Johnson would declare that he wanted "to be the President who educated young children to the wonders of their world."[45] The child in this imagination is wholesome.

There remains, however, another resonance to be pointed to: the fearsome black man-child, the queer body, and the undesirable woman—all beyond the grasp of such rescue. Whereas the unquestionably denuded antiblack Dwight Eisenhower's hand was forced to deploy the National Guard for the protection of the Little Rock Nine, the president was obstinately silent in the face of David Jackson's infamous photograph of Emmett Till's mother looking at the mutilated corpse of her fourteen-year-old son. This image of a dead child galvanized the black community for the battles to come, but Eisenhower endorsed the FBI's conclusion that Till was not an innocent child but an instrument for communist subversion. (He had, in fact, given J. Edgar Hoover the National Security Medal just three months prior.)[46] Children in the mold of Till strain for legibility and do not garner the same sympathy as those imagined as wholesome. James Baldwin would speak of such children in a 1981 article for *Playboy* that was later expanded into his last book-length nonfiction work (*The Evidence of Things Not Seen*). Written in tandem with the then-burgeoning Reagan era, it reflects on what would be called the Atlanta Child Murders, which saw the death of twenty-seven children and two adults between 1979 and 1981. As the great majority of the victims came from Atlanta's black underclass, Baldwin's analysis centers on a remaining relative nonpresence of certain black bodies in what he understood as the American imagination. Early in the work, Baldwin presents the first thirteen of these particular twenty-nine bodies in a sparse roll call: *Name, age. Date last seen. Date body was found. Cause of death, if known.*[47] Baldwin stops at thirteen because, though the authorities would ultimately claim a pattern led to the conviction of Wayne Williams, it was only after the thirteenth murder that there was a legible, "(official) hue and cry."[48] Baldwin was confused—or, rather, infuriated that he was not confused—by the fact that it took so long for the terror of Atlanta's underclass to register in the city's imagination. Baldwin is primarily interested in pointing out the case's dubious nature in order to use it as a vivid metaphor for how the myth of social progress functions to placate the larger society and, ultimately, to underline who gets left behind in this myth-making process. What finally made present this obscene collection of bodies, at that point all children between seven and fourteen years old? And the reverse: What had allowed the vanishing of the first twelve for such a protracted time? It is a meditation on the nature of the barrier that floats between these two questions. Baldwin is coming up against the germinal stages of a postracial imaginary and arguing that the case demonstrates that the United States' psychological apparatus desperately needed to understand the movement for full civil rights as complete and wholly successful. In other words, in light of evidence to the contrary, Atlanta, famously dubbed the "city too busy to hate" and an unquestioned emblem of the movement's success, had to *move* on. And the child, or rather the dead unwholesome child, was not to be a part of this.[49]

The idea of the child has remained fraught as the liberal postracial imaginary has continued to develop. In the court case of seventeen-year-old Trayvon Martin's slaying on February 26, 2012, photographic evidence drawing on age and innocence (or lack thereof) was a gravitational centerpiece. The most prominently distributed image of Martin is an appeal to that innocence, showing him as a smiling thirteen- or fourteen-year-old boy. The lawyers for George Zimmerman, Martin's killer, attempted to combat this image by bringing into evidence photographs substantiating their portrayal of a more menacing Martin smoking marijuana. Though declared inadmissible by the judge, this evidence nonetheless became part of the larger public discourse.[50]

President Obama attached himself to the boyish image when speaking after the ruling that cleared Zimmerman from any wrongdoing. Importantly, this was before Ferguson and before the Black Lives Matter movement would galvanize around the dead body of Martin and the ensuing acquittal of Zimmerman. Obama would claim at the time that Martin "could have been my son" or himself "35 years ago."[51] He framed his comments around "boys" and a belief that, while we are not quite there, we are much closer to an idea of a "postracial society" that the liberal imagination clung to in their push to bring him to office.[52] It is an appeal to the sentimental register, a cry for peace in the name of the wholesome child.

As legible police violence has continued, however, the force of the figure of the child in the liberal imagination of the nation has diminished significantly. This is most evident in the events surrounding the murder of Tamir Rice by a Cleveland police office on November 22, 2014. No anachronistic gymnastics involving photographs to appeal to our better angels were needed with Tamir Rice: he *was* twelve years old. Yet despite the traditional markers bespeaking legibility and pushing the agenda of an acknowledged (if not marginal) politics, Rice's body seems to be in the process of becoming, archivally speaking, dark, not to be recovered in the collective liberal psychic apparatus but relentlessly pulled toward that nigrescent beyond.

If one were to construct such an archive, one would be hard pressed to find anything more symbolic than the Obama White House Archives. The website is framed by words drawn from the president's farewell address: "Yes, we did. Yes, we can . . . You were the change. You answered people's hopes, and because of you, by almost every measure, America is a better, stronger place than it was when we started."[53] On this same page you are reminded that this archive "is historical material 'frozen in time.' "[54] It is a collection of information to be carried forward, a repository of what we will be heir to. Yet and still, there is contained within not one direct remark from Obama on the body of Tamir Rice. Three weeks after the shooting of Rice, Obama would be interviewed by Jeff Johnson on Black Entertainment Television (BET). It was framed as an opportunity to speak to the black community, at least those who tune in to BET, and underscore his compassion for victims of police violence and allay fears that his administration was not making a strong enough effort addressing this violence. One particular exchange deserves significant space:

> JEFF JOHNSON: We talked about having 15-year-old daughters. And at one point those daughters may have children. What's the vision that you have—not necessarily as President of the United States, but as Barack Obama, the man—for those children that's different than what Mike Brown, Tamir Rice and others have had to face?
>
> BARACK OBAMA: I want my children to be seen as the individuals that they are, and I want them to be judged based on the content of their character and their behavior and their talents and their

> gifts. I don't want them to be objects of fear simply because of misguided attitudes.
>
> Part of what I think is so heartbreaking and frustrating for a lot of folks when they watch this is the recognition that simply by virtue of color you've got less margin for error. And that's particularly true for black boys. Young men, teenage boys—sometimes they're going to do stupid stuff. That's true whether they're white, black, Hispanic. It doesn't matter. You did stupid stuff. I did stupid stuff. Most of the time it's harmless. Sometimes it's careless. And then we grow and we progress, and we become, hopefully, solid citizens and men who are contributing to our society. And so it's not simply that we want to make sure that the perfect young man is treated okay. We also want a boy who's a boy, or a young man who maybe is a little confused, maybe makes a mistake—we want them to be given the same benefit of the doubt as any other man would, or any other boy would be given . . . I guess the answer to your question is pretty simple: I want my grandsons to be treated like anybody else's grandsons. If they're messing up, I think they should be corrected—they'll first be corrected by me or their mother or their father. But I don't want them to be subjected to the kind of constant bias that makes them feel as if this is not their home, and that they're not safe in their own neighborhoods, or that they cannot trust the institutions that are put in place supposedly to serve and protect them. And I think that can be achieved.[55]

Not only is Barack Obama's response bound by a troublingly simple framing of masculinity, his daughters' primary legibility in this response is as the reproducers of wholesome "boys [who] will be boys." Despite Tamir Rice's name being mentioned by Johnson in two questions, Obama cannot utter his name. At one time he refers to "the Cleveland case." Though doubtful, this could be referring to Malissa Williams and Timothy Russell, who were killed after police shot 137 rounds into their vehicle during a high-speed chase almost two years to the day prior to Rice's murder. This is the limit of legibility offered to the liberal imagination. "The Cleveland case" is the closest one gets to a surfacing of Tamir Rice in the Obama archive. This is telling: the twelve-year-old-toy-gun-carrying-boys-will-be-boys Rice—even this child, a potential bastion of an acknowledged politics whose killing was caught on videotape—is lost to the archive.[56]

The bodies explicitly connected to the foundations of the Black Lives Matter movement are clear examples that carry forward both this strain for legibility and an ever-increasing vanishing in the liberal imagination. Though the Black Lives Matter movement is appropriately characterized as a decentralized push for systemic change, Alicia Garza, Patrisse Cullors, and Opal Tometi, are certainly the most qualified and deserving to put forward how we got here. The most recognized website of the movement (blacklivesmatter.com) frames the work of these activists as a "Herstory." Telling, from my perspective, is the absence of history within this guiding document. While appeals to both systematic racism and failures in the scope of prior black liberation movements do gesture to a past, the work this document encourages is nevertheless overwhelmingly present and grants insight into the movement's understanding of itself in a way that usually aligns with what P. Khalil Saucier and Tryon Woods critique as black feminism's tendency to be "depicted as occurring ahistorically outside of the black radical tradition."[57] Garza, writing in October 2014 in an essay featuring very similar language, expands on this slightly by remarking that the movement "was a response to the anti-Black racism that permeates our society and also, unfortunately, our movements."[58] However, regardless of Garza's reading of black radical history, as this is not the focus here, the movement's foundations were intended to be constructed as both decidedly feminist and queer. And this certainly lends to much of its illegibility. Beyond Tamir Rice, for example, Tanisha Anderson, Mya Hall, Walter Scott, Sandra Bland, and Michael Brown are the black bodies used by the architects of the movement to articulate BLM's official Herstory.[59] And they, too, are nearly invisible in Obama's archive of the acknowledged politics of the liberal imagination. In this universe, there is not one mention of Mya Hall, the twenty-seven-year-old trans woman who died after police riddled the car she was driving with bullets, leading to a fatal car crash a stone's throw from the National Security Agency's headquarters in Baltimore. Given her marginal status—as a trans and queer body, as a sex worker, and as socioeconomically disadvantaged—her illegibility is not surprising. But there are others. Tanisha Anderson, the thirty-seven-year-old woman who stopped breathing after being slammed to the concrete by police, does not surface in this archive. And absent is the name of Sandra Bland, the twenty-eight-year-old woman found hanged in her jail cell three days after being arrested for a traffic stop in Texas. The vanishings of Anderson and Bland are perhaps similarly unsurprising, especially in light of Obama's blinding focus on men/boys and police violence. As Audre Lorde reminds us, if black men are the nightmare, "even worse than the nightmare is the blank. And Black women are the blank."[60] There is no space within the bounds of this imagination for Hall, Anderson, or Bland and the countless blank bodies existing beneath this register. This frightening yet predictable absence led the African American Policy Forum to begin the #SayHerName social movement in 2015. Both Sandra Bland and Maya Hall figure prominently in their initial statements.[61]

In the end, Michael Brown is the only body from BLM's Herstory to have a presence in Obama's archive. But this presence is ultimately indicative of this mounting gravitational pull. Reacting to the shooting death of Brown, on August 12, 2014, Obama released a statement, quoted in full, titled "Statement by the President on the Passing of Michael Brown":

> The death of Michael Brown is heartbreaking, and Michelle and I send our deepest condolences to his family and his community at this very difficult time. As Attorney General Holder has indicated, the Department of Justice is investigating the situation along with local officials, and they will continue to direct resources to the case as needed. I know the events of the past few days have prompted strong passions, but as details unfold, I urge everyone in Ferguson, Missouri, and across the country, to remember this young man through reflection and understanding. We should comfort each other and talk with one another in a way that heals, not in a way that wounds. Along with our prayers, that's what Michael and his family, and our broader American community, deserve.[62]

Though Brown is referred to as "passing" in the statement's title, there is no hint of a violent death at the hands of law enforcement in the 129 words that follow. Furthermore, these words come three days after the shooting, when the unrest in Ferguson was clearly not dissipating. His focus is peace and not the circumstances surrounding the death itself. His statement after the grand jury's decision to not indict Brown's killer can be characterized in a similar fashion.[63] The sentimental, once the only register available for legible black life and death, is also unaccounted for in both statements. In fact, reading the archived notes, one would have no idea that Brown's life was cut short at eighteen years old, just one year older than Martin.

The information I have presented here is by no means novel. BLM and its sinews are in many ways governed by this illegibility. Samaria Rice, mother of Tamir Rice, has on multiple occasions given voice to this critique of the administration. During an MSNBC interview eighteen months after her son was murdered, she would say of Obama: "I don't know what you are doing. I don't know how you are able to sleep at night. And just sleep and wake up and see that another murder has happened on behalf of the government and nobody is getting any justice at the Department of Justice."[64] What is novel here, however, is how this progression of illegibility in relation to an idea of the liberal archive is being understood. From my perspective, this represents not a mere ebb and flow of data in and out of the archive but, rather the early stages of an irrecoverable erosion of a psychic border.

So while select ideas of blackness are slowly being made material in the collective Mexican psyche, the opposite appears to be the case in the United States. However, radical ideas of blackness, that psychic matter that lies beyond a counting, beyond archiving, are suffering similar fates in both nations. And though we in the United States have yet to accumulate the generations of such information loss, I have proposed that the collective liberal imagination is moving in this direction. For this reason, Mexico has provided and continues to provide a framework that can inform a critical practice of reading that the preceding work has endeavored to model. This practice must be added to the evolving architecture of hemispheric black studies to enhance its capacity to think past projects of retrieval, even fragmented retrieval, and to mobilize anxieties that point to the contours of this ongoing recession, which finds ideas of radical blackness accelerating toward the nigrescent beyond, that unthought region developing within portions of the liberally oriented collective psyche of the United States.

Afterword

✦

Nigrescent Futures

> By the time those two sisters of mystery from just outside of town got to Arizona, there was not enough to decipher.
>
> —Author unknown

> It did rain. It had been raining pretty much constantly since that day. At the window of the conference room, Mark Spitz looked out into a solemn nigrescence.
>
> —Colson Whitehead, *Zone One*

In a work that has been focused on reading from south to north, it is fitting that while I began in the introduction with the science fiction of Eduardo Urzaiz and his imagined Villautopia in the year 2218, in this afterword I move to the domain of Afrofutures. In a certain sense, the preceding pages can be read as scouring the intersection of ideas of utopia and blackness in order to understand this intersection's relationship to the development of what has been described here as transgenerational intrapsychic gaps. The ever-growing gravitational force of these gaps draws in radical ideas of blackness that would otherwise compromise the stability of these psychic structures. Because I have argued that what is within these gaps will always be unavailable, my effort is in many respects ultimately a work of theoretically oriented speculative fiction. And because the coming utopia is always impelling, it must confront ideas of futurity. In deference to these admissions, in conclusion I look directly toward a portion of the future-oriented borders of black thought in the United States.

A pronounced turn away from utopian discourses has long been felt across multiple academic registers—aspects of queer theory rejecting futurity, portions of the radical left adopting a similar politics of no future, and scholars in black studies debating the idea of an Afro-pessimism, to name just a few examples. This accumulation of tragic thought brings the question: Does the utopian text no longer hold any value in the development of alternative political thought? Responding to this in the context of Latin America, Erin Graff Zivin, with whom I communicated in the second chapter, stands out because of her demand for a dismissal of the utopian *and* tragic or dystopian registers on the assumption that neither can offer a viable alternative to contemporary political thought, as both are based on the idea of a predetermined future.[1] Confronting the idea of a future that is dependent on the constructed stability of unburied truths, this well-articulated logic desires an an-archaeological approach that seeks "a relation with the past that does not annihilate futurity" in order to discover an enclave in thought that leaves room for the unforeseen and the incalculable.[2] I propose here, however, that a rejection of the utopian and the tragic need not occur to support such thinking. More specifically, the utopian register itself can, in some cases, contain the tragic and, as such, is quite capable of pointing us toward a theoretically rich and productively indeterminate futurity.

Much of this, of course, rests on one's definition of the utopian register. Fredric Jameson's work from the perspective of science fiction is instructive here, specifically his separation of the utopian impulse from the utopian text. The former, an attempt to explain uncritical and future-oriented aspects of the everyday, is structured by a predetermined logic of futurity. Utopian texts, by contrast, critically engage with that impulse. And for Jameson, within the bounds of the utopian text there exists a capacity to demonstrate failed utopias that exceeds the possibilities offered by a mere dystopian reversal. Though clearly all utopian texts do not attempt to demonstrate such failures, those that do and do so "most comprehensively," according to Jameson, bring with them the possibility of activating an awareness of "our mental and ideological imprisonment."[3] Jameson labels the text that succeeds in presenting such failure "anti-anti-utopian."

Carlos Fuentes's ruminations on utopia connect with Jameson's and are articulated from the perspective of Latin America and thus serve as a more focused entrance point to this conversation. In an essay revolving around José Lezama Lima in *Valiente mundo nuevo*, Fuentes expands on the notion of the Neobaroque as a form of counterconquest in a way that further addresses my question concerning the status of the utopian text. Here he calls on those born "de la catástrofe de la conquista, nosotros, los indo-afro-iberoamericanos . . . ver nuestra historia como un conflicto de valores en el cual ninguno es destruido por su contrario sino que, trágicamente, cada uno se resuelve en el otro. La tragedia sería así, prácticamente, una definición de nuestro mestizaje" (of the catastrophe of the conquest, we, the *indo-afro-iberoamericanos* . . . to view our history as a conflict of values in which no value is destroyed by its opposite but rather that, tragically, each one is resolved in the other. This tragedy would also be, practically, a definition of our mestizaje).[4] Fuentes is working against the traditional understanding of tragedy that, being unequivocally oriented toward destruction, would see the mutual extinction of these values. The seeds of Fuentes's idiosyncratic understanding are to be discovered in the founding of America—in the gulf between the utopian idea of America itself and the violence of its conquest. Heavily influenced by Américo Castro's push to bring to light the multiethnic (Jewish/Islamic) composition of Spain, Fuentes views the concept of tragedy as capable of maintaining the antagonistic relation between the key components of Latin America's mestizaje (European, indigenous, and African) without giving in to a depoliticized homogenization.[5] Fuentes terms the disruptive capacity of such a resistance to synthesis the "tragic opportunity"[6]—an enclave in thought that aligns with Jameson's anti-anti-utopianism and the desire for a governing principle of absolute indeterminacy. This is the understanding of tragedy that will be adopted and explored here in my closing thoughts that are framed by Colson Whitehead's postapocalyptic zombie novel *Zone One* (2011).

Whitehead's novel is the story of Mark Spitz in the final three days of a walled portion of a future-yet-undated New York City—once the avant-garde of the reconstruction of the United States in the wake of a zombie incursion. Spitz, part of the armed, three-person Omega Unit, is responsible for patrolling beyond the walls and slowly regaining the city. Sunday, the last day, begins with the failure of Zone One's principal barrier:

> When the wall fell, it fell quickly, as if it had been waiting for this moment, as if it had been created for the very instant of its failure. Barricades collapsed with haste once *they* were exposed for the riddled and rotten things *they* had always been. Beneath that façade of stability *they* were as ethereal as the society that created *them*.[7]

Whitehead invests these lines with an extraordinary ambivalence. On the first read, the pronoun "they" is used to describe the barricades themselves; true to the genre, *Zone One* is a story of barricades and breaches. As one of the lieutenants of the reconstruction effort notes: "The barricade is the only metaphor left in this mess. The last one standing . . . There are small barricades—across the apartment door, then a whole house nailed up—and then we have the bigger barricades. The camp. The settlement. The city. We work our way to bigger walls."[8] Thus, *Zone One* is a text that on a topographical level is designed to demonstrate what *permeates*, or breaks through, this or that side to the other.

But the repetition of "they" beginning in the second sentence suggests a certain vacillation that allows for the word to be read as signifying the surviving humans themselves—*Barricades collapsed with haste once humans were exposed for the riddled and rotten things they had always been*—or the zombies of the coming horde—*Beneath that façade of stability the zombies were as ethereal as the society that created them*. This collapsing of the possibility of otherness forces the inference that the zombies are within us, the conception of the human, and what is breaking through the barrier can and should be described as an internal leak, a secretion from some intrapsychic structure.

This striking indeterminacy is seen again later in the novel when Spitz and the two other members of his crew (Kaitlyn and Gary), having survived the repercussions of the initial rupture, find themselves among the living, but not for long: "They fired until all that needed to be killed had been killed, and they stood numbly looking into the darkness for more, the next apparitions hiding in the wings, for surely *they were not finished. They were human beings*, after all, and full of things that needed to be put down."[9] Having been gifted with the previous anxiety, we are left productively unsure of who exactly is not finished and what is being classified as human.

Pages before the zombies will assert their dominance, as is both expected and allowed in this genre, Spitz stands above the walls of Zone One peering through the glass window in a conference room that has been repurposed as one of the military nerve centers of the reconstruction. He looks out into what is described as a "solemn nigrescence."[10] In this instance, nigrescence clearly references the darkening night but also renders the looming zombie threat as one of becoming dark. When anachronistically paired with the reading above that will come two days later, we realize that Spitz is now, on Friday, observing, perhaps unaware, his own nigrescence.

It is not the first time that Whitehead has taken cover within a genre novel to find a surprising freedom for an oblique social commentary. In *The Intuitionist* (1999), his debut, the former MacArthur Fellow uses the noir detective genre to explore the nexus of race and social change via the prism of warring schools of thought in the elevator inspection community (Intuitionists and Empiricists). All of this is set in another undated, Gotham-like city. Now as then, his humor, satire, and knack for corralling a seemingly disparate accumulation of cultural references are presented front and center. This is the same Whitehead, after all, who in 2009 penned a *New York Times* op-ed, "The Year of Living Postracially," where he announced his tongue-in-cheek candidacy for Obama's secretary of postracial affairs, satirizing the notion that centuries of "institutionalized dehumanization" could be so easily cast away.[11]

The particular levity of *Zone One* is undoubtedly related to these meditations. The recovering New York City we are introduced to is, from all signs, not only postapocalypse but also postidentity, and fully embracing of a vacant and insignificant multiculturalism. Fort Wonton, for example, is the name of a military staging area beyond the walls of Zone One that was once a Chinese restaurant. Spitz is the everyman hero for this postidentity world, having already on his own accord survived the initial zombie onslaught and the interregnum that followed. This uncommon feat is attributed to him being a specimen of "unrivaled mediocrity," someone who "had led a mediocre life exceptional only in the magnitude of its unexceptionality."[12] This postdistinguishability is further set off by the fact that Mark Spitz is a nickname earned for his inability to swim—the name borrowed from the swimmer who once won seven gold medals for the United States in the 1972 Munich Olympics. But, as Whitehead tells us, this is only "one of the subordinate ironies" in his naming.[13] The other, which is only confirmed toward the end of the novel, is that he is phenotypically black and thus aligns with the stereotype that black folk can't swim.

But it is a stereotype that has lost most of its resonance within the novel. And if one returns to Spitz's introduction earlier in the novel armed with knowledge of his racial background, we learn that while he may have found some objection to his naming in a previous time, that time has passed: "They called him Mark Spitz nowadays. He didn't mind."[14] The fact that his racial identity is of no other consequence to a narrative that features no other visible blackness confirms a certain commitment on Whitehead's behalf to the visualization of a postracial world.

This is all very clever, but it is a zombie novel and there are darker things afoot. At one point, trapped in a nostalgic reverie, Whitehead's protagonist strolls through a part of the city that has remained untouched by the markings of the horde:

> It was any city block on a normal day of that expired calendar, five minutes before dawn, say, when most of the city was still sleeping it off . . . Nothing had been boarded up, there were no firefight traces or other signs of mayhem, and a finicky wind had kicked all the litter around the corner. From time to time Mark Spitz happened on these places in Zone One, where he strolled down a movie set, earning scale as an extra in a piece about the dead world.
>
> The swiftness of the evac, and the fact *the island* hadn't endured a major engagement—been firebombed like Oakland or nuked like St. Augustine or whatever the hell happened in Birmingham—meant that entire stretches of the city were pristine.[15]

It is a portrait of New York, the center of civilization, as an isolated island that was given the benefit of all available resources. Oakland, Birmingham, and St. Augustine are described as standing-apart, almost-unregistered sites of violence, even in the violent apocalypse. When read through the nexus of state-sponsored violence and radical blackness, the cities mentioned form a list that is by no means random. The addition of St. Augustine, Florida, in particular, the site of a more obscure rebellion in 1964, calls attention to the fact that Whitehead both summons three critical sites of the violent repression of the black radical movement of the 1960s and points to a weakened resonance. It is the registration of that which can no longer be fully registered, though secretions nonetheless emerge.

To give language to such secretions, it is constructive to return to my work with black holes and collective psyches and consider how it intersects with the discourse of Afrofuturism's apparent embrace of recoverability.[16] So much of our present contemplation of Afrofutures is indebted to the space(s) conjured by John Akomfrah and Edward George's *The Last Angel of History*. Their vision is very much structured by the invention of a Data Thief, the backward glancing figure positioned in the future. A refashioning of the Akan idea of *sankofa*, the Data Thief can be read as putting in its place, or blackening, Walter Benjamin's reading of Paul Klee's *Angelus Novus* and placing on the table the concept of a prophetic black countermemory. Seven years after *The Last Angel of History*, Kodwo Eshun, also featured in the 1996 film, reanimates the critical possibilities of such an Afrofuturism. In place of the Data Thief, Eshun describes a "team of African archaeologists from the future." Representing the United States of Africa (USAF), these scholars are described as "sifting patiently" through damaged but identifiable fragments, charged with "excavating a site, a museum from their past."[17] Eshun considers his idea of Afrofuturism as undercutting a neoliberal "futures industry" aiming to predict and produce an Africa, and the matter connected to its orbit, as a site of perpetual dystopia. This industry is not unlike the Mexican culture industries and their restrictive articulations of Afro-Mexican identity discussed in the previous chapter. Eshun's Afrofuturism, however, comfortably understands itself as heir to an Afrocentric revisionist logic, and as extending such logic through the insertion of an anachronistic element. While nodding to the evidence of potentially problematic "totalizing reversals of Stolen Legacy–style Afrocentricity," it nonetheless assumes a relatively discrete and stable separation between the liberal (and neoliberal) imagination(s) and the collective imagination governed by ideas of Afrofuturism.[18] Toni Morrison is a key figure, for Eshun, in constructing this stability:

> Her argument that the African slaves that experienced capture, theft, abduction, and mutilation were the first moderns is important for positioning slavery at the heart of modernity. The cognitive and attitudinal shift demanded by her statement also yokes philosophy together with brutality, and binds cruelty to temporality. The effect is to force together separated systems of knowledge, so as to disabuse apparatuses of knowledge of their innocence.
>
> Afrofuturism can be understood as an elaboration upon the implications of Morrison's revisionary thesis.[19]

Eshun is gleaning from Paul Gilroy's "Living Memory: A Meeting with Toni Morrison," which was first published in 1988 in the magazine *City Limits* and later collected in his 1993 book *Small Acts: Thoughts on the Politics of Black Cultures*.[20] However, in *Playing in the Dark*, Morrison's collection of a series of lectures given at Harvard in 1990, she expressly states that she does "not want to encourage those totalizing approaches to African-American scholarship which have no drive other than the exchange of dominations—dominant Eurocentric scholarship *replaced* by dominant Afrocentric scholarship."[21] Hers is the desire to force a dwelling in and constant interrogation of one's awareness of and relation to the *yoke*. While I realize it would be hyperbolic to describe the discourse of Afrofurism as definitively tending toward the types of "Africanist idiom[s that are] used to establish difference" that she draws attention to in her study of aspects of the Western literary canon, is there not a debilitating trace here?[22] Returning to her own words, might she be inclined to say that an Afrofuturist logic framed in this way, while a psychic comfort, necessitates what she describes as a "willful critical blindness"?[23] Digging up evidence, imagined or otherwise, to counter the institutional archive is crucial for Eshun and the strand of Afrofuturism conditioned by his thought. This critical expression of Afrofuturism has remained tethered, with a few exceptions, to a male- and Western-dominated conceit of archaeological penetration.[24]

If we are to accept that the psychic processes discussed in my work on Mexico are beginning to describe, in some form, portions of the American collective imagination(s) (this is certainly where intellectual paths may diverge), why must we find our space within a theoretical scaffolding so conditioned by archaeology? For it is undeniable that such an archaeological rhetoric has been carried forward as relatively solid ground in a project that looks to unsettle ground. The artist is crucial in this carrying forward, as, according to Eshun, they might "work on the exposure and reframing of [these] futurisms . . . and reassemble the predatory futures that insist the next 50 years will be ones of unmitigated despair."[25] But is there always a capacity for such exposure and reassemblage? This is not to suggest that the spectrum of Afrofuturism is not aware of the archaeological nature of the discourse in which it sits, or that its formative gestures are not in many ways productively transforming this space. That said, I still believe we will benefit from the addition of a decidedly an-archaeological rhetoric to our toolkit. For if Afrofuturism remains focused on how to unsettle a future that wishes to disappear us, it is imperative for us to examine how a multidecade (sometimes blind) devotion to an archaeological mind-set has compromised the range of our visions. In doing so, I believe we in black studies must ask ourselves how the irrecoverable has been inherited in a way that Afrofuturism and similarly entangled frameworks cannot unsettle. Or, more precisely, what does a literature moving against archaeology look like?

The final scene in Whitehead's story, which tells of the day the Zone was overrun, is helpful in addressing this question. It is introduced by the following epigraph: "Move as a team, never move alone: Welcome to the Terrordome." The quote is only credited extratextually, on the copyright page, where the unfamiliar reader is introduced to Public Enemy.[26] That it comes from the group's song "Welcome to the Terrordome" from the album *Fear of a Black Planet* is left unstated. As many of my generation know, the song confronts the liberal narrative of the civil disturbances that occurred in the summer of 1989 at Greekfest in Virginia Beach, a Labor Day beach party attracting thousands of black youths and celebrities. The festivities were centered around "The Dome," a large Virginia Beach entertainment facility. Because crowds had been growing each year since its inception in 1986, the city and its largely white inhabitants had begun to express concern. In 1989, it all came to a head with hundreds of arrests, claims of police brutality, and the destruction of local businesses. In the song, Chuck D speaks not only of what became known as the "Greekfest Riots" but also of the racially motivated shooting of Yusef Hawkings in the Bensonhurst neighborhood of Brooklyn. He raps of his lack of patience in waiting "for the state to decide the fate" and warns of a coming "subordinate terror." However, by separating this lyric from its context, Whitehead's deployment only activates a subtle antagonism. This strategy intuits that what lies beneath can no longer only be described as a *slumbering volcano*, to borrow language from Frederick Douglass's influential 1849 speech warning northern white liberals of the looming threat of black violence if the injustices of slavery were not addressed. By presenting even the nonthreatening, mainstream activism found in the Public Enemy lyric as he does the zombie—as something that has passed a barrier but nonetheless works against the assimilation into a full understanding—Whitehead has given light to an extratextual element that can itself be read as a metaphor for what escapes the nigrescent beyond and the apparent horizon that governs it. In Whitehead's speculative future, this accumulation has reached a critical mass: the sea of the dead.

This sea is representative of a certain Eliot-inspired wasteland, and Whitehead sees theoretical value in embracing this dead zone as is:

> It was not the dead that passed through the barrier but the wasteland itself, the territory he had kept at bay since the farmhouse. It embraced him; he slid inside it . . . The black tide had rolled in everywhere, no place was spared this deluge, everyone was drowning. Of course he was smiling. This is where he belonged.[27]

This embodiment has given Spitz what Whitehead calls "wastelanded" eyes capable of viewing the nature of the barricade:[28]

> Mark Spitz saw it clearly: Kaitlyn's implacable march through a series of imaginative and considered birthday parties—her parents were so thoughtful, here was a blessing bestowed from one generation to the next—each birthday party transcending the last and approaching a kind of birthday-party perfection that once accomplished would usher in an exquisite new age of bourgeois utopia. They strove, they plotted, they got the e-mail of that new magician in town with his nouveau prestidigitations. Maybe, he thought one night, it wasn't utopia they worked toward after all, and it was Kaitlyn herself that summoned the plague: as she cut into the first slice of cake at her final, perfect birthday party, history had come to an end.[29]

The plague is imagined to be somehow "summoned" by a collective utopian impulse, but there is an underlying banality here: birthday cakes and magic shows. Kaitlyn is shown as one of the summoners. Her prior inoffensive life—described at one point as "bioengineered in the birthing vats of a sanctified midwestern principality, an upper-middle-class Kingdom of Bruiselessness"—has nonetheless led to this fall.[30] Or, rather, the horde of similarly inoffensive lives has led to this fall. Whitehead has provided a subtle critique on the nature of the "dangerously disoriented human being[s]"—to borrow from Baldwin—that now flood our present moment.[31] It is the *we* that imagines even the more legible sites of violence such as those at Greekfest in 1989, or the countless bodies presently being worked through in public discourse, as both an outrage and quite distant from our own realities.

Perhaps a similar awareness washes over Mark Spitz as he stands at the conference room window watching his own solemn nigrescence; "solemn" bringing its myriad interpretations: grave, sober, holy, grim, earnest, dignified. Or perhaps his awareness has not been conditioned by a vague knowledge of the fact that what is beyond is within. We cannot read this. All we do know is that at the conclusion of the novel, Spitz, Whitehead's "last man," is faced with the potential of finally being overrun. Instead of resisting, he opens the door to where he had been hiding and simply walks "into the sea of the dead."[32]

Whitehead, aided by the expectations of the zombie genre, has long prepared the reader for the fact that this is how it would end, perhaps never more clearly than in a flashback where the reader is briefly introduced to a character by the name of Quiet Storm. She is part of a unit responsible for clearing cars off one of the main highways into New York City. Had things ended differently, the highway would have made way for commerce as the nation was rebuilt. Those who work alongside her are baffled by her insistence on arranging cars on the highway's shoulder in the oddest ways. But they let her persist, assuming it is just a quirky manifestation of her PASD, or Post-Apocalyptic Stress Disorder. Later, Whitehead's narrative uses this instance to further explore ideas of information loss that govern the apparent horizon:

> [Spitz] told his unit how he'd discovered the clandestine heart of the Quiet Storm's maneuvers. He was aboard the chopper on his way to the Zone . . . He finally saw it from above, what she had carved into the interstate . . . The *grammar* lurked in the numbers and colors, the meaning encoded in the spaces between the vehicular syllables, half a mile, quarter mile. Five jeeps lined up south by southwest on a north-south stretch of highway . . . Ten sport-utility vehicles arranged one-eighth of a mile apart east-west were the fins of an eel slipping through silty depths, or the fletching on an arrow aimed at—what? Tomorrow? What readers?[33]

What had Spitz discovered? In the banter of disinterested soldiers, Spitz, Kaitlyn, and Gary discuss the nature of this indecipherability as they sweep the storefront of a fortune-teller beyond the wall. Spitz contends that it is some emblem from the future that "we don't [yet] know how to read" but nevertheless need to "pay witness" to; he thinks to himself that perhaps it is a warning.[34] Kaitlyn proffers that it may be an invitation, while Gary, unimpressed by such musings, claims to have known a man in one of the camps who "wrote Bible verses in his own shit."[35] With this, the conversation is dropped. What remains is left indecipherable—a subtle anxiety that only recalls the absence of a grammar. It is a re-visioning of the Data Thief and the archaeologists from the USAF, and an acceptance of, as the example of Mexico has given new language to, a delicate and destabilizing embrace of the impossibility of black wholes.

NOTES

Introduction

1. Eduardo Urzaiz, *Eugenia: A Fictional Sketch of Future Customs; A Critical Edition*, ed. and trans. Sarah A. Buck Kachaluba and Aaron Dziubinskyj (Madison: University of Wisconsin Press, 2016), xx–xxvi.

2. Urzaiz, *Eugenia*, 27.

3. Urzaiz, *Eugenia*, 28, 32.

4. Beyond the scholarship contained in the 2016 critical edition, see Aaron Dziubinskyj, "Eduardo Urzaiz's 'Eugenia': Eugenics, Gender, and Dystopian Society in Twenty-Third-Century Mexico," *Science Fiction Studies* 34, no. 3 (2007): 463–72; Miguel García, "Eugenia en su context: Utopía y proyecto alterno de nación," *Alambique: Revista académica de ciencia ficción y fantasía* 4, no. 1 (2016): article 6. García does briefly present the hypothesis that the black characters in the novel might be read as surrogates for the indigenous population of then-contemporary Mexico. Though this idea is interesting, I am inclined to disagree, as I read Eugenia herself as representative, however mysteriously, of that identity.

5. Brian Hamnett, *A Concise History of Mexico*, 3rd ed. (Cambridge: Cambridge University Press, 2019), 112.

6. Colin Palmer, *Slaves of the White God: Blacks in Mexico, 1570–1650* (Cambridge, Mass.: Harvard University Press, 1976), 2.

7. Ben Vinson, "Fading from Memory: Historiographical Reflections on the Afro-Mexican Presence," *Review of Black Political Economy* 33, no. 1 (2005): 59–72.

8. Herman L. Bennett, *Africans in Colonial Mexico: Absolutism, Christianity, and Afro-Creole Consciousness, 1570–1640* (Bloomington: Indiana University Press, 2005), 1; Gonzalo Aguirre Beltrán, *La población negra de México: Estudio etnohistórico* (1946; repr., Mexico City: Fondo de Cultura Económica, 1972), 214–19.

9. Bennett, *Africans in Colonial Mexico*, 1; Aguirre Beltrán, *La población negra de México*, 232–34.

10. For a reference to this state-engendered commitment to the recognition of a pluricultural composition, see "Article 2," Constitución política de los Estados Unidos Mexicanos, 1917, Orden Jurídico Nacional, http://www.ordenjuridico.gob.mx/Constitucion/cn16.pdf.

11. In *The Impure Imagination: Toward a Critical Hybridity in Latin American Writing* (Minneapolis: University of Minnesota Press, 2006) Lund hosts a conversation that involves both Brazil and Mexico, but blackness is similarly not discussed significantly in the context of Mexico.

12. Juliet Hooker, *Theorizing Race in the Americas: Douglass, Sarmiento, Du Bois, and Vasconcelos* (New York: Oxford University Press, 2017), 22.

13. See Alejandro Solomianski, *Identidades secretas: La negritud Argentina* (Buenos Aires: Beatriz Viterbo, 2003).

14. See Eduardo Bonilla-Silva and David R. Dietrich, "The Latin Americanization of US Race Relations: A New Pigmentocracy," in *Shades of Difference: Why Skin Color Matters*, ed. Evelyn Glenn (Palo Alto, Calif.: Stanford University Press, 2009).

15. Frank B. Wilderson III, *Red, White, and Black: Cinema and the Structure of U.S. Antagonisms* (Durham, N.C.: Duke University Press, 2010), 4. In Wilderson's visioning, this erosion is complete, as embodied blackness is discussed as being disavowed and "doubly foreclosed" in the production of cinema. In traditional cinema, even that which attempts the articulation of a purportedly radically black position, the demand for a narrative movement from "equilibrium to disequilibrium to equilibrium" only strengthens this disavowal (26). Nonetheless, what Wilderson refers to as the "grammar of antagonism" is understood to interrupt "the mendacity of conflict" by way of the more peripheral cinematic strategies of "lighting, camera angles, image composition, and acoustic design" (4–5).

16. Wilderson, *Red, White, and Black*, 28. The italics are a refashioning of Wilderson's question, "How does a film tell the story of a being that has no story?"

17. William E. Cross Jr., at the intersection of black studies and clinical psychology, has devoted his career to thinking through the idea of nigrescence as it relates to the individual's transition from Negro to black in order to establish and interrogate what he understands as a psychology of black liberation. See Cross, "The Negro-to-Black Conversion Experience," *Black World* 20 (July 1971): 13–27; Cross, *Shades of Black: Diversity in African-American Identity* (Philadelphia: Temple University Press, 1991).

18. "Herstory," Black Lives Matter, accessed November 20, 2019, https://blacklivesmatter.com/about/herstory/.

19. Homepage, Obama White House Archives, https://obamawhitehouse.archives.gov.

20. James Baldwin, *Nobody Knows My Name: More Notes of a Native Son* (New York: Dell, 1961), 117.

21. This question is greatly informed by Christina Sharpe's demand that we "become undisciplinded [in order to discover] new ways of entering and leaving the archives of slavery." See Christina Sharpe, *In the Wake: On Being and Blackness* (Durham, N.C.: Duke University Press, 2016), 13.

Chapter 1

1. The epigraph translation and all other translations not credited in the notes are my own. All Spanish presented in this book preserves the language of the original texts regardless of how that language may or may not adhere to contemporary customs.

2. David M. Davidson, "Negro Slave Control and Resistance in Colonial Mexico, 1519–1650," in *Maroon Societies: Rebel Slave Communities in the Americas*, ed. Richard Price (New York: Anchor Books, 1973), 90–92; and, in the same volume, José L. Franco, "Maroons and Slave Rebellions in the Spanish Territories," 35–37.

3. Yanga is alternatively referred to as Ñanga and Ñaga throughout the historical records of New Spain.

4. "Las condiciones que piden los Negros cimarrones de esta comarca," (Mexico City: Archivo General de la Nación), Inquisición 1608, vol. 283, file 26, fols. 186–87. All eleven points are reproduced in the original Spanish here: (1) que sean libres todos los que se han huido hasta el mes de septiembre próximo pasado y los de entonces acá se vuelven a sus dueños; (2) que han de tener justicia mayor que no sea mestizo ni criollo ni letrado sino de capa y espada; (3) que no ha de haber casa ni morada de español dentro del pueblo sino fuere a fueren a los tiangues lunes y jueves que le harán en su pueblo; (4) que han de tener los regidores y forma de cabildo; (5) que el capitán Ñaga que es el mayoral de ellos ha de ser gobernador y después de él sus hijos y descendientes; (6) que los negros que huyeren de los puertos acá se obliguen a traerlos a sus dueños con tal que por el trabajo les den doce pesos a los negros que los fueren a buscar y mientras no los volvieron a sus dueños les darán otros de los suyos que les sirvan y que si no los volvieren que pagaran lo que valen; (7) que dentro de un año y medio se les han de dar estas capitulaciones confirmadas por su majestad y sino que se volverán a su primer estado; (8) que han de fundar su pueblo entre Río Blanco y las haciendas de Ribadeneira a donde ellos señalaren; (9) que pagaran los tributos a su majestad como todos los demás negros y mulatos horros de las indias; (10) la última condición que piden en que los administre frailes franciscanos y no otros ningunos y que los ornamentos se han de hacer a costa de su majestad para la iglesia; (11) que asistirán a sus armas todos los negros que su majestad tuviese necesario de estas para defender la tierra.

5. San Lorenzo de los Negros was also named San Lorenzo de Cerralvo after the Franciscan friar who lived in the community. The presnt-day municipality has had the name Yanga since 1932.

6. Jane Landers, "*Cimarrón* and Citizen: African Identity, Corporate Identity, and the Evolution of Free Black Towns in the Spanish Circum-Caribbean," in *Slaves, Subjects, and Subversives: Blacks in Colonial Latin America*, ed. Jane Landers and Barry Robinson (Albuquerque: University of New Mexico Press, 2006), 144n60, 129–32.

7. Joy James, "Afrarealism and the Black Matrix: Maroon Philosophy at Democracy's Border," *Black Scholar* 43, no. 2 (2013): 125. The term "world line" is borrowed from the field of physics, which demands for the trajectory of an object to be calculated in the spatial as well as temporal dimension, what is called spacetime. Ian Ridpath, Oxford Dictionary of Astronomy, 2nd ed. (Oxford: Oxford University Press, 2012), s.v. "world line."

8. Jared Sexton, *Amalgamation Schemes: Antiblackness and the Critique of Multiracialism* (Minneapolis: University of Minnesota Press, 2008), 17.

9. *Triunfos de la fe* is the abbreviated title of *Historia de los triunfos de nuestra santa fe entre las gentes más bárbaras y fieras del nuevo orbe: Conseguidos por los soldados de la milicia de la Compañía de Jesús en las misiones de la Nueva España*.

10. Juan Antonio Mateos, Manuel Payno, and Rafael Martínez de la Torre are the other contributors.

11. This process of censorship has been noted in the introduction to the 1896 edition of this text. See Andrés Pérez de Ribas, *Crónica y historia religiosa de la*

Provincia de la Compañía de Jesús de México en Nueva España, vol. 2 (1654; repr., Mexico City: Imprenta del Sagrado Corazón de Jesús, 1896), iii.

12. Pérez de Ribas, *Crónica y historia religiosa*, 290.

13. Pérez de Ribas, *Crónica y historia religiosa*, 284.

14. Pérez de Ribas, *Crónica y historia religiosa*, 284–85.

15. Pérez de Ribas, *Crónica y historia religiosa*, 285.

16. Though it comes from the same Latin root, this is not to be confused with Spanish verb for "denigrate" (*denigrar*), as in "to defame or offend." *Denegrir* does not carry with it a moral judgment. This distinction is not maintained in English, as "to denigrate," at one point, accommodated both definitions. *Diccionario de la lengua española, RAE* (23rd ed.), s.v. "denegrir," "denigrar," https://dle.rae.es; Dictionary.com unabridged, s.v. "denigrate," https://www.dictionary.com.

17. Pérez de Ribas, *Crónica y historia religiosa*, 285.

18. Pérez de Ribas, *Crónica y historia religiosa*, 289.

19. Vicente Riva Palacio and Manuel Payno, "Los treinta y tres negros," in Vicente Riva Palacio, Manuel Payno, Juan A. Mateos, and Rafael Martínez de la Torre, *El libro rojo, 1520–1867* (1870; repr., Mexico City: A. Polo, 1905), 1:67.

20. Riva Palacio and Payno, "Los treinta y tres negros," 1:66.

21. Riva Palacio and Payno, "Los treinta y tres negros."

22. William F. Hanks, *Converting Words: Maya in the Age of the Cross* (Berkeley: University of California Press, 2010), 2.

23. Hanks turns to Sebastián de Covarrubias's definition in the *Tesoro de la lengua castellana o española* (1611), where both *reducción* and *reducido* are defined with the verb *convencer(se)*. Its proper etymological roots can be traced to the idea of restoration or "leading back" from the Latin *reducere*. See Francisco Del Rosal, *Diccionario etimológico: Alfabeto primero de origen y etimología de todos los vocablos originales de la lengua castellana* (Madrid: Consejo Superior de Investigaciones Científicas, 1992), 534.

24. Hanks, *Converting Words*, 2–3.

25. Pérez de Ribas, *Crónica y historia religiosa*, 285.

26. Pérez de Ribas, *Crónica y historia religiosa*, 292–93.

27. Another suspicious rhetorical decision that draws attention to potential historical inaccuracies within the account is the temporal frame Pérez de Ribas choses for his narrative. The text asserts that the battles between the Spanish colonial authority and Yanga's community began on February 22. And by Laurencio's accounting, we know that the on-again, off-again battles lasted several days, and most likely more than a few weeks, as there had to be time enough for him to be recalled to the distant Mexico City and for another priest to travel to replace him. In Pérez de Ribas's summary, however, he maintains that there was a prolonged period between when the new priest had joined the troops and when the agreement was reached: "Duró algún tiempo el acabar de limpiar esta tierra de negros bandoleros para dejarla quieta, y los caminos seguros para trajinar por ellos, en que se trabajó mucho" (It took some time and hard work to finish ridding this land of black bandits and leave it quiet, and the roads secure enough for transportation) (292). While this prolonged struggle helps to underline the arduous but valuable work of the Jesuit mission that Pérez de Ribas's larger project seeks to bring attention to, it does not conform well to the fact that, as noted

above, the surviving treaty is dated March 8, just two weeks after the combat is said to have begun. There is also the curiously specific request in the San Lorenzo treaty for a priest from the Franciscan order (read: not Jesuit). See note 4 in this chapter.

28. Riva Palacio and Payno, "Los treinta y tres negros," 67.

29. Riva Palacio and Payno, "Los treinta y tres negros," 68.

30. Davidson, "Negro Slave Control and Resistance in Colonial Mexico," 98, 98n14. Davidson's archival work substantiates Riva Palacios's claim that the threat of black violence and retribution for enslavement, whether real or imagined, continued to be felt and recorded throughout New Spain.

31. Riva Palacio and Payno, "Los treinta y tres negros," 68.

32. Riva Palacio and Payno, "Los treinta y tres negros."

33. Riva Palacio and Payno, "Los treinta y tres negros."

34. Landers, "*Cimarrón* and Citizen," 132. In the case of Cuijla, located in the present-day Mexican state of Guerrero, no treaty has been discovered. Both Gonzalo Aguirre Beltrán's (*Cuijla: Esbozo etnográfico de un pueblo negro* [Mexico City: Fondo de Cultura Económica, 1985]) and Patrick Carroll's archival research notes it as a maroon stronghold since the sixteenth century. In 1792 they are recognized as "free black tributaries, indicating that the maroons had officially received their liberty, and that their town had a royal charter." See Patrick J. Carroll, "Mandinga: The Evolution of a Mexican Runaway Slave Community, 1735–1827," *Comparative Studies in Society and History* 19, no. 4 (1977): 493.

35. Carroll, "Mandinga," 497.

36. Carroll, "Mandinga."

37. Carroll, "Mandinga."

38. Carroll, "Mandinga," 498–99.

39. Landers, "*Cimarrón* and Citizen," 130, 145n68.

40. Landers, "*Cimarrón* and Citizen," 112.

41. Carroll, "Mandinga," 499.

42. Shelby McCloy, *The Negro in the French West Indies* (Louisville: University of Kentucky Press, 1969), 240.

43. A maroon community in Brazil is often referred to as a *mocambo* or *quilombo*. According to Eduardo Silva, the term was adopted after the colonial period, while *mocambo*, originating from the Ambundu (a people located in what is now Angola) word for "hideout" (*mu-kambo*), can be traced back to the early colonial period in Brazil. See Silva, "Black Abolitionists in the *Quilombo* de Leblon, Rio de Janeiro," in *Beyond Slavery: The Multilayered Legacy of Africans in Latin America and the Caribbean*, ed. Darién J. Davis (Lanham, Md.: Rowman and Littlefield, 2007), 111. The word *quilombo* has since migrated into the Spanish as slang for both "brothel" and "racket" (as in noise) and is especially common in South America. Its earliest recorded usage for this purpose was in Argentina at the end of the nineteenth century. Slang expressions for "to frequent brothels" (*quilombear*) and "one who frequents brothels" (*quilombero*) have also developed. *Diccionario de la lengua española*, *RAE* (23rd ed.), s.v. "quilombo."

44. R. K. Kent, "Palmeras: An African State in Brazil," in Price, *Maroon Societies*, 170–85; Carroll, "Mandinga," 491.

45. Kent, "Palmeras," 184–87.

46. As is customary, the word "maroon" is capitalized when referring specifically to the Leeward and Windward Maroons of Jamaica.

47. Carroll, "Mandinga," 491–92.

48. Orlando Patterson, "Slavery and Slave Revolts: A Sociohistorical Analysis of the First Maroon War, 1665–1740," in Price, *Maroon Societies*, 246.

49. Barbara Klamon Kopytoff, "The Maroons of Jamaica: An Ethnohistorical Study of Incomplete Polities, 1655–1905" (Ph.D. diss., University of Pennsylvania, 1973), 366, 378, 80.

50. Kopytoff, "The Maroons of Jamaica," 379, 382–83, 371, 375.

51. Kopytoff, "The Maroons of Jamaica," 375, 370

52. Kopytoff, "The Maroons of Jamaica," 151, 275.

53. "Las condiciones."

54. Kopytoff, "The Maroons of Jamaica," 380.

55. Kopytoff, "The Maroons of Jamaica," 369. Quao's agreement contains the same intent with adjusted language: "Captain Quao, and his people, shall be ready on all commands the governor, or his commander in chief for the time being, shall send him, to suppress and destroy all other party or parties of rebellious negroes, that now are or shall from time to time run away from their respective owners" (379).

56. Kopytoff, "The Maroons of Jamaica," 373.

57. For a discussion of maroon communities in the United States, see Sylviane Diouf, *Slavery's Exiles: The Story of the American Maroons* (New York: New York University Press, 2014). Many of the enslaved from the United States escaped and found refuge in Spanish Florida. In many instances, these communities were granted a relative degree of freedom due to their positions as allies of Spain in the protection of Spanish territories by settlers encroaching from the United States and as allies of Great Britain in both the Revolutionary War and the War of 1812. See Virginia Bergman Peters, *The Florida Wars* (Hamden, Conn.: Archon Books, 1979); Nathaniel Millett, *The Maroons of Prospect Bluff and Their Quest for Freedom in the Atlantic World* (Gainesville: University Press of Florida, 2013).

58. Patterson, "Slavery and Slave Revolts."

59. Paul Gilroy, *The Black Atlantic: Modernity and Double Consciousness* (Cambridge, Mass.: Harvard University Press, 1993), 46.

60. For collections of work addressing this, see Alasdair Pettinger, ed., *Always Elsewhere: Travels of the Black Atlantic* (London: Cassell, 1998); Walter Goebel and Saskia Schabio, eds., *Beyond the Black Atlantic: Relocating Modernization and Technology* (Abingdon, UK: Routledge, 2006); David Lloyd and Peter D. O'Neill, eds., *The Black and Green Atlantic: Cross-Currents of the African and Irish Diasporas* (London: Palgrave Macmillan, 2009).

61. Gilroy, *The Black Atlantic*, 16.

62. Gilroy, *The Black Atlantic*, 49.

63. Gilroy, *The Black Atlantic*, 4. This oversight impoverishes Gilroy's brief analysis of Richard Wright's *Pagan Spain* that comes later in the book. In this work of nonfiction, Wright is sorting through his impressions of Spain in the time of Francisco Franco. In Wright's own words, it is a meditation on the question of whether "being Western [was] something so absolutely different from Spanish life and civilization to be of another genus? Or was that difference a mere nuance,

an angle of vision, a point of view?" By not dealing with New Spain previously, Gilroy is forced to quickly read past much of the potentially interesting detail in Wright's work. See Gilroy, The Black Atlantic, 162–63. For a more thorough conversation between Gilroy and Wright's text, see Chris Schmidt-Nowara, "'This Rotting Corpse': Spain between the Black Atlantic and the Black Legend," *Arizona Journal of Hispanic Studies* 5 (2001): 149–60.

64. María Elena Martínez, *Genealogical Fictions: Limpieza de Sangre, Religion, and Gender in Colonial Mexico* (Palo Alto, Calif.: Stanford University Press, 2011), 15.

65. Martínez, *Genealogical Fictions*, 161.

66. Nicolas Abraham and Maria Torok, *The Shell and the Kernel: Renewals of Psychoanalysis*, vol. 1, trans. Nicholas Rand (Chicago: University of Chicago Press, 1994), 125.

67. Abraham and Maria Torok, *The Shell and the Kernel*, 129. Emphasis added.

68. Abraham and Maria Torok, *The Shell and the Kernel*, 130.

69. Abraham and Maria Torok, *The Shell and the Kernel.*

70. Abraham and Maria Torok, *The Shell and the Kernel*, 134.

71. Abraham and Maria Torok, *The Shell and the Kernel*, 132.

72. Abraham and Maria Torok, *The Shell and the Kernel*, 159.

73. Merrill Cole, "Nat Turner's Thing," in *The Psychoanalysis of Race*, ed. Christopher Lane (New York: Columbia University Press, 1999), 270.

74. Cole, "Nat Turner's Thing."

75. Cole, "Nat Turner's Thing," 272.

76. Though brief, Suzanne Yang's "A Question of Accent: Ethnicity and Transference" does give nuanced recognition to the ability of Abraham and Torok's theories to speak to a "folding inward" of race that is both "impossible to see" and "impossible to forsake." Yang, "A Question of Accent," in Lane, *Psychoanalysis of Race*, 140.

77. The transferring of Abraham and Torok's theories from the individual to the broader communal or national contexts specifically is also by no means new. My mobilization of their theories is similar to that of Esther Rashkin in *Unspeakable Secrets and the Psychoanalysis of Culture* (Albany: State University of New York Press, 2009), where she works to remedy what she perceives as the field of cultural studies' allergy to both psychoanalysis and close reading. She leans on their theories to "provide a conceptual base from which to shift the psychoanalysis of the unspeakable into the realm of cultural and ideological analysis" (16). We share a particular interest in cultural instances where there remains an absolute and unconscious denial that any secreting has occurred.

78. Arthur Howard Noll and A. Phillip McMahon, *The Life and Times of Miguel Hidalgo y Costilla* (Chicago: A. C. McClurg, 1910), 1, 7.

79. Landers, "*Cimarrón* and Citizen," 145n72.

80. Noll and McMahon, *The Life and Times of Miguel Hidalgo*, 10; Landers, "*Cimarrón* and Citizen," 132, 145n72.

81. Miguel Hidalgo, "Bando de Miguel Hidalgo, 6 de diciembre de 1810," Orden Jurídico Nacional, http://www.ordenjuridico.gob.mx/Constitucion/1810.pdf.

82. Carroll, "Mandinga," 503.

83. Carroll, "Mandinga."

84. José María Morelos, "Sentimientos de la nación, 14 de septiembre de 1813," Orden Jurídico Nacional, http://www.ordenjuridico.gob.mx/Constitucion/1813.pdf.

85. *Diccionario de la lengua española, RAE* (23rd ed.), s.v. "proscribir."

86. José Martí, *Nuestra América* (Barcelona: Linkgua, 2011), 61. Before the first federal constitution of Mexico, the conservative Agustín de Iturbide would form a short-lived alliance with Vicente Guerrero and Guadalupe Victoria. The Plan of Iguala laid the foundation for the First Mexican Empire (1821–23) and would use similarly utopian language in reference to racial distinction: "Todos los habitantes de la Nueva España, sin distinción alguna de europeos, africanos ni indios, son ciudadanos de esta monarquía con opción á todo empleo, según su mérito y virtudes" (All inhabitants of New Spain, without any distinction between Europeans, Africans, or Indians, are citizens of this monarchy with the right to full employment according to their merits and virtues). See "Plan de Iguala, 24 de febrero de 1821," Orden jurídico nacional, http://www.ordenjuridico.gob.mx/Constitucion/1821A.pdf.

87. Constitución federal de los Estados Unidos Mexicanos, 1824, Orden Jurídico Nacional, http://www.ordenjuridico.gob.mx/Constitucion/1824B.pdf.

88. Guerrero's decree also had to do with the precarious position of Texas, then a Mexican state, as settlers from the United States were bringing enslaved persons into the territory. Under pressure from local government administrators who felt such a decree would undermine Mexico's social control in the region, Guerrero would go on to exempt Texas from this decree. See Timothy E. Anna, *Forging Mexico, 1821–1835* (Lincoln: University of Nebraska Press, 2001), 503, 227.

89. Article 2, Constitución federal de los Estados Unidos Mexicanos, 1857, Orden Jurídico Nacional, http://www.ordenjuridico.gob.mx/Constitucion/1857.pdf.

90. Article 2, Constitución federal de los Estados Unidos Mexicanos, 1857. The 1917 federal constitution carries forward very similar language in relation to slavery. See Constitución política de los Estados Unidos Mexicanos, 1917, Orden Jurídico Nacional, http://www.ordenjuridico.gob.mx/Constitucion/1917.pdf.

91. The Mexican-American War, concluded less than a decade prior, led to the United States eventually assuming (either via purchase or annexation) territories that include all or part of the following present-day states: Texas, Nevada, Colorado, New Mexico, Arizona, California, Kansas, and Oklahoma. The Wilmot Proviso, legislation attempting to ban slavery in these newly acquired states, was unable to pass and thus made the crossing of enslaved persons from the United States to Mexico a real issue to be dealt with. See Roger L. Ransom, *Conflict and Compromise: The Political Economy of Slavery, Emancipation and the American Civil War* (Cambridge: Cambridge University Press, 1989), 97–100.

92. Claudio Lomnitz-Adler, *Exits from the Labyrinth: Culture and Ideology in the Mexican National Space* (Berkeley: University of California Press, 1992), 9.

93. Lomnitz-Adler, *Exits from the Labyrinth*, 276.

94. Lomnitz-Adler, *Exits from the Labyrinth*, 277, 281.

95. Rashkin, *Unspeakable Secrets*, 15.

96. Abraham and Torok, *The Shell and the Kernel*, 173.

97. Abraham and Torok, *The Shell and the Kernel* .

98. Abraham and Torok, *The Shell and the Kernel*, 178.
99. Rashkin, *Unspeakable Secrets*, 95.
100. Rashkin, *Unspeakable Secrets*.
101. Abraham and Torok, *The Shell and the Kernel*, 174.
102. Abraham and Torok, *The Shell and the Kernel*.
103. Abraham and Torok, *The Shell and the Kernel*, 174–75. Emphasis added.
104. Abraham and Torok, *The Shell and the Kernel*, 175.
105. Abraham and Torok, *The Shell and the Kernel*.
106. Abraham and Torok, *The Shell and the Kernel*, 181.
107. *Blacks in Latin America*, episode 4, "Mexico and Peru: The Black Grandma in the Closet," produced by Henry Louis Gates. Aired May 11, 2011, PBS.
108. Abraham and Torok, *The Shell and the Kernel*, 157.
109. Abraham and Torok, *The Shell and the Kernel*, 180.
110. This notion of the irrevocably interwoven comes from Achille Mbembe's discussion of freedom and death in "Necropolitics," trans. Libb Meintjes, *Public Culture* 15, no. 1 (2003): 38.

Chapter 2

1. My use of the word "creole" is a translation of the Spanish term *criollo/a*, understood to be a person of Spanish descent born in the New World. In English, while this definition does transfer, it can also be used to refer to a person of mixed African and European heritage.
2. Lomnitz-Adler, *Exits from the Labyrinth*, 9.
3. Adriana Williams, *Covarrubias* (Austin: University of Texas Press, 1994), 87.
4. José Vasconcelos, *La raza cósmica / The Cosmic Race* (Baltimore: Johns Hopkins University Press, 1997), 72, 32.
5. Carrie C. Chorba, *Mexico, from Mestizo to Multicultural: National Identity and Recent Representations of the Conquest* (Nashville: Vanderbilt University Press, 2007), 9.
6. Octavio Paz, *El laberinto de la soledad* (Mexico City: Fondo de Cultura Económica, 1959), 26; Paz, "The Labyrinth of Solitude," in *The Labyrinth of Solitude and Other Writings* (New York: Grove Press, 1985), 29.
7. Octavio Paz, *Posdata* (Mexico City: Siglo Veinteuno Editors, 1970), 11–12.
8. Paz, "The Other Mexico," in *The Labyrinth of Solitude and Other Writings*, 216.
9. Paz, *Posdata*, 109; Paz, "The Other Mexico," 287.
10. Paz, *Posdata*, 111; Paz, "The Other Mexico," 289.
11. Paz, *Posdata*, 10; Paz, "The Other Mexico," 215.
12. Paz, "The Other Mexico," 321.
13. Paz, *Posdata*, 153; Paz, "The Other Mexico," 323–24.
14. Lomnitz-Adler, *Exits from the Labyrinth*, 3.
15. Roger Bartra, *The Cage of Melancholy: Identity and Metamorphosis in the Mexican Character* (New Brunswick, N.J.: Rutgers University Press, 1992), 2–3.
16. Bartra, *The Cage of Melancholy*, 2. Emphasis added.
17. Bartra, *The Cage of Melancholy*, 6.
18. Octavio Paz, introduction to *Massacre in Mexico*, by Elena Poniatowska, trans. Helen Lane (Columbia: University of Missouri Press, 1992), xi.

19. Paz, introduction.

20. Paz, introduction, xii.

21. Edmundo O'Gorman, "Sobre los inconvenientes de vivir los indios en el centro de la ciudad," *Boletín del Archivo General de la Nación* 9, no. 1 (1938): 1–34.

22. Anna More, *Baroque Sovereignty: Carlos de Sigüenza y Góngora and the Creole Archive of Colonial Mexico* (Philadelphia: University of Pennsylvania Press, 2012), 8.

23. More, *Baroque Sovereignty*, 15.

24. Paz, introduction, xii. Paz has offered his own translation of the Spanish rather than rely on Irving Leonard's 1929 English translation. The following is Romero de Terreros's Spanish edition of the same passage: "Por aquella calle donde yo estaba (y por cuantas otras desembocaban a las plazas sería lo propio) venían atropellándose bandadas de hombres. Traían desnudas sus espadas los españoles y, viendo lo mismo que allí me tenía suspenso, se detenían; pero los negros, los mulatos y todo lo que es plebe gritando: '¡Muera el Virrey y cuantos lo defendieren!', y los indios: '¡Mueran los españoles y gachupines (son los venidos de España) que nos comen nuestro maíz!,' y exhortándose unos a otros a tener valor, supuesto que ya no había otro Cortés que los sujetase, se arrojaban a la plaza a acompañar a los otros y a tirar piedras." Carlos de Sigüenza y Góngora, *Relaciones históricas*, ed. Manuel Romero de Terreros (Mexico City: Ediciones de la Universidad Nacional Autónoma de México, 1954), 152.

25. R. Douglas Cope, *The Limits of Racial Domination: Plebeian Society in Colonial Mexico City, 1660–1720* (Madison: University of Wisconsin Press, 1994), 155–58.

26. Paz, introduction, xii.

27. Paz, introduction.

28. Carlos de Sigüenza y Góngora, *Seis obras* (Caracas: Biblioteca Ayacucho, 1984), iv; Paz, introduction, x.

29. Irving A. Leonard, *Baroque Times in Old Mexico: Seventeenth-Century Persons, Places, and Practices* (1959; repr., Ann Arbor: University of Michigan Press, 1966), 229n6, 246.

30. While in the catalogue of Sigüenza's writing in Leonard's original 1929 work the letter is referenced using this language, it does not become the title of the letter until *Baroque Times*. In *Seis obras*, the same retroactive titling of his own 1932 book occurs in the notes and bibliography (136n1, 427).

31. Irving Leonard, "An Interview with Irving Leonard," by John J. Tepaske, *Hispanic American Historical Review* 63, no. 2 (1983): 239.

32. Noteworthy examples include José Rabasa, *Without History: Subaltern Studies, the Zapatista Insurgency, and the Specter of History* (Pittsburgh: University of Pittsburgh Press, 2010); Rabasa, "Pre-Columbian Pasts and Indian Presents in Mexican History," *Disposito* 19, no. 46 (1994): 245–70; Kathleen Ross, *The Baroque Narrative of Carlos de Sigüenza y Góngora: A New World Paradise* (New York: Cambridge University Press, 1993). Ross does not make this error when referencing the letter within an earlier essay where she relies on the text as edited by Romero de Terreros. See Ross, "Alboroto y motín de México: Una noche triste criollo," *Hispanic Review* 56, no. 2 (1988): 181–90.

33. Irving Albert Leonard, *Don Carlos de Sigüenza y Góngora: A Mexican Savant of the Seventeenth Century* (Berkeley: University of California Press, 1929), 240.

34. Carlos de Sigüenza y Góngora, *Alboroto y motín de México, del 8 de junio 1692: Relación de Don Carlos de Sigüenza y Góngora en una carta dirigida al Almirante Don Andrés de Pez*, ed. Irving A. Leonard (Mexico City: Talleres Gráficos del Museo Nacional de Arqueología, Historia y Etnografía, 1932), 51. All of the errors and or linguistic idiosyncrasies of Leonard's transcription are maintained in this quotation.

35. Ilona Katzew, *Casta Painting: Images of Race in Eighteenth-Century Mexico* (New Haven, Conn.: Yale University Press, 2004), 44.

36. Katzew, *Casta Painting*.

37. More, *Baroque Sovereignty*, 192.

38. Sigüenza y Góngora, *Relaciones históricas*, 133; Sigüenza y Góngora, *Seis obras*, 113; Irving A. Leonard, *Don Carlos de Sigüenza y Góngora: Un sabio mexicano del siglo XVII* (Mexico City: Fondo de Cultura Económica, 1984), 243.

39. Rabasa, *Without History*, 29.

40. Vinson, "Fading from Memory," 67.

41. Herskovitz is the American anthropologist who played a role in introducing the academic disciplines of African and African American Studies in the United States.

42. Aguirre Beltrán, *La población negra de México*, 12.

43. Alberto Moreiras, "Common Political Democracy: The *Marrano* Register," in *Impasses of the Post-global: Theory in the Era of Climate Change*, vol. 2, ed. Henry Sussman (Ann Arbor, Mich.: Open Humanities Press, 2012), 175; Erin Graff Zivin, "Beyond Inquisitional Logic, or, Toward an An-archaeological Latin Americanism," *CR: The New Centennial Review* 14, no. 1 (2014): 200. Moreiras's marranismo has its origin in the figure of the marrano in Spanish and Portuguese history. The marrano was a Jew who converted to Christianity to avoid persecution but nonetheless continued their prior religious practices in secret. As the crypto-Jew is the origin of the theorizations collected under the umbrella of a "marrano register," my own borrowing via Graff Zivin will steer away from the idea of haunting and its resonances to the crypt and the cemetery. Graff Zivin's turn to archaeology is helpful in this separation. For a more detailed explanation of this reasoning, see the previous chapter's discussion of a similar move with regard to Abraham and Torok's notion of the crypt.

44. Graff Zivin, "Beyond Inquisitional Logic," 200.

45. Graff Zivin, "Beyond Inquisitional Logic," 201.

46. Ridpath, *Oxford Dictionary of Astronomy*, s.v. "black hole."

47. Stephen Hawking, "Information Preservation and Weather Forecasting for Black Holes," Kavli Institute for Theoretical Physics (Santa Barbara, California, August 2013), 3, https://arxiv.org/pdf/1401.5761.pdf.

48. Hawking, "Information Preservation and Weather Forecasting for Black Holes," 1.

49. Ridpath, *Oxford Dictionary of Astronomy*, s.v. "accretion disk."

50. This borrowing remains fully aware that Hawking's thesis has yet to gain general acceptance by those most invested in this area of the cosmos. However,

it remains productive both despite and because of this anxiety, as both articulations share a tentative embrace of their especially nascent theorizations of the unthought. Additionally, this grand oscillation between astrophysics and national psychological apparatuses that will be carried through the remaining pages of this book serves as a reminder that all is reading.

51. This process was overseen by the Comisión Nacional de Libros de Texto Gratuitos.

52. Luis González y González, *Viaje por la historia de México*, ed. Andrea Citlapiltzin (Mexico City: Conaculta, 2010), 3.

53. González y González, *Viaje por la historia de México*.

54. González y González, *Viaje por la historia de México*, 22.

55. González y González, *Viaje por la historia de México*, 33.

56. González y González, *Viaje por la historia de México*, 24.

Chapter 3

1. Lindon W. Barrett, *Racial Blackness and the Discontinuity of Western Modernity*, ed. Justin A. Joyce, Dwight A. McBride, and John Carlos Rowe (Champaign: University of Illinois Press, 2013), 72.

2. Morelos, "Sentimientos de la nación, 14 de septiembre de 1813."

3. Abraham Lincoln, "Preliminary Emancipation Proclamation," September 22, 1862, National Archives and Records Administration, http://www.archives.gov/exhibits/american_originals_iv/sections/transcript_nonjava_preliminary_emancipation.html.

4. In *Abraham Lincoln*, Michael Burlingame picks up on the "curious" omission of the word "forever" when the following statement is reiterated in the final Emancipation Proclamation: "shall be then, thenceforward, and forever free" turns to "are, and henceforward shall be free" (2:463). Both phrases are present in the document, as two paragraphs from the preliminary Emancipation Proclamation were included verbatim in the final version. Burlingame supposes that perhaps Lincoln "may have feared that the courts would take a dim view of such an extravagant claim" (2:463). In either case, it points to the delicate nature of language as this idea was finding its form.

5. Alexander Tsesis, *The Thirteenth Amendment and American Freedom: A Legal History* (New York: New York University Press, 2004), 35.

6. Abraham Lincoln, "Second Annual Message," December 1, 1862, American Antiquarian Society, https://www.americanantiquarian.org/Freedmen/Manuscripts/lincolnsecondannual.html.

7. Lincoln, "Second Annual Message." This is a somewhat veiled reference to the ultimately failed colonization project in the Chiriquí region of Panama that I discuss later in the chapter.

8. Phillip W. Magness and Sebastian N. Page, *Colonization after Emancipation: Lincoln and the Movement for Black Resettlement* (Columbia: University of Missouri Press, 2011), 1; Burlingame, *Abraham Lincoln*, 2:385; Charles Tuckerman, "President Lincoln and Colonization," *Magazine of American History with Notes and Queries* 16 (1886): 332.

9. Burlingame, *Abraham Lincoln*, 2:394.

10. Michael Vorenberg, "Abraham Lincoln and the Politics of Black Colonization," *Journal of the Abraham Lincoln Association* 14, no. 2 (1993): 22;

Burlingame, *Abraham Lincoln*, 2:395–96; Abraham Lincoln, "Proclamation 99—Repudiation of an Agreement with Bernard Kock," April 16, 1863, American Presidency Project, https://www.presidency.ucsb.edu/documents/proclamation-99-repudiation-agreement-with-bernard-kock.

11. Tuckerman, "President Lincoln and Colonization," 330–31; Burlingame, *Abraham Lincoln*, 2:396. For insight into the man that Lincoln felt decidedly more comfortable working with than Kock, here is a portion of Tuckerman's recollections of the disaster made for the *Magazine of American History* in 1886: "No sooner were the survivors landed and the necessity for manual labor on their part apparent, than the lowest characteristics of the negro—indolence, discontent, insubordination, and finally open revolt prevailed. Mistaking liberty for license, they refused to work, and raised preposterous demands for luxuries to which they were wholly unaccustomed during servitude. History repeats itself" (330–31).

12. Magness and Page, *Colonization after Emancipation*, 55.

13. Magness and Page, *Colonization after Emancipation*, 60, 86–89.

14. Magness and Page, *Colonization after Emancipation*, 8–9.

15. Perhaps the most famous of such statements comes from his fourth debate with Stephen Douglas during his 1858 campaign for the U.S. Senate. Though Lincoln did not approve of the expansion of slavery, he did not envision social and political equality for blacks and whites: "I will say then that I am not, nor ever have been in favor of bringing about in any way the social and political equality of the white and black races—that I am not nor ever have been in favor of making voters or jurors of negroes, nor of qualifying them to hold office, nor to intermarry with white people; and I will say in addition to this that there is a physical difference between the white and black races which I believe will forever forbid the two races living together on terms of social and political equality. And inasmuch as they cannot so live, while they do remain together there must be the position of superior and inferior, and I as much as any other man am in favor of having the superior position assigned to the white race . . . Judge Douglas has said to you that he has not been able to get from me an answer to the question whether I am in favor of negro-citizenship. So far as I know, the Judge never asked me the question before. He shall have no occasion to ever ask it again, for I tell him very frankly that I am not in favor of negro citizenship." Rodney Davis and Douglas Wilson, *The Lincoln-Douglas Debates: The Lincoln Studies Center Edition* (Champaign: University of Illinois Press, 2014), 131, 164.

16. Chris Cillizza, "Donald Trump Ranked Himself 2nd on a List of Most 'Presidential' Presidents," CNN.com, July 26, 2017, https://www.cnn.com/2017/07/26/politics/donald-trump-abe-lincoln/index.html.

17. Phillip Rucker, "Obama Inspired by, Compared to Lincoln," *Washington Post*, November 19, 2008.

18. Abraham Lincoln, "Inaugural Address: March 4, 1861," American Presidency Project, http://www.presidency.ucsb.edu/ws/index.php?pid=25818.

19. Michelle Boorstein, "Obama to Take Oath on Bibles Used by Martin Luther King Jr., Lincoln," *Washington Post*, January 10, 2013.

20. Allen C. Guelzo, *Lincoln's Emancipation Proclamation: The End of Slavery in America* (New York: Simon and Schuster, 2006), 2.

21. Barack Obama, "Presidential Proclamation—150th Anniversary of the Emancipation Proclamation," White House, December 31, 2012, https://www.whitehouse.gov/the-press-office/2012/12/31/presidential-proclamation-150th-anniversary-emancipation-proclamation.

22. Refer to note 4 in this chapter to see how Obama has chosen to restore the language of the preliminary version: "*shall be then, thenceforward, and forever free*" instead of "are, and henceforward shall be free."

23. Sumner's first appearance is in the reception line for a party where he is waiting to greet Mary Todd Lincoln. His one line in the film is of no significance as he is interrupted so that she may direct her attention to the other guests. He is later visible in the balcony when the vote on the Thirteenth Amendment is read.

24. Amy Dru Stanley, "Instead of Waiting for the Thirteenth Amendment: The War Power, Slave Marriage, and Inviolate Human Rights," *American Historical Review* 115, no. 3 (2010): 740–42.

25. Stanley, "Instead of Waiting for the Thirteenth Amendment," 742.

26. Stanley, "Instead of Waiting for the Thirteenth Amendment."

27. Stanley, "Instead of Waiting for the Thirteenth Amendment"; Michael Vorenberg, *Final Freedom: The Civil War, the Abolition of Slavery, and the Thirteenth Amendment* (Cambridge: Cambridge University Press, 2001), 107.

28. Stanley, "Instead of Waiting," 742.

29. John C. Waugh, *Reelecting Lincoln: The Battle for the 1864 Presidency* (Boston: Da Capo Press, 2001), 162.

30. Their convention was held a week prior to the National Union Party's and included in their platform the call for a constitutional amendment abolishing slavery. This would eventually make it into the Republican Party platform a week later.

31. Joshua Zeitz, "Fact-Checking 'Lincoln': Lincoln's Mostly Realistic; His Advisers Aren't," *Atlantic*, November 12, 2012, https://www.theatlantic.com/entertainment/archive/2012/11/fact-checking-lincoln-lincolns-mostly-realistic-his-advisers-arent/265073/.

32. Rucker, "Obama Inspired by, Compared to Lincoln."

33. Harold Holzer, "Reel vs. Real: Was Thaddeus Stevens as Angry and Abrasive as He's Portrayed in Spielberg's *Lincoln*?," *Civil War Times* 52, no. 2 (April 2013): 48.

34. Vorenberg, *Final Freedom*, 200–201.

35. Vorenberg, "Spielberg's Lincoln: The Great Emancipator Returns," *Journal of the Civil War Era* 3, no. 4 (2013): 567.

36. Michael Shank, "'Lincoln': Where Was Frederick Douglass?," *Washington Post*, November 28, 2012.

37. Harold K. Bush, "What Historians Think about Spielberg's *Lincoln*," *Cineaste* 38, no. 2 (2013): 18.

38. Bush, "What Historians Think about Spielberg's *Lincoln*."

39. *Lincoln Unite*, DreamWorks Pictures, October 3, 2012, https://www.youtube.com/watch?v=F_PfTl63qQQ.

40. The civil rights activists shown in the photo are Ralph Abernathy, James Foreman, Reverend Jesse Douglass, and John Lewis.

41. "Suffragette Parade in Brooklyn," The Monticello Digital Classroom, https://classroom.monticello.org/media-item/suffragette-parade-in-brooklyn/.

42. Burlingame, *Abraham Lincoln*, 1:104; Eric Foner, *The Fiery Trial: Abraham Lincoln and American Slavery* (New York: W. W. Norton, 2010), 291; Wendy Hamand Venet, *Neither Ballots nor Bullets: Women Abolitionists and the Civil War* (Charlottesville: University of Virginia Press, 1991), 120.

43. Foner, *The Fiery Trial*, 291; Venet, *Neither Ballots nor Bullets*, 120. This pressure would also be added to in the months after by the threat of the more radical Butler or Frémont usurping Lincoln's bid for a second term.

44. "About Us," Participant Media, accessed November 25, 2018, http://www.participantmedia.com/about-us.

45. "About Us."

46. Ann Hornaday, "Participant Media Invents an Activist Aesthetic," *Washington Post*, May 10, 2012.

47. Wilderson, *Red, White, and Black*, 26; Hornaday, "Participant Media Invents an Activist Aesthetic."

48. Hornaday. "Walk It Back" is the song playing.

49. *Lincoln: A Cinematic and Historical Companion* (New York: Disney Editions, 2012).

50. Shank, "'Lincoln'"; Vorenberg, "Spielberg's Lincoln"; Kate Masur, "In Spielberg's 'Lincoln,' Passive Black Characters," *New York Times*, November 12, 2012.

51. Burlingame, *Abraham Lincoln*, 2:398.

52. Frederick Douglass, *Frederick Douglass: Selected Speeches and Writings*, ed. Phillip S. Foner and Yuval Taylor (Chicago: Chicago Review Press, 2000), 506.

53. Richard Striner, *Father Abraham: Lincoln's Relentless Struggle to End Slavery* (New York: Oxford University Press, 2006), 168–70.

54. Vorenberg, "Spielberg's Lincoln," 567.

55. Doris Kearns Goodwin, *Team of Rivals: The Political Genius of Abraham Lincoln* (New York: Simon and Schuster, 2005), 394.

56. Goodwin, *Team of Rivals*, 470.

57. Goodwin, *Team of Rivals*.

58. Goodwin, *Team of Rivals*, 207.

59. Goodwin, *Team of Rivals*, xv.

60. Goodwin, *Team of Rivals*.

61. Goodwin, *Team of Rivals*, 22.

62. Douglass, *Selected Speeches*, 615, 618.

63. Douglass, *Selected Speeches*, 618

64. Douglass, *Selected Speeches*.

65. Douglass, *Selected Speeches*.

66. Douglass, *Selected Speeches*, 619.

67. Douglass, *Selected Speeches*, 616.

68. Douglass, *Selected Speeches*, 715.

69. Striner, *Father Abraham*, 63–64. Emphasis added.

70. More, *Baroque Sovereignty*, 8.

71. Goodwin, *Team of Rivals*, 470.

72. Eric Foner, "*Lincoln*'s Use of Politics for Noble Ends," *New York Times*, November 26, 2012.

73. Saidiya Hartman, *To Lose Your Mother: A Journey along the Atlantic Slave Route* (New York: Farrar, Straus and Giroux, 2007).

74. Hawking, "Information Preservation and Weather Forecasting for Black Holes," 4.

75. Abraham and Torok, *The Shell and the Kernel*, 171. The word "haunts" is used in place of "emanates" in the original text.

Chapter 4

1. David C. Grove, *Discovering the Olmecs: An Unconventional History* (Austin: University of Texas Press, 2014), 5–16.

2. José María Melgar y Serrano, "Estudio sobre la antigüedad y el origen de la cabeza colosal de tipo etiópico que existe en Hueyapan en el cantón de los Tuxtlas," in *Boletín de la Sociedad Mexicana de Geografía y Estadística*, época 2, III (Mexico City: Imprenta del Gobierno, 1871), 6. At this time, the adjective *etiópico/a* described something African in nature.

3. Melgar y Serrano, "Estudio," 8.

4. Melgar y Serrano, "Estudio," 12.

5. Bennetta Jules-Rosette, *Josephine Baker in Art and Life: The Icon and the Image* (Champaign: University of Illinois Press, 2007), 61, 130; Harriet Beecher Stowe, *Uncle Tom's Cabin* (New York: Limited Editions Club, 1938).

6. His relationship with Carl Van Vechten, a patron of the Harlem Renaissance, was particularly important as he negotiated the space of Harlem. Van Vechten, himself a writer and a photographer, produced work that was similarly drawn to the exotic nature of black life and similarly influenced the archive that we have received of that era. In an early essay on the black theatrical production *My Friend from Kentucky* (1913), for example, Van Vechten would famously applaud "how the darkies danced, sang, and cavorted. Real nigger stuff, this, done with spontaneity and joy in the doing." See Carl Van Vechten, "The Negro Theatre," in *In the Garret* (New York: Knopf, 1920), 316. And while his thoughts on race may be argued to have developed as he matured, pro and con reactions to his 1926 fictional portrayal of Harlem life, *Nigger Heaven*, from black luminaries (Hughes, W. E. B. Du Bois, and Countee Cullen, among others) spoke to his legibility and his power within the black community. Covarrubias would gift a caricature to Van Vechten, entitled "A Prediction," with the famous patron drawn as a black man. See Archivo Miguel Covarrubias, Universidad de las Américas, Puebla, http://catarina.udlap.mx/xmLibris/projects/covarrubias/browse/item.jsp?id=caricaturas_ii&key=amc_caricaturas_ii_090.xml.

7. Williams, *Covarrubias*, 12, 255.

8. Williams, *Covarrubias*.

9. Miguel Covarrubias, *Indian Art of Mexico and Central America* (New York: Knopf, 1957), 62; Richard Diehl, *The Olmecs: America's First Civilization* (London: Thames and Hudson, 2004), 98.

10. Diehl, *The Olmecs*, 98.

11. *Mayas y olmecas: segunda Reunión de mesa redonda sobre problemas antropológicos de México y Centro América* (Tuxtla Gutiérez, Chiapas: Sociedad Mexicana de Antropología, 1942).

12. Miguel Covarrubias, *Mexico South: The Isthmus of Tehuantepec* (New York: Knopf, 1946), 96, 89.

13. Diehl, *The Olmecs*, 112.

14. Ivan Van Sertima, *They Came Before Columbus: The African Presence in Ancient America* (New York: Random House, 2003), 3.

15. Ivan Van Sertima, "African Presence in Early America," in *Race, Discourse, and the Origin of the Americas: A New World View*, ed. Vera Lawrence Hyatt and Rex Nettleford (Washington, D.C.: Smithsonian Institution Press, 1995), 66.

16. Van Sertima, "African Presence in Early America," 73.

17. Van Sertima, "African Presence in Early America," 68.

18. Van Sertima, "African Presence in Early America."

19. David Kelley, "An Essay on Pre-Columbian Contacts between the Americas and Other Areas, with Special Reference to the Work of Ivan Van Sertima," in *Race, Discourse, and the Origin of the Americas: A New World View*, ed. Vera Lawrence Hyatt and Rex Nettleford (Washington, D.C.: Smithsonian Institution Press, 1995), 107.

20. Kelley, "An Essay," 104.

21. Kelley, "An Essay," 107, 114. Kelley also opens the door for the potential of contact from a non-African black population with the Olmec culture.

22. Kelley, "An Essay," 114.

23. Kelley, "An Essay."

24. Gabriel Haslip-Viera, Bernard Ortiz de Montellano, and Warren Barbour, "Robbing Native American Cultures: Van Sertima's Afrocentricity and the Olmecs," *Current Anthropology* 38, no. 3 (June 1, 1997): 419–41. Montellano had in fact published a book chapter entitled "Afrocentric Pseudoscience: The Miseducation of African Americans," in *The Flight from Science and Reason*, ed. Paul R. Gross, Norman Levitt, and Martin W. Lewis (New York: New York Academy of Sciences, 1997), 561–572.

25. Haslip-Viera, Montellano, and Barbour, "Robbing Native American Cultures," 421.

26. Haslip-Viera, Montellano, and Barbour, "Robbing Native American Cultures," 420.

27. Haslip-VieraMontellano, and Barbour, "Robbing Native American Cultures," 422.

28. Haslip-Viera, Montellano, and Barbour, "Robbing Native American Cultures," 431.

29. Haslip-Viera, Montellano, and Barbour, "Robbing Native American Cultures," 432. Emphasis added.

30. Martin Bernal, "On 'Robbing Native American Cultures,'" *Current Anthropology* 39, no. 4 (1998): 513, 512.

31. Bernal, "On 'Robbing Native American Cultures,'" 513.

32. Kelley, "Pre-Columbian Contacts," 106.

33. Richard Callaghan, "Drift Voyages across the Mid-Atlantic," *Antiquity* 89, no. 345 (2015): 724.

34. Callaghan, "Drift Voyages across the Mid-Atlantic," 725.

35. Callaghan, "Drift Voyages across the Mid-Atlantic," 729.

36. Callaghan, "Drift Voyages across the Mid-Atlantic."

37. See Stephen Jett, *Ancient Ocean Crossings: Reconsidering the Case for Contacts with the Pre-Columbian Americas* (Tuscaloosa: University of Alabama Press, 2017).

38. Haslip-Viera, Montellano, and Barbour, "Robbing Native American Cultures," 431.

39. Van Sertima's Rutgers degree information was confirmed by the School of Arts and Sciences and the Department of Africana Studies at Rutgers University. All of his other advanced degrees are honorary.

40. Williams, *Covarrubias*, 5. As Adriana Williams notes, it was in an incident where Covarrubias, perhaps accidentally, struck one of his clerical teachers with a stick and fractured his skull (5).

41. Williams, *Covarrubias*, 168.

42. *Mexico South* was not translated into Spanish until 1980, bringing into question the idea of audience.

43. Diehl, *The Olmecs*, 112, 108.

44. Diehl, *The Olmecs*, 109.

45. Diehl, *The Olmecs*, 127.

46. Michael Coe, "The Olmec Heartland: Evolution and Ideology," in *Regional Perspectives on the Olmec*, ed. Robert Sharer and David C. Grove (Cambridge: Cambridge University Press, 1989), 68; Michael Coe and Rex Koontz, *Mexico: From the Olmecs to the Aztecs* (London: Thames and Hudson, 2013), 50.

47. Kathleen Berrin and Virginia Fields, eds., *Olmec: Colossal Masterworks of Ancient Mexico* (New Haven, Conn.: Yale University Press, 2010), 20.

48. Berrin and Fields, *Olmec*, 25.

49. Van Sertima, *They Came Before Columbus*, plates 27 and 31.

50. Covarrubias, *Mexico South*, plate 1.

51. Haslip-Viera, Montellano, and Barbour, "Robbing Native American Cultures," 423.

52. Grove, *Discovering the Olmecs*, 52.

53. Diehl, *The Olmecs*, 29.

54. Coe and Koontz, *Mexico*, 91.

55. Diehl, *The Olmecs*, 108.

Chapter 5

1. *Encuesta Intercensal 2015: Cuestionario para viviendas particulares habitadas y población* (Mexico City: Instituto Nacional de Estadística y Geografía, 2015), 5–6.

2. *Perfil sociodemográfico de la población afrodescendiente en México* (Mexico City: Instituto Nacional de Estadística y Geografía, 2017), 3.

3. *Perfil sociodemográfico de la población afrodescendiente en México.*

4. *Perfil sociodemográfico de la población afrodescendiente en México*, 57. The six municipalities with the largest Afro-descendant population are Santiago Tapextla (83.7 percent), Santo Domingo Armenta (76.1 percent), San Juan Bautista Lo de Soto (68.3 percent), Santa María Cortijo (53.7 percent), Santa María Huazolotitlán (49.4 percent), and Santiago Llano Grande (49.2 percent).

5. Randal Archibold, "Negro? Prieto? Moreno? A Question of Identity for Black Mexicans," *New York Times*, October 25, 2014.

6. "Info Note: International Year for People of African Descent," United Nations Human Rights Office, 2011, http://www2.ohchr.org/english/issues/racism/groups/african/docs/Info_note_IYPAD.pdf.

7. *Guía para la acción pública contra la discriminación y para la promoción de igualdad e inclusión de la población afrodescendiente en México* (Mexico City: Consejo Nacional para Prevenir la Discriminación, 2011), 62.
8. *Guía para la acción pública*, 86–87.
9. *Guía para la acción pública*, 15–16.
10. *Guía para la acción pública*, 9.
11. *Guía para la acción pública*, 61.
12. *Guía para la acción pública*, 9, 54, 40–43.
13. *Guía para la acción pública*, 43.
14. *Guía para la acción pública*.
15. Tianna Paschel, "'The Beautiful Faces of My Black People': Race, Ethnicity and the Politics of Colombia's 2005 Census," *Ethnic and Racial Studies* 36, no. 10 (2013): 1549–50.
16. Emiko Saldívar, "'It's Not Race, It's Culture': Untangling Racial Politics in Mexico," *Latin American and Caribbean Ethnic Studies* 9, no. 1 (2014): 89.
17. Emiko Saldívar and Casey Walsh, "Racial and Ethnic Identities in Mexican Statistics," *Journal of Iberian and Latin American Research* 20, no. 3 (2014): 472.
18. Saldívar, "It's Not Race," 102.
19. Emiko Saldívar Tanaka, "La representación estadística de la negritud en México: Entre el dato duro y la realidad," presented at the "Coloquio Nacional ¿Cómo queremos llamarnos? Horizonte INEGI 2020," May 30, 2017, https://www.youtube.com/watch?v=elaYc1h-RJs.
20. Saldívar Tanaka, "La representación estadística de la negritud en México."
21. See two works by Mónica G. Moreno Figueroa and Emiko Saldívar Tanaka: "Comics, Dolls and the Disavowal of Racism: Learning from Mexican Mestizaje," in *Creolizing Europe: Legacies and Transformations*, ed. Encarnación Gutiérrez Rodríguez and Shirley Anne Tate (Liverpool: Liverpool University Press, 2015); "'We Are Not Racists, We Are Mexicans': Privilege, Nationalism and Post-race Ideology in Mexico," *Critical Sociology* 42, nos. 4–5 (July 1, 2016): 515–33.
22. See Christine Arce's chapter "The Music of the Afro-Mexican Universe and the Dialectics of *Son*" in *México's Nobodies: The Cultural Legacy of the Soldadera and Afro-Mexican Women* (Albany: State University of New York Press, 2017) for a nuanced discussion of this musical landscape.
23. See Micaela Díaz-Sánchez and Alejandro Hernández, "The *Son Jarocho* as Afro-Mexican Resistance Music," *Journal of Pan African Studies* 6, no. 1 (2013): 187–209.
24. Hettie Malcomson, "New Generations, Older Bodies: *Danzón*, Age and 'Cultural Rescue' in the Port of Veracruz, Mexico," *Popular Music* 31, no. 2 (2012): 217–30.
25. Christina Sue, *The Land of the Cosmic Race: Race Mixture, Racism, and Blackness in Mexico* (New York: Oxford University Press, 2013), 144.
26. Laura Lewis, *Chocolate and Corn Flour: History, Race, and Place in the Making of Black Mexico* (Durham, N.C.: Duke University Press, 2012), 155–57.
27. Claudia Rankine and Beth Loffreda, introduction to *The Racial Imaginary: Writers on Race in the Life of the Mind*, ed. Claudia Rankine, Beth Loffreda, and Cap Max King (Albany, N.Y.: Fence Books, 2015), 14; James Baldwin,

"Everybody's Protest Novel," in *Notes of a Native Son* (Boston: Beacon Press, 1955), 10. Baldwin's essay contains the famous critique of the work of both Harriet Beecher Stowe and Richard Wright. Rankine's project, relying heavily on Baldwin, testifies to the fact that his thought conditions conversations on race in the present moment.

28. An almost identical explanatory note is present in the census of 1900. Tzendal is added as a legible potential indigenous language choice. Both explanatory notes' enumeration of potential indigenous languages (1895 and 1900) end with "etc.," underlining the possibility of positions beyond those conceptualized by the document.

29. Interest and anxiety in relation to international migration, existing on the forms themselves, is not analyzed in my work.

30. Barack Obama, "Barack Obama at Annual NCLR Conference," July 12, 2008, https://www.youtube.com/watch?v=M6LuA_S5sP4.

31. Amanda Holpuch, "US Census Bureau Drops 'Negro' as Option for Respondents on Race," *Guardian*, February 25, 2013.

32. Jilian Fama, "Census Dropping the Term, 'Negro,'" ABC News, February 25, 2013, http://abcnews.go.com/Politics/OTUS/us-census-bureau-drops-negro-surveys/story?id=18591761.

33. Holpuch, "US Census Bureau Drops 'Negro' as Option for Respondents"; Fama, "Census Dropping the Term, 'Negro.'" See Jens Manuel Krogstad and D'Vera Cohn, "U.S. Census Looking at Big Changes in How It Asks about Race and Ethnicity," Pew Research Center, March 14, 2015, http://www.pewresearch.org/fact-tank/2014/03/14/u-s-census-looking-at-big-changes-in-how-it-asks-about-race-and-ethnicity/; "The Black Population: 2010," U.S. Census Bureau, September, 2011, https://www.census.gov/prod/cen2010/briefs/c2010br-06.pdf. The U.S. Census Bureau's public reversal seems designed to signal both a progressive evolution and an attempt to restore any faith lost in the science of its counting. However, this incredible instability is, of course, not limited to the "Negro." Take another aspect of the 2010 accounting of the "Black or African American" population in the United States. Imagine, for example, that when presented with the choice to identify your race, you were uncomfortable with checking the "Black, African Am., or Negro" box because of your Nigerian ancestry. You could have decided to self-identify in the write-in space allotted for "Some Other Race." Given that Asians are required to identify themselves racially by national origin (Chinese, Korean, Filipino, etc.), it might not at all feel strange for you to self-identify as Nigerian. Though no indication of how self-identified responses will be *read* is provided on the form itself, this response in 2010 would have nonetheless been counted as "Black or African American" because, as is made clear in the Census Briefs released in the year following the 2010 Census, "Sub-Saharan African entries are classified as Black or African American" ("The Black Population," 2). That is, as one might or might not expect, "with the exception of [those identifying as] Sudanese and Cape Verdean" who were counted as separate "because of their complex, historical heritage" ("The Black Population," 2). And if you self-identified by way of a North African nation, you, perhaps unknowingly, identified yourself as "White" regardless of your reasoning for not checking the "White" box in the first place. All of this is dictated by the standards of the U.S. Office of Management and Budget.

34. "Census Questionnaires (1790–2010)," U.S. Census Bureau, https://www.census.gov/history/www/through_the_decades/questionnaires/.

35. Sexton, *Amalgamation Schemes*, 12.

36. "Questions Asked: The 2020 Census is easy. The questions are simple," U.S. Census Bureau, https://2020census.gov/en/about-questions.html. In July of 2019, Donald Trump backed down from his insistence on having a question regarding citizenship on the 2020 Census (seen in the previously noted document). See Andrew Prokop, "Trump's census citizenship Question Fiasco, Explained: The president admitted defeat on his push to add the question to the," *Vox*, July 11, 2019, https://www.vox.com/2019/7/11/20689015/census-citizenship-question-trump-executive-order.

37. "About the American Community Survey," U.S. Census Bureau, https://www.census.gov/programs-surveys/acs/about.html.

38. Lee Edelman, *No Future: Queer Theory and the Death Drive* (Durham, N.C.: Duke University Press, 2004), 3.

39. *Cooper v. Aaron*, 358 U.S. 1 (1958).

40. Taylor Branch and Haley Sweetland Edwards, "The Second Emancipation," *Washington Monthly*, January/February 2013.

41. Branch and Edwards, "The Second Emancipation."

42. Lyndon Johnson, "Remarks upon Signing the Civil Rights Act," American Presidency Project, http://www.presidency.ucsb.edu/ws/index.php?pid=28799. The following is a portion of Johnson's address to the nation: "We believe that all men are created equal. Yet many are denied equal treatment . . . We believe that all men have certain unalienable rights. Yet many Americans do not enjoy those rights . . . We believe that all men are entitled to the blessings of liberty. Yet millions are being deprived of those blessings—not because of their own failures, but because of the color of their skin . . . The reasons are deeply imbedded in history and tradition and the nature of man. We can understand—without rancor or hatred—how this all happened . . . But it cannot continue. Our Constitution, the foundation of our Republic, forbids it. The principles of our freedom forbid it. Morality forbids it. And the law I will sign tonight forbids it . . . The only limit to a man's hope for happiness, and for the future of his children, shall be his own ability . . . Let us close the springs of racial poison . . . Let us hasten that day when our unmeasured strength and our unbounded spirit will be free to do the great works ordained for this Nation by the just and wise God who is the Father of us all."

43. Johnson, "Remarks upon Signing the Civil Rights Act."

44. Lyndon Johnson, "Special Message to Congress: The American Promise [on the Voting Rights Act 3/15/65]," LBJ Presidential Library, http://www.lbjlibrary.org/lyndon-baines-johnson/speeches-films/president-johnsons-special-message-to-the-congress-the-american-promise.

45. Johnson, "Special Message to Congress."

46. Dwight Eisenhower, "Citation and Remarks at Presentation of the National Security Medal to J. Edgar Hoover," May 27, 1955, American Presidency Project, http://www.presidency.ucsb.edu/ws/index.php?pid=10244.

47. James Baldwin, *The Evidence of Things Not Seen* (New York: Henry Holt, 1985), 39–40.

48. Baldwin, *The Evidence of Things Not Seen*, 40.

49. Baldwin, *The Evidence of Things Not Seen*, 4.

50. Russell Goldman, "Trayvon Martin Drug Photos Can't Be Mentioned, Says Judge," ABC News, May 28, 2013, https://abcnews.go.com/US/trayvon-martin-drug-photos-mentioned-judge/story?id=19271093.

51. Barack Obama, "Remarks by the President on Trayvon Martin," Obama White House Archives, July 19, 2013, https://obamawhitehouse.archives.gov/the-press-office/2013/07/19/remarks-president-trayvon-martin.

52. Obama, "Remarks by the President on Trayvon Martin."

53. "Homepage," Obama White House Archives, https://obamawhitehouse.archives.gov.

54. "Homepage," Obama White House Archives.

55. Barack Obama and Jeff Johnson, "Transcript: BET's Exclusive Interview with President Obama," BET.com, December 12, 2014, https://www.bet.com/news/national/2014/12/12/transcript-bet-s-exclusive-interview-with-president-obama.html?cid=facebook.

56. Walter Scott, the fifty-year-old man shot in 2015 on the anniversary of Martin Luther King Jr.'s assassination after being pulled over for a minor traffic violation, despite indictments of his killer at both the state and federal level during Obama's second term, is also absent in the archive. His death, like that of Rice, was caught on videotape. Christina Sharpe examines Obama's February 15, 2013 speech at the Hyde Park Academy in Chicago and similarly speaks to how his oratory appears to "suffer from dysgraphia: the inability of language to cohere around the bodies and the suffering of [Black people]" See *In the Wake*, 96.

57. P. Khalil Saucier and Tryon P. Woods, "What Is the *Danger* in Black Studies and Can We Look at It Again (and Again)?," in *On Marronage: Ethical Confrontations with Antiblackness*, edited by P. Khalil Saucier and Tryon P. Woods (Trenton: Africa World Press, 2015), 9.

58. Alicia Garza, "A Herstory of the #BlackLivesMatter Movement," *The Feminist Wire*, October 7, 2014, https://www.nfg.org/news/herstory-blacklivesmatter-movement.

59. "Herstory," Black Lives Matter.

60. Audre Lorde and James Baldwin, "Revolutionary Hope: A Conversation between James Baldwin and Audre Lorde," MoCADA, http://mocada-museum.tumblr.com/post/73421979421/revolutionary-hope-a-conversation-between-james.

61. "#SayHerName: Resisting Police Brutality Against Black Women," African American Policy Forum, July 16, 2015, https://aapf.org/sayhernamereport.

62. Barack Obama, "Statement by the President on the Passing of Michael Brown," Obama White House Archives, August 12, 2014, https://obamawhitehouse.archives.gov/the-press-office/2014/08/12/statement-president-passing-michael-brown.

63. Barack Obama, "Remarks by the President after Announcement of the Decision by the Grand Jury in Ferguson, Missouri," Obama White House Archives, November 24, 2014, https://obamawhitehouse.archives.gov/the-press-office/2014/11/24/remarks-president-after-announcement-decision-grand-jury-ferguson-missou.

64. "Tamir Rice's Mom 'Very Disappointed' with President Obama," MSNBC, July 18, 2016, https://www.youtube.com/watch?v=lKsk1PuPWEU.

Afterword

1. Graff Zivin, "Beyond Inquisitional Logic," 200–201.

2. Zivin, "Beyond Inquisitional Logic," 197.

3. Fredric Jameson, *Archaeologies of the Future: The Desire Called Utopia and Other Science Fictions* (London: Verso, 2007), xiii.

4. Carlos Fuentes, *Valiente mundo nuevo: Épica, utopía y mito en la novela hispanoamericana* (Mexico City: Fondo de Cultura Económica, 1990), 217.

5. Fuentes's output is marked by this interest in unsettling the single narrative of the Mexican nation by paying particular attention to repressed histories and identities. He remains, for example, one of the few Mexican novelists who have engaged critically and openly with Mexico's Afro-descendant heritage in their own work. True to his construction of the *indo-afro-iberoamericano*, *Terra Nostra* (Mexico City: Alfaguara, 2013) issues perhaps his most elaborate challenge to a world that presents itself as "univocal in its normativity." Carlos Fuentes, "Cervantes, or the Critique of Reading," in *Myself with Others: Selected Essays* (New York: Farrar, Straus and Giroux, 1990), 69.

6. Fuentes, "Cervantes, or the Critique of Reading," 214.

7. Colson Whitehead, *Zone One* (New York: Anchor Books, 2012), 275. Emphasis added.

8. Whitehead, *Zone One*, 121.

9. Whitehead, *Zone One*, 267. Emphasis added.

10. Whitehead, *Zone One*, 124.

11. Colson Whitehead, "The Year of Living Postracially," *New York Times*, November 4, 2009.

12. Whitehead, *Zone One*, 322, 183.

13. Whitehead, *Zone One*, 287.

14. Whitehead, *Zone One*, 9.

15. Whitehead, *Zone One*, 79. Emphasis added.

16. I am not alone in seeing the relevance of the discourse of Afrofuturism in a comparative work that manages blackness in the United States and Mexico. Juliet Hooker, in a portion of her book *Theorizing Race in the Americas*, uses this framework to read W. E. B. Du Bois's speculative fictions managing race mixture alongside Vasconcelos.

17. Kodwo Eshun, "Further Considerations of Afrofuturism," *CR: The New Centennial Review* 3, no. 2 (2003): 287.

18. Eshun, "Further Considerations of Afrofuturism," 297.

19. Eshun, "Further Considerations of Afrofuturism."

20. Gilroy, "Living Memory," *City Limits*, March 31–April 7, 1988, 10–11; Gilroy, *Small Acts: Thoughts on the Politics of Black Cultures* (London: Serpent's Tail, 1993), 175–82.

21. Toni Morrison, *Playing in the Dark: Whiteness and the Literary Imagination* (New York: Vintage, 1993), 8.

22. Morrison, *Playing in the Dark*, 52.

23. Morrison, *Playing in the Dark*, 18. For a similar critique launched in a more comic register, see Martine Syms, "The Mundane Afrofuturist Manifesto," *Rhizome*, December 17, 2013, https://rhizome.org/editorial/2013/dec/17/mundane-afrofuturist-manifesto/.

24. For evidence of the continued influence of this strand of Afrofuturism, see Reynaldo Anderson, "Afrofuturism 2.0 & The Black Speculative Arts Movement: Notes on a Manifesto," *Obsidian: Literature in the African Diaspora* 42, no. 1–2 (2016): 230–71. For an analysis that both works within and complicates this intellectual inheritance, see Kara Keeling's examination of Arthur Jafa's short film *Love Is the Message, the Message Is Death* (2016) in *Queer Times, Black Futures* (New York: New York University Press, 2019), 137–44.

25. Eshun, "Further Considerations," 293.

26. Whitehead has similarly repurposed quotes from Walter Benjamin and Ezra Pound to open the first and second sections, respectively, and this aligns with his take on the genre that constantly mashes up supposedly "high" and "low" cultural references.

27. Whitehead, *Zone One*, 283. Underlining his own investment in Eliot's work, Whitehead uses this term and its related iterations ("wastelanders" and "wastelanded") twenty-two times throughout the novel.

28. Whitehead, *Zone One*, 305.

29. Whitehead, *Zone One*, 58.

30. Whitehead, *Zone One*, 57.

31. Baldwin, *The Evidence of Things Not Seen*, 31.

32. Baldwin, *The Evidence of Things Not Seen*, 322.

33. Baldwin, *The Evidence of Things Not Seen*, 288–89. Emphasis added.

34. Baldwin, *The Evidence of Things Not Seen*, 290.

35. Baldwin, *The Evidence of Things Not Seen*.

BIBLIOGRAPHY

Abraham, Nicolas, and Maria Torok. *The Shell and the Kernel: Renewals of Psychoanalysis*. Vol. 1. Translated by Nicholas Rand. Chicago: University of Chicago Press, 1994.

Aguirre Beltrán, Gonzalo. *Cuijla: Esbozo etnográfico de un pueblo negro*. Mexico City: Fondo de Cultura Económica, 1985.

———. *La población negra de México: Estudio etnohistórico*. 1946. Reprint, Mexico City: Fondo de Cultura Económica, 1972.

Anna, Timothy E. *Forging Mexico, 1821–1835*. Lincoln: University of Nebraska Press, 2001.

Arce, Christine. *México's Nobodies: The Cultural Legacy of the Soldadera and Afro-Mexican Women*. Albany: State University of New York Press, 2017.

Archibold, Randal. "Negro? Prieto? Moreno? A Question of Identity for Black Mexicans." *New York Times*, October 25, 2014.

Baldwin, James. "Atlanta: The Evidence of Things Not Seen." *Playboy* (December 1981): 140–42, 308–16.

———. "Everybody's Protest Novel." In *Notes of a Native Son*. Boston: Beacon Press, 1955.

———. *The Evidence of Things Not Seen*. New York: Henry Holt, 1985.

———. *Nobody Knows My Name: More Notes of a Native Son*. New York: Dell, 1961.

Barrett, Lindon W. *Racial Blackness and the Discontinuity of Western Modernity*. Edited by Justin A. Joyce, Dwight A. McBride, and John Carlos Rowe. Champaign: University of Illinois Press, 2013.

Bartra, Roger. *The Cage of Melancholy: Identity and Metamorphosis in the Mexican Character*. New Brunswick, N.J.: Rutgers University Press, 1992.

Bennett, Herman L. *Africans in Colonial Mexico: Absolutism, Christianity, and Afro-Creole Consciousness, 1570–1640*. Bloomington: Indiana University Press, 2005.

Bernal, Martin. "On 'Robbing Native American Cultures.' " *Current Anthropology* 39, no. 4 (1998): 512–14.

Berrin, Kathleen, and Virginia M. Fields, eds. *Olmec: Colossal Masterworks of Ancient Mexico*. New Haven, Conn.: Yale University Press, 2010.

Bonilla-Silva, Eduardo, and David R. Dietrich. "The Latin Americanization of US Race Relations: A New Pigmentocracy." In *Shades of Difference: Why Skin Color Matters*, edited by Evelyn Glenn, 40–60. Palo Alto, Calif.: Stanford University Press, 2009.

Boorstein, Michelle. "Obama to Take Oath on Bibles Used by Martin Luther King Jr., Lincoln." *Washington Post*, January 10, 2013.

Branch, Taylor, and Haley Sweetland Edwards. "The Second Emancipation." *Washington Monthly*, January/February 2013.

Burlingame, Michael. *Abraham Lincoln*. 2 vols. Baltimore: Johns Hopkins University Press, 2012.

Bush, Harold K. "What Historians Think about Spielberg's *Lincoln*." *Cineaste* 38, no. 2 (2013): 13–19.

Callaghan, Richard. "Drift Voyages across the Mid-Atlantic." *Antiquity* 89, no. 345 (2015): 724–31.

Carroll, Patrick J. "Mandinga: The Evolution of a Mexican Runaway Slave Community, 1735–1827." *Comparative Studies in Society and History* 19, no. 4 (1977): 488–505.

Chorba, Carrie. *Mexico, from Mestizo to Multicultural: National Identity and Recent Representations of the Conquest*. Nashville: Vanderbilt University Press, 2007.

Coe, Michael. "The Olmec Heartland: Evolution and Ideology." In *Regional Perspectives on the Olmec*, edited by Robert Sharer and David C. Grove, 68–82. Cambridge: Cambridge University Press, 1989.

Coe, Michael, and Rex Koontz. *Mexico: From the Olmecs to the Aztecs*. London: Thames & Hudson, 2013.

Cole, Merrill. "Nat Turner's Thing." In Lane, *Psychoanalysis of Race*, 261–81.

"Las condiciones que piden los Negros cimarrones de esta comarca." Mexico City: Archivo General de la Nación. Inquisición 1608, vol. 283, file 26, fols. 186–87.

Cope, R. Douglas. *The Limits of Racial Domination: Plebeian Society in Colonial Mexico City, 1660–1720*. Madison: University of Wisconsin Press, 1994.

Covarrubias, Miguel. *Indian Art of Mexico and Central America*. New York: Knopf, 1957.

———. *Island of Bali*. New York: Random House, 1937.

———. *Mexico South: The Isthmus of Tehuantepec*. New York: Knopf, 1946.

———. *Negro Drawings*. Preface by Ralph Barton. Introduction by Frank Crowninshield. New York: A. A. Knopf, 1927.

Cross, William E., Jr. "The Negro-to-Black Conversion Experience." *Black World* 20 (July 1971): 13–27.

———. *Shades of Black: Diversity in African-American Identity*. Philadelphia: Temple University Press, 1991.

Davidson, David M. "Negro Slave Control and Resistance in Colonial Mexico, 1519–1650." In Price, *Maroon Societies*, 82–103.

Davis, Rodney, and Douglas Wilson. *The Lincoln-Douglas Debates: The Lincoln Studies Center Edition*. Champaign: University of Illinois Press, 2014.

Del Rosal, Francisco. *Diccionario etimológico: Alfabeto primero de origen y etimología de todos los vocablos originales de la lengua castellana*. Madrid: Consejo Superior de Investigaciones Científicas, 1992.

Díaz-Sánchez, Micaela, and Alejandro Hernández. "The *Son Jarocho* as Afro-Mexican Resistance Music." *Journal of Pan African Studies* 6, no. 1 (2013): 187–209.

Diehl, Richard. *The Olmecs: America's First Civilization*. London: Thames & Hudson, 2004.

Diouf, Sylviane. *Slavery's Exiles: The Story of the American Maroons*. New York: New York University Press, 2014.

Douglass, Frederick. *Frederick Douglass: Selected Speeches and Writings*. Edited by Phillip S. Foner and Yuval Taylor. Chicago: Chicago Review Press, 2000.

Dziubinskyj, Aaron. "Eduardo Urzaiz's 'Eugenia': Eugenics, Gender, and Dystopian Society in Twenty-Third-Century Mexico." *Science Fiction Studies* 34, no. 3 (2007): 463–72.

Edelman, Lee. *No Future: Queer Theory and the Death Drive*. Durham, N.C.: Duke University Press, 2004.

Encuesta Intercensal 2015: Cuestionario para viviendas particulares habitadas y población. Mexico City: Instituto Nacional de Estadística y Geografía, 2015.

Eshun, Kodwo. "Further Considerations of Afrofuturism." *CR: The New Centennial Review* 3, no. 2 (2003): 287–302.

Fanon, Frantz. *Black Skin, White Masks*. Translated by Richard Philcox. New York: Grove Press, 2008.

Figueroa, Mónica G. Moreno, and Emiko Saldívar Tanaka. "Comics, Dolls and the Disavowal of Racism: Learning from Mexican Mestizaje." In *Creolizing Europe: Legacies and Transformations*, edited by Encarnación Gutiérrez Rodríguez and Shirley Anne Tate, 175–201. Liverpool: Liverpool University Press, 2015.

———. "'We Are Not Racists, We Are Mexicans': Privilege, Nationalism and Post-race Ideology in Mexico." *Critical Sociology* 42, nos. 4–5 (July 1, 2016): 515–33. https://journals.sagepub.com/doi/abs/10.1177/0896920515591296.

Foner, Eric. *The Fiery Trial: Abraham Lincoln and American Slavery*. New York: W. W. Norton, 2010.

———. "*Lincoln*'s Use of Politics for Noble Ends." *New York Times*, November 26, 2012.

Franco, José L. "Maroons and Slave Rebellions in the Spanish Territories." In Price, *Maroon Societies*, 35–48.

Fuentes, Carlos. "Cervantes, or the Critique of Reading." In *Myself with Others: Selected Essays*, 49–71. New York: Farrar, Straus and Giroux, 1990.

———. *Terra Nostra*. Mexico City: Alfaguara, 2013.

———. *Valiente mundo nuevo: Épica, utopía y mito en la novela hispanoamericana*. Mexico City: Fondo de Cultura Económica, 1990.

García, Miguel. "'Eugenia' en su contexto: Utopía y proyecto alterno de nación." *Alambique: Revista académica de ciencia ficción y fantasía* 4, no. 1 (2016): article 6.

Garza, Alicia. "A Herstory of the #BlackLivesMatter Movement." *The Feminist Wire*, October 7, 2014. https://www.nfg.org/news/herstory-blacklivesmatter-movement.

Gilroy, Paul. *The Black Atlantic: Modernity and Double Consciousness*. Cambridge, Mass.: Harvard University Press, 1993.

———. "Living Memory: A Meeting with Toni Morrison." In *Small Acts: Thoughts on the Politics of Black Cultures*, 175–82. London: Serpent's Tail, 1993.

Goebel, Walter, and Saskia Schabio, eds. *Beyond the Black Atlantic: Relocating Modernization and Technology*. Abingdon, U.K.: Routledge, 2006.

González y González, Luis. *Viaje por la historia de México*. Edited by Andrea Citlapiltzin. Mexico City: Conaculta, 2010.

Goodwin, Doris Kearns. *Team of Rivals: The Political Genius of Abraham Lincoln*. New York: Simon & Schuster, 2005.

Graff Zivin, Erin. "Beyond Inquisitional Logic, or, Toward an An-archaeological Latin Americanism." *CR: The New Centennial Review* 14, no. 1 (Spring 2014): 195–211.

Grove, David C. *Discovering the Olmecs: An Unconventional History*. Austin: University of Texas Press, 2014.

Guelzo, Allen C. *Lincoln's Emancipation Proclamation: The End of Slavery in America*. New York: Simon and Schuster, 2006.

Guía para la acción pública contra la discriminación y para la promoción de igualdad e inclusión de la población afrodescendiente en México. Mexico City: Consejo Nacional para Prevenir la Discriminación, 2011.

Hamnett, Brian. *A Concise History of Mexico*. 3rd ed. Cambridge: Cambridge University Press, 2019.

Hanks, William F. *Converting Words: Maya in the Age of the Cross*. Berkeley: University of California Press, 2010.

Hartman, Saidiya. *Scenes of Subjection: Terror, Slavery, and Self-Making in Nineteenth-Century America*. New York: Oxford University Press, 1997.

———. *To Lose Your Mother: A Journey along the Atlantic Slave Route*. New York: Farrar, Straus and Giroux, 2007.

Haslip-Viera, Gabriel, Bernard Ortiz de Montellano, and Warren Barbour. "Robbing Native American Cultures: Van Sertima's Afrocentricity and the Olmecs." *Current Anthropology* 38, no. 3 (June 1, 1997): 419–41.

Hawking, Stephen. "Information Preservation and Weather Forecasting for Black Holes." Kavli Institute for Theoretical Physics, Santa Barbara, California, August 2013. https://arxiv.org/pdf/1401.5761.pdf.

Hofstadter, Richard. *The American Political Tradition and the Men Who Made It*. New York: Vintage Books, 1989.

Holpuch, Amanda. "US Census Bureau Drops 'Negro' as Option for Respondents on Race." *Guardian*, February 25, 2013.

Holzer, Harold. "Reel vs. Real: Was Thaddeus Stevens as Angry and Abrasive as He's Portrayed in Spielberg's *Lincoln*?" *Civil War Times* 52, no. 2 (April 2013): 48–53.

Hooker, Juliet. *Theorizing Race in the Americas: Douglass, Sarmiento, Du Bois, and Vasconcelos*. New York: Oxford University Press, 2017.

Hornaday, Ann. "Participant Media Invents an Activist Aesthetic." *Washington Post*, May 10, 2012.

Hyatt, Vera Lawrence, and Rex Nettleford, eds. *Race, Discourse, and the Origin of the Americas: A New World View*. Washington, D.C.: Smithsonian Institution Press, 1995.

James, Joy. "Afrarealism and the Black Matrix: Maroon Philosophy at Democracy's Border." *Black Scholar* 43, no. 4 (2013): 124–31.

Jameson, Fredric. *Archaeologies of the Future: The Desire Called Utopia and Other Science Fictions*. London: Verso, 2007.

Jett, Stephen. *Ancient Ocean Crossings: Reconsidering the Case for Contacts with the Pre-Columbian Americas*. Tuscaloosa: University of Alabama Press, 2017.

Jules-Rosette, Bennetta. *Josephine Baker in Art and Life: The Icon and the Image.* Champaign: University of Illinois Press, 2007.

Katzew, Ilona. *Casta Painting: Images of Race in Eighteenth-Century Mexico.* New Haven, Conn.: Yale University Press, 2004.

Keeling, Kara. *Queer Times, Black Futures.* New York: New York University Press, 2019.

Kelley, David. "An Essay on Pre-Columbian Contacts between the Americas and Other Areas, with Special Reference to the Work of Ivan Van Sertima." In Hyatt and Nettleford, *Race, Discourse, and the Origin of the Americas*, 103–22.

Kent, R. K. "Palmeras: An African State in Brazil." In Price, *Maroon Societies*, 170–90.

Kopytoff, Barbara Klamon. "The Maroons of Jamaica: An Ethnohistorical Study of Incomplete Polities, 1655–1905." Ph.D. diss., University of Pennsylvania, 1973.

Kushner, Tony. *Lincoln: The Screenplay.* New York: Theatre Communications Group, 2013.

Landers, Jane. "*Cimarrón* and Citizen: African Identity, Corporate Identity, and the Evolution of Free Black Towns in the Spanish Circum-Caribbean." In *Slaves, Subjects, and Subversives: Blacks in Colonial Latin America*, edited by Jane Landers and Barry Robinson, 111–45. Albuquerque: University of New Mexico Press, 2006.

Lane, Christopher, ed. *Psychoanalysis of Race.* New York: Columbia University Press, 1999.

Leonard, Irving Albert. *Alboroto y motín de México, del 8 de junio 1692: Relación de Don Carlos de Sigüenza y Góngora en una carta dirigida al Almirante Don Andrés de Pez.* Mexico City: Talleres Gráficos del Museo Nacional de Arqueología, Historia y Etnografía, 1932.

———. *Baroque Times in Old Mexico: Seventeenth-Century Persons, Places, and Practices.* 1959. Reprint, Ann Arbor: University of Michigan Press, 1966.

———. *Don Carlos de Sigüenza y Góngora: A Mexican Savant of the Seventeenth Century.* Berkeley: University of California Press, 1929.

———. *Don Carlos de Sigüenza y Góngora: Un sabio mexicano del siglo XVII.* Mexico City: Fondo de Cultura Económica, 1984.

———. "An Interview with Irving Leonard." By John J. Tepaske. *Hispanic American Historical Review* 63, no. 2 (1983): 233–53.

———. Review of *Obras históricas* by Carlos de Sigüenza y Góngora. *Hispanic American Historical Review* 26, no. 2 (1946): 203–4.

Lewis, Laura. *Chocolate and Corn Flour: History, Race, and Place in the Making of Black Mexico.* Durham, N.C.: Duke University Press, 2012.

Lincoln: A Cinematic and Historical Companion. New York: Disney Editions, 2012.

Lloyd, David, and Peter D. O'Neill, eds. *The Black and Green Atlantic: Cross-Currents of the African and Irish Diasporas.* London: Palgrave Macmillan, 2009.

Lomnitz-Adler, Claudio. *Exits from the Labyrinth: Culture and Ideology in the Mexican National Space.* Berkeley: University of California Press, 1992.

Lorde, Audre and James Baldwin. "Revolutionary Hope: A Conversation between James Baldwin and Audre Lorde." The Museum of Contemporary

African Diasporan Arts (MoCADA). http://mocada-museum.tumblr.com/post/73421979421/revolutionary-hope-a-conversation-between-james.

Lund, Joshua. *The Impure Imagination: Toward a Critical Hybridity in Latin American Writing*. Minneapolis: University of Minnesota Press, 2006.

Magness, Phillip W., and Sebastian N. Page. *Colonization after Emancipation: Lincoln and the Movement for Black Resettlement*. Columbia: University of Missouri Press, 2011.

Malcomson, Hettie. "New Generations, Older Bodies: *Danzón*, Age and 'Cultural Rescue' in the Port of Veracruz, Mexico." *Popular Music* 31, no. 2 (2012): 217–30.

Margeirsson, Veigar. "Dawn of the Titans." *Universal Trailer Series—Heaven and Hell*. Universal, 2014.

Martí, José. *Nuestra América*. Barcelona: Linkgua, 2011.

Martínez, María Elena. *Genealogical Fictions: Limpieza de Sangre, Religion, and Gender in Colonial Mexico*. Palo Alto, Calif.: Stanford University Press, 2011.

Masur, Kate. "In Spielberg's 'Lincoln,' Passive Black Characters." *New York Times*, November 12, 2012.

Mayas y olmecas: segunda Reunión de mesa redonda sobre problemas antropológicos de México y Centro América. Tuxtla Gutiérrez, Chiapas: Sociedad Mexicana de Antropología, 1942.

Mbembe, Achille. "Necropolitics." Translated by Libb Meintjes. *Public Culture* 15, no. 1 (2003): 11–40.

McCloy, Shelby. *The Negro in the French West Indies*. Louisville: University of Kentucky Press, 1969.

Melgar y Serrano, José María. "Estudio sobre la antigüedad y el origen de la cabeza colosal de tipo etiópico que existe en Hueyapan en el cantón de los Tuxtlas." *Boletín de la Sociedad Mexicana de Geografía y Estadística*, series 2, vol. 3, 104–9. Mexico City: Imprenta del Gobierno, 1871.

Mendoza, Antonio de. "Carta de D. Antonio de Mendoza, Virrey de Nueva España, al Emperador, dándole cuenta de varios asuntos de su gobierno." In *Colección de documentos inéditos, relativos al descubrimiento, conquista y colonización de las posesiones españoles en América y Oceanía*, edited by Joaquín Pacheco, Francisco de Cárdenas, and Luis Torres de Mendoza, 2:179–211. Madrid: J. M. Pérez, 1864.

Millett, Nathaniel. *The Maroons of Prospect Bluff and Their Quest for Freedom in the Atlantic World*. Gainesville: University Press of Florida, 2013.

More, Anna. *Baroque Sovereignty: Carlos de Sigüenza y Góngora and the Creole Archive of Colonial Mexico*. Philadelphia: University of Pennsylvania Press, 2012.

Moreiras, Alberto. "Common Political Democracy: The *Marrano* Register." In *Impasses of the Post-global: Theory in the Era of Climate Change*, vol. 2, edited by Henry Sussman, 175–93. Ann Arbor, Mich.: Open Humanities Press, 2012. http://dx.doi.org/10.3998/ohp.10803281.0001.001.

Morrison, Toni. *Playing in the Dark: Whiteness and the Literary Imagination*. New York: Vintage, 1993.

Noll, Arthur Howard, and A. Phillip McMahon. *The Life and Times of Miguel Hidalgo y Costilla*. Chicago: A. C. McClurg, 1910.

O'Gorman, Edmundo. "Sobre los inconvenientes de vivir los indios en el centro de la ciudad." *Boletín del Archivo General de la Nación* 9, no. 1 (1938): 1–34.

Palmer, Colin A. *Slaves of the White God: Blacks in Mexico, 1570–1650*. Cambridge, Mass.: Harvard University Press, 1976.

Paschel, Tianna. "'The Beautiful Faces of My Black People': Race, Ethnicity and the Politics of Colombia's 2005 Census." *Ethnic and Racial Studies* 36, no. 10 (2013): 1544–63.

Patterson, Orlando. "Slavery and Slave Revolts: A Sociohistorical Analysis of the First Maroon War, 1665–1740." In Price, *Maroon Societies*, 246–92.

———. *Slavery and Social Death: A Comparative Study*. Cambridge, Mass.: Harvard University Press, 1982.

Paz, Octavio. *El laberinto de la soledad*. Mexico City: Fondo de Cultura Económica, 1959.

———. "The Labyrinth of Solitude." In *The Labyrinth of Solitude and Other Writings*. New York: Grove Press, 1985.

———. Introduction to *Massacre in Mexico*, by Elena Poniatowska, translated by Helen Lane. Columbia: University of Missouri Press, 1992.

———. "The Other Mexico." Translated by Lysander Kemp. In *The Labyrinth of Solitude and Other Writings*, 213–325. New York: Grove Press, 1985.

———. *Posdata*. Mexico City: Siglo Veintiuno Editores, 1970.

Pérez de Ribas, Andrés. *Crónica y historia religiosa de la Provincia de la Compañía de Jesús de México en Nueva España*. Vol. 2. 1654. Reprint, Mexico City: Imprenta del Sagrado Corazón de Jesús, 1896.

Perfil sociodemográfico de la población afrodescendiente en México. Mexico City: Instituto Nacional de Estadística y Geografía, 2017.

Peters, Virginia Bergman. *The Florida Wars*. Hamden, Conn.: Archon Books, 1979.

Pettinger, Alasdair, ed. *Always Elsewhere: Travels of the Black Atlantic*. London: Cassell, 1998.

Powell, Richard, and David Bailey. *Rhapsodies in Black: Art of the Harlem Renaissance*. Berkeley: University of California Press, 1997.

Price, Richard. "Introduction: Maroons and Their Communities." In Price, *Maroon Societies*, 1–32.

———, ed. *Maroon Societies: Rebel Slave Communities in the Americas*. New York: Anchor Books, 1973.

Rabasa, José. "Pre-Columbian Pasts and Indian Presents in Mexican History." *Disposito* 19, no. 46 (1994): 245–70.

———. *Without History: Subaltern Studies, the Zapatista Insurgency, and the Specter of History*. Pittsburgh: University of Pittsburgh Press, 2010.

Rankine, Claudia, and Beth Loffreda. Introduction to *The Racial Imaginary: Writers on Race in the Life of the Mind*, edited by Claudia Rankine, Beth Loffreda, and Cap Max King, 13–22. Albany, N.Y.: Fence Books, 2015.

Ransom, Roger L. *Conflict and Compromise: The Political Economy of Slavery, Emancipation and the American Civil War*. Cambridge: Cambridge University Press, 1989.

Rashkin, Esther. *Unspeakable Secrets and the Psychoanalysis of Culture*. Albany: State University of New York Press, 2009.

Riva Palacio, Vicente, and Manuel Payno. "Los treinta y tres negros." In Vicente Riva Palacio, Manuel Payno, Juan A. Mateos, and Rafael Martínez de la

Torre, *El libro rojo, 1520–1867*, 1:351–68. 1870. Reprint, Mexico City: A. Polo, 1905.

Ross, Kathleen. "Alboroto y motín de México: Una noche triste criollo." *Hispanic Review* 56, no. 2 (1988): 181–90.

———. *The Baroque Narrative of Carlos de Sigüenza y Góngora: A New World Paradise*. New York: Cambridge University Press, 1993.

Rucker, Philip. "Obama Inspired by, Compared to Lincoln." *Washington Post*, November 19, 2008.

Saldívar, Emiko. "'It's Not Race, It's Culture': Untangling Racial Politics in Mexico." *Latin American and Caribbean Ethnic Studies* 9, no. 1 (2014): 89–108.

Saldívar, Emiko, and Casey Walsh. "Racial and Ethnic Identities in Mexican Statistics." *Journal of Iberian and Latin American Research* 20, no. 3 (2014): 455–75.

Saucier, P. Khalil, and Tryon P. Woods. "What Is the *Danger* in Black Studies and Can We Look at It Again (and Again)?" In *On Marronage: Ethical Confrontations with Antiblackness*, edited by P. Khalil Saucier and Tryon P. Woods, 1–32. Trenton: Africa World Press, 2015.

Scovel, James. "Thaddeus Stevens." *Lippincott's Monthly Magazine* (April 1898): 548–50.

Sexton, Jared. *Amalgamation Schemes: Antiblackness and the Critique of Multiracialism*. Minneapolis: University of Minnesota Press, 2008.

Shank, Michael. "'Lincoln': Where Was Frederick Douglass?" *Washington Post*, November 28, 2012.

Sharpe, Christina. *In the Wake: On Blackness and Being*. Durham, N.C.: Duke University Press, 2016.

Sigüenza y Góngora, Carlos de. *Alboroto y motín de México, del 8 de junio 1692: Relación de Don Carlos de Sigüenza y Góngora en una carta dirigida al Almirante Don Andrés de Pez*. Edited by Irving A. Leonard. Mexico City: Talleres Gráficos del Museo Nacional de Arqueología, Historia y Etnografía, 1932.

———. *Relaciones históricas*. Edited by Manuel Romero de Terreros. Mexico City: Ediciones de la Universidad Nacional Autónoma de México, 1954.

———. *Seis obras*. Caracas: Biblioteca Ayacucho, 1984.

Silva, Eduardo. "Black Abolitionists in the *Quilombo* de Leblon, Rio de Janeiro." In *Beyond Slavery: The Multilayered Legacy of Africans in Latin America and the Caribbean*, edited by Darién J. Davis, 109–22. Lanham, Md.: Rowman & Littlefield, 2007.

Solomianski, Alejandro. *Identidades secretas: La negritud Argentina*. Buenos Aires: Beatriz Viterbo, 2003.

Spielberg, Steven, dir. *Lincoln*. DreamWorks Pictures, 2012.

Stanley, Amy Dru. "Instead of Waiting for the Thirteenth Amendment: The War Power, Slave Marriage, and Inviolate Human Rights." *American Historical Review* 115, no. 3 (2010): 732–65.

Stowe, Harriet Beecher. *Uncle Tom's Cabin*. New York: Limited Editions Club, 1938.

Striner, Richard. *Father Abraham: Lincoln's Relentless Struggle to End Slavery*. New York: Oxford University Press, 2006.

Sue, Christina Sue. *The Land of the Cosmic Race: Race Mixture, Racism, and Blackness in Mexico*. New York: Oxford University Press, 2013.

Tsesis, Alexander. *The Thirteenth Amendment and American Freedom: A Legal History*. New York: New York University Press, 2004.

Tuckerman, Charles. "President Lincoln and Colonization." *Magazine of American History with Notes and Queries* 16 (1886): 329–32.

Urzaiz, Eduardo. *Eugenia: A Fictional Sketch of Future Customs; A Critical Edition*. Edited and translated by Sarah A. Buck Kachaluba and Aaron Dziubinskyj. Madison: University of Wisconsin Press, 2016.

Van Sertima, Ivan. "African Presence in Early America." In Hyatt and Nettleford, *Race, Discourse, and the Origin of the Americas*, 66–102.

———. *They Came Before Columbus: The African Presence in Ancient America*. 1976; reprint, New York: Random House, 2003.

Van Vechten, Carl. "The Negro Theatre." In *In the Garret*. New York: Knopf, 1920.

Vasconcelos, José. *La raza cósmica / The Cosmic Race*. Baltimore: Johns Hopkins University Press, 1997.

Venet, Wendy Hamand. *Neither Ballots nor Bullets: Women Abolitionists and the Civil War*. Charlottesville: University of Virginia Press, 1991.

Vinson, Ben. "Fading from Memory: Historiographical Reflections on the Afro-Mexican Presence." *Review of Black Political Economy* 33, no. 1 (2005): 59–72.

Vorenberg, Michael. "Abraham Lincoln and the Politics of Black Colonization." *Journal of the Abraham Lincoln Association* 14, no. 2 (1993): 22–45.

———. *Final Freedom: The Civil War, the Abolition of Slavery, and the Thirteenth Amendment*. Cambridge: Cambridge University Press, 2001.

———. "Spielberg's Lincoln: The Great Emancipator Returns." *Journal of the Civil War Era* 3, no. 4 (2013): 549–72.

Waugh, John C. *Reelecting Lincoln: The Battle for the 1864 Presidency*. Boston: Da Capo Press, 2001.

Whitehead, Colson. "The Year of Living Postracially." *New York Times*, November 4, 2009.

———. *Zone One*. New York: Anchor Books, 2012.

Wilderson, Frank B., III. *Red, White, and Black: Cinema and the Structure of U.S. Antagonisms*. Durham, N.C.: Duke University Press, 2010.

Williams, Adriana. *Covarrubias*. Austin: University of Texas Press, 1994.

Yang, Suzanne. "A Question of Accent: Ethnicity and Transference." In Lane, *Psychoanalysis of Race*, 261–81.

INDEX

Note: page numbers followed by *f* refer to figures.